Utopianism in Eighteenth-century Ireland

Utopianism in Eighteenth-century Ireland

Deirdre Ní Chuanacháin

CORK **cup** UNIVERSITY PRESS

Published in 2016 by
Cork University Press
Youngline Industrial Estate
Pouladuff Road, Togher
Cork, Ireland

© Deirdre Ní Chuanacháin

British Library Cataloguing in Publication Data

A CIP catalogue record for this book is available from the British Library

ISBN: 978-1-78205-168-8

Typeset by Dominic Carroll, Ardfield, County Cork
Printed in Malta by Gutenberg Press

www.corkuniversitypress.com

The land sustaining us seemed to hold firm
Only when we embraced it in extremis.
All I believed that happened there was vision.
> Seamus Heaney, 'The Disappearing Island'

Our arrivals at meaning and at value are momentary
pauses in the ongoing dialogue with others from which
meaning and value spring.
> Gary Tomlinson, *Music in Renaissance Magic*

Contents

List of Illustrations

Select Chronology of Key Late Seventeenth-century and Eighteenth and Nineteenth-century Works of Irish Utopian Literature and Thought

1663   Richard Head, *Hic et Ubique: or, the humours of Dublin*

1673   Richard Head, *The Floating Island: or, a new discovery relating the strange adventure on a late voyage from Lambethana to Villa Franca, alias Ramallia, to the eastward of Terra del Templo, by three ships, viz. the* Pay-naught, *the* Excuse, *the* Least-in-Sight, *under the conduct of Captain Robert Owe-much: describing the nature of the inhabitants, their religion, laws and customs. Published by Franck Careless* [pseud], *one of the discoverers*

1674   Richard Head, *The Western Wonder: or, O Brazeel, an inchanted island discovered; with a relation of two ship-wracks in a dreadful sea-storm in that discovery. To which is added, a description of a place, called, Montecapernia, relating the nature of the people, their qualities, humours, fashions, religion*

1675   Richard Head, *O-Brazile, or the Inchanted Island: being a perfect relation of the late discovery and wonderful dis-inchantment of an island on the north of Ireland: with an account of the riches and commodities thereof. Communicated by a letter from London-Derry, to a friend in London*

c. 1703   Domhnall Ó Colmáin, *Párliament na mBan* [*The Parliament of Women*]

1726   Jonathan Swift, *Gulliver's Travels. Travels into several remote nations of the world. In four parts. By Lemuel Gulliver*

1728   Murtagh McDermot, *A Trip to the Moon. Containing some observations and reflections, made by him during his stay in that planet, upon the manners of the inhabitants*

1733   Samuel Madden, *Memoirs of the Twentieth Century. Being original letters of state, under George the Sixth: relating to the most important events in Great-Britain and Europe, as to Church and state, arts and sciences, trade, taxes, and treaties, peace, and war: and characters of the greatest persons of those times; from the middle of the eighteenth, to the end of the twentieth century, and the world. Received and revealed in the year 1728; and now published, for the instruction of all eminent* statesmen, churchmen, patriots, politicians, projectors, papists and Protestants* (6 vols)

1735 George Berkeley, *The Querist Containing Several Queries, Proposed to the Consideration of the Public*

1737 Timothy Plaine, *Tom Tell-Truth, of the Island of Utopia's Letter to Mr. Nobody. Num. 1. Newly translated from the Utopian language*

1747 Henry Lewis Younge, *Utopia: or, Apollo's golden days*

1750 Micheál Coimín, *Laoi Oisín ar Tír na nÓg* [*The Lay of Oisín in the Land of Youth*]

1752? *Old Ireland's Misery at an end: or, the English empire in the Brazils restored. Being the second appearance of the inchanted lady, who appeared the 5th day of June, 1752, in the form of a mermaid, on a sand bank, in the harbour of Lougres, and parish of Endeskeale, north-west of the County of Donegall, in Ireland, as was seen and heard by Thomas White, John Brown, and William Cunningham, who were coming up the channel in a small fishing boat* [the author may have been Revd James MacSparran (1693–1757)]

1752 Manus O'Donnel, *A Voyage to O'Brazeel: or, the sub-marine island. Giving a brief description of the country; and a short account of the customs, manners, government, law, and religion of the inhabitants*

1759 Oliver Goldsmith, 'The Proceedings of Providence vindicated. An eastern tale', *Royal Magazine*, no. 1 (December 1759)

1764–65 Francis Gentleman, *A Trip to the Moon. Containing an account of the island of Noibla. Its Inhabitants, religious and political customs, &c. by Sir Humphrey Lunatic, Bart.* [pseud], 2 vols

1770 Oliver Goldsmith, *The Deserted Village*

1782 Anon., *A History of the Customs, Manners, and Religion of the Moon. To which are annexed several specimens of lunar poetry; and the characters of the most distinguished personages*

1784 Anon., *Oppression Unmasked: being a narrative of the proceedings in a case between a great corporation, and a little fishmonger, relative to some customs for fish, demanded by the former as legal, but refused by the latter, as exactions and extortions. By an advocate for justice*

1790 Theobald Wolfe Tone, *Sandwich Islands Memorandum*

1813 Edward Mangin, *Utopia Found: being an apology for Irish absentees. Addressed to a friend in Connaught. By an absentee, residing in Bath*

1824 John Banim, *Revelations of the Dead-alive*

1827 William Maginn, *Whitehall or the Days of George IV*

Acknowledgements

I cannot thank enough Professor Tom Moylan; his interest in my work and his advice and guidance on everything from source material on utopian studies to approaching different aspects of the subject matter were second to none. I also wish to thank Dr Michael Griffin, who was always ready with advice and encouragement around my research. I want especially to thank Dr Joachim Fischer for the crucial and catalysing guidance he provided in regard to my Irish-language research, as well as for expediting funding for this aspect of my study. This book was researched with the kind assistance of several librarians in Cork City Library, in the Special Collections Departments of University of Limerick and University College, Cork, and in the Royal Irish Academy; I wish to thank all the staff in these institutions, especially Ken Bergin, Jean Turner, Pattie Punch and Pauric Dempsey. I am grateful to the staff of University of Limerick: Dr Michael Kelly, Dr David Coughlan, Niamh Lenahan and the Postgraduate Office, and Lawrence Cleary of the Writing Centre, who were always ready with advice and guidance. Thanks also to Éamonn de Búrca of De Búrca Rare Books for all his help and interest. For assistance in and around my research, I owe debts to Kerby A. Miller, Anne Markey, Toby Barnard, Ruth Levitas, Antonis Balasopoulos, David Lee, Barbara Freitag, Breandán MacSuibhne, Hoda Zaki and Catherine Gilchrist. A very special thanks to Lyman Tower Sargent, who answered innumerable questions and who, while researching his own subjects, managed to uncover material pertaining to mine. His interest in my research has been of enormous help to me. I must thank my two dissertation examiners, Professor Tadhg Foley and Professor Vince Geoghegan, who inspired me and helped me to think about my writing in unexpected ways. My thanks also to the anonymous reviewers of the manuscript at Cork University Press for their helpful comments. Finally, my deepest appreciation goes to Seán Blake and my special brother Brian Ó Cuanacháin, who have supported me every step of the way. *Buíochas mór daoibh go léir.*

CHAPTER 1

Introduction: The Utopian Propensity

There is a way I am fain to go
To the mystical land where all are young,
Where the silver branches have buds of snow.
And every leaf is a singing tongue.

Ethna Carbery[1]

It is indeed the Land of Youth –
And maiden's truth I've ever told –
No joy or bliss I've promised thee
But thou shalt see this land doth hold!

Micheál Coimín[2]

At low tide we might wade out to an island,
Hy-Brasil, the Land of Youth.

Paul Muldoon[3]

Tá Tír na nÓg ar chúl an tí,
Tír álainn trína chéile.

Seán Ó Ríordáin[4]

I n a satirical pamphlet entitled *A Dialogue Between Dean Swift and Thomas Prior, Esq. in the Isles [sic] of St Patrick's Church, Dublin, on That Memorable Day, October 9th, 1753*, an imagined conversation between the ghosts of its long-serving dean, the late Jonathan Swift (1667–1745), and the animator of the Dublin Society, Thomas Prior (1681–1751), allegorises the impoverished and melancholy circumstances of contemporary Ireland.[5] While alive,

Swift's indignation and satire had savagely exposed moral vices and intellectual pretensions. Meanwhile, Prior and his contemporaries, moulded by a spirit of nationalism, had transformed their tangible and worthwhile efforts into the formation of the Dublin (subsequently Royal Dublin) Society. Swift's ghost in a most satirical mood finds evident enjoyment in ridiculing Prior for his many schemes for improving the lot of the Irish people. The pamphlet's exhortations in the final pages reveal both Swift and Prior as disparate characters while foregrounding the sometimes ambiguous representations of Utopia in eighteenth-century Irish utopian writing in English. Prior's utopian vision for improving Irish society, his hopeful vision of a *better* society, is tempered by Swift's baleful pessimism about the state of his country:

> Here is a fine Bundle of Hopes for a Man in Despair to live comfortably on! But pray now Tom, have you done reckoning up all your mighty Projects to make Ireland another Utopia? I am almost at the End of my Patience, for to say Truth, Tom, the List of the Ships in Homer's *Iliad* is not more tedious.[6]

Swift's ghostly nocturnal perambulations through the aisles of the cathedral result from his discomfort about the present state of Ireland. Such discombobulation keeps him from his eternal sleep: 'Tis my Country keeps me walking! why who can lie still? I don't believe there are many ghosts now, that have any share of understanding, or any regard for Ireland, that are to be found in their graves at midnight.'[7] Swift recounts that he had been 'earthed' for eight years, but worry about the state of Ireland has caused him unease and led to his nightly ramblings. In addition, the ghost of Prior was similarly to be found walking the aisles of St Patrick's; he describes his having slept for months like a dormouse until thoughts of Ireland entered his head; his distress strengthened and caused him to waken. Swift recounts that when he gets into a certain train of thought, or, as he puts it, 'considers the present situation of our Country, it makes me as uneasy in my coffin as a rat shut up in a trap'.[8] Swift is as perplexed about the state of Ireland as if he were still alive and living in the deanery.

Moreover, Prior, grieved at the ill circumstances of Ireland, concludes that 'the World seems resolved they shall never mend; and, I think so, by their treating all true Patriots in the most unhandsome manner. This is as mad a measure, as imprisoning the physicians in an epidemical sickness would be.'[9] Prior is concerned about the treatment of patriots in Ireland, that their zeal and motives are suspected. He clearly sees himself as having formerly been such a living patriot, and says he could not have ceased to write what he had written because he always maintained the hope of doing good by his pen. This, in turn, sheds light on Prior's work during his lifetime, which coexists with his ghostly concerns in 1753, where he speaks of a life spent in the service of his fellow citizens, the concern for whom has followed him beyond the grave. He observes: 'I profess I writ whatever I publish'd, barely for the Joy I had in doing some service to my Country, and with so little a view to reputation, that I would have done it, if there had been no such thing as Fame in the world',[10] and he continues: 'I troubled the world with a deal of Tracts on publick subjects; and, I thank Heaven, my heart is as little asham'd of it, now I am dead, as I was proud of it when I was living.'[11] He argues that he saw writing as an absolute necessity, a moral obligation towards the well-being of what he calls the 'most neglected Nation under Heaven'.[12] He notes that he had received rebukes from those with whom he had disagreed. Parallel with this, Swift claims that over a hundred pamphlets had been written against him full of both vitriol and scandal – indeed, enough to fill a library.

Swift explains his philosophy as 'to do Good in an evil world. I don't see anything very desirable in the greatest talents, or in the largest affluence of fortune, unless they are in some measure employed in the Publick Service, and if they be, it truly dignifies them.'[13] When Prior comments that all the bile directed towards Swift must have been a wounding grief to his 'generous Mind',[14] Swift responds that this made no impression on him: 'What harm did all their ribaldry do me? I Neither eat, nor drunk, nor slept the worse for it.'[15] He confirms that he 'wrote for Truth and Reason, for Liberty, and the Rights of my Country and Fellow-Subjects; and it gave me Joy, to see the Minions of a Court, and the Slaves of Power, stare at the dextrous boldness of my Pen'.[16] His perceived absence of preferment or advancement in the Church did not bother him, but gave him an enlarged power of doing good, while he saw 'so many bad men pass for good; so many fools for wise; so many ignorants for learned; and so many knaves for honest, and rewarded accordingly, that I was rather provok'd, than mortified'.[17] Prior concedes that he thought when he died that his country was left 'in a very improving way, and on the mending hand, by my writings and my constant labours in its service, and had I liv'd a little longer, I would have wrote some Tracts, that would have prevented some distresses, which I hear, are likely to fall heavy on her'.[18] In a satirical mode, Swift concludes that Ireland was also in a tolerably improved way when he died: 'I have heard indeed, from the Ghosts of some half-starved silk-weavers, and some manufacturers of Irish woollen goods that died of hunger and poverty, that I—d was vastly improved, as to the elegance of taste in her gentry, as to eating and drinking.'[19]

Prior points out that he had seen several considerable improvements in the country that had given him to say she was on 'the mending hand'.[20] He notes improvements such as advances in the linen trade; he refers to the increase in the number of acres sowed with flaxseed and in the number of spinners who manufacture it. Swift agrees, but argues that caution is required: 'are there no fears to balance these growing hopes, and mighty prospects?'[21] Prior mentions the Dublin Society and its premiums:

> they gave Premiums, to heighten the Manufacture and Dying of our Woollen Cloths; of our Silks, and our Velvets; of our Blankets; of our Worsteds; of our Cottons; of our Coffoys; Buffs, Lutherines and Fustians; of our Stockings, and our Carpets, with surprising success: In our Husbandry they did wonders also; as to Wheat and Barley; as to Liming, Marling, and Sanding of Land; as to planting of hops, draining of bogs; as to raising Liquorish, Saffron and Madder. They raised the manufactures of our finest hats, to a surprising degree; and they did the same by our window glass, and made so great a progress in our paper business, and building of mills for carrying it on, as if they had got the mines of Peru, or the industry of China, to assist in their undertakings.[22]

Swift concludes that 'all the Dublin Society did, was to show what we wanted, and to set an example, of what might be done, to help our dreadful ailments'.[23] He believes these ideas are doomed due to the impoverished funds of the Dublin Society, and tells Prior 'you might as well expect to work miracles, and to feed thousands like our Saviour, with a few loaves, as to retrieve a Nation'.[24] He views Prior as a projector, cheating himself with his own dreams. However, Swift's fears for the future prosperity of Ireland are based on his concerns about the factions that divide its countrymen. The first great division among them are the disputes on spiritual matters among Protestants and Catholics. What alarms him is that this causes an indisposition to unity and mutual affection by which means the country of Ireland is lessened in its strength because of the divisions that exist within it. He uses a corporeal analogy to make his case: 'while we seem to drag like a Man in a palsy one half of our Body after the other, which ought to co-operate with it'.[25]

Prior believes that such a situation can only be resolved when their Catholic neighbours get priests with better principles who will not have, or pass on, the 'inhuman prejudices'[26] towards Protestants. Swift believes that this will be difficult to achieve as the Catholics in his opinion retain their superstitious pilgrimages, nunneries, yearly Lents, and weekly fasts that, as he argues, in the words of the prophet 'eat up the sins of the people, keep them very low, and unable, as well as unwilling to join us in serving the Nation'.[27] Apart from these circumstances, Swift refers to what he calls 'another ill-omened circumstance to our welfare … the terrible Parties and Factions among Protestants'[28] that will, he believes, add further difficulties to what he calls Ireland's 'natural infirmities'.[29] Indeed, he quotes from verses he says he had written while residing in England in the last four stormy years of Queen Anne's reign (he claims he never had them printed). They are on the topic of High and Low Church, and Swift believes they could be applied to Ireland on this occasion:

> For as two sawyers in a pit,
> Toiling a massy Beam to
> Slit,
> A like their Skill and Prowess show,
> While one draws High and t'other Low.
> So WHIG and TORY, BRITAIN
> tear Asunder, and her strength impair.
> While Factions all their Arts renew,
> To cut the Nation into Two.[30]

Even then, Swift shows how divisions and factions, both in religion and in politics, simply serve to impair a nation's strength. Prior, in defending the Dublin Society, aims to show how its strength has not been impaired by either divisions or factions but strengthened by the fact that people will join together in pursuance of the public good:

> I allow all this would hold true, if the great and admirable effects of the Society's Premiums, did not make it highly probable, that I should have prevailed with several of our worthiest Countrymen, to have assisted so great and so successful an Undertaking. When Men see they have it in their Power, if they will join together, to deliver their Country from all its calamitous distresses.[31]

Prior suggests that he would in general have doubled the premiums and, indeed, in some of the most important improvements and manufactures he would have trebled them; faster progress would therefore have been made in a few years if the skill and industry of people had been given every incentive. It brought joy to his heart to see the enlarging and improving of tillage, the encouraging and heightening of old decaying manufactures, and the setting up of new ones, and with it extending the strength and force of the society. He would have brought over foreign workmen of all trades and professions; he would have set up glass manufacturing of all kinds near collieries. He would have established earthenware production, and if possible would have brought over skilled workers in that trade from Birmingham. He would also have wanted to see improvements in silk and thread bone lace, and in the paper and sugar businesses in Ireland.

To this end, we find that Swift's response, as quoted at the beginning of this chapter – the 'mighty projects to make Ireland another Utopia' – is not, in Prior's view, to be chided and ridiculed. He insists on recounting the success of the Dublin Society, particularly regarding the advances in silk manufacturing and tapestry, and saying he would have, among other things, encouraged salt works, shipbuilding and fisheries. He admonishes Swift, saying frankly: 'I never saw or heard any eminent proofs of your extraordinary skill as a politician, except a vast crowd of pamphlets; and what are they but the mere cobwebs of politicks.'[32] Prior avows that Swift was a good patriot but too much the politician, and that if only his political secrets had become known, he would have been revealed as a Jacobite. Swift rejects this, leading Prior to quote some words he had written previously, contending that they could be applied to Swift 'with all the Graces, all the faults of Wit, You both adorn'd and blemished all you writ'.[33] To ease the wrath of Prior, Swift offers a proposal that he hopes will assist him in laying aside his resentment about Swift's admonishing his schemes, and he says he will lay forth a clearly utopian spirited plan which, 'if it ever comes to be embraced, will make Ireland one of the fortunate islands'.[34]

As Swift saw it, the Dublin Society should not be dependent on private contributions for its funding, and Parliament should resolve to provide financial assistance. Ultimately, societies should be founded in every county in Ireland, or at least in every considerable county. As Prior accepts Swift's sentiments, he notes that many would look on such plans of theirs 'as Dreams and Visions',[35] but that 'the active and virtuous, and the disinterested, know their real worth, and wish and labour, to have them spread as widely and as forcibly among Men'.[36] And so, the ghosts of both Swift and Prior urge a renewal of Ireland through the improving visions of the Dublin Society, and recognise the great need for an infusion of utopian perspectives in contemporary political practice. Their conversation ends as a curate and three elderly women start to light candles for the morning service, causing both Swift and Prior to return to their uneasy rest.

The anonymous author of this pamphlet ventriloquises the voices of Swift and Prior so as to portray the economic, cultural and political interests of these eighteenth-century characters with their differing visions of how contemporary Ireland could be improved. However, through the figures of Swift and Prior, he does reveal how visions for a *better* society arise from the conflicts, crises and hopes of the society from which both the author and those he ventriloquises emerge. The pamphlet's publication coincided with a rich phase of utopianism in eighteenth-century Ireland. *A Dialogue* captures some of the disparate elements of Irish utopian writing in English: satire, improvement, patriotism, national feeling and the wider colonial, anti-colonial, political and religious concerns. The aim of this book is to fill the lacuna in our knowledge of utopianism in eighteenth-century Ireland. It is essentially a work of recovery, or reconfiguring, of literary works and documents that have remained obscured from view or whose histories are ambiguous.

As I began to draw the threads together, a picture of eighteenth-century Ireland was revealed, especially at the interface between the languages, Irish and English, between the Catholic and Protestant communities and their respective cultures, and between colonial and anti-colonial writings. But if we are to discover the societal significance of utopianism in eighteenth-century Ireland, some guiding principles are required: first, to establish what utopianism means, and, second, to identify the common factors that draw these works together. In the case of the former, the dominant traditions in British, European and American utopianism have been recognised, and they are also relevant in the Irish instance. The later eighteenth-century stages of Irish republicanism were a repository for French, American and English influences, while also containing elements of ancient Gaelic culture. The radical utopianism of the Society of United Irishmen's *Northern Star* newspaper, with its recurring references to James Harrington's *The Commonwealth of Oceana* (1656) as an exemplar, heralds that confluence of the international and the national. To identify the common factors that drew these works together is more complex. Many had similar points of reference emerging out of eighteenth-century political and cultural contexts, the genesis of which began, as

I observe, much earlier in Irish historical life. To that end, what follows in this chapter, 'The Utopian Propensity', surveys specific definitions and discussions on utopianism. I then apply them in context in chapter 2, 'Utopian Geographies', to pre-eighteenth-century and eighteenth-century Irish utopian forms. These include the tradition of the *aisling*, or vision poetry, narratives around the journey to, and topos of, Hy Brasil, the Celtic Otherworld of the Land of Youth (Tír na nÓg), and Richard Head's seventeenth-century drama *Hic et Ubique: or, the humours of Dublin*.

While Plato and Thomas More imagined alternative ways of organising society, in chapter 3, 'Improving Visions: The Early Philosophical Societies and the Dublin Society', I look at those eighteenth-century Irish modes of imagining alternative ways of organising society. I focus on the origins and philosophy of the early philosophical societies, and particularly on the Dublin Society, which is one of two that originated in the eighteenth century and which has survived in a continuing history up to the present, the other being the Royal Irish Academy. These societies originated during a dynamic phase in associational life in eighteenth-century Ireland. It is important to view them in a wide context, with linkages to developments in Britain, the American colonies, France and elsewhere. I contend that they amount to a practical demonstration of utopianism and, indeed, in certain instances, of patriotism. To be sure, it has been cogently argued by commentators such as James Livesey that the Dublin Society contributed to what Jürgen Habermas has called 'the growth of the public sphere'[37] alongside, but distinct from, the formal political realm of Parliament, the Dublin administration and municipal corporations.

Chapter 4, 'George Berkeley's New World Utopia and the Pacific Utopia in the Writings of Theobald Wolfe Tone', expands upon the connections between Ireland and the wider world. First, I focus on George Berkeley's life, which is marked by differing utopian causes. However, I emphasise his utopian Bermuda project (1722–31) and its legacy, and his subsequent work of practical philanthropy, *The Querist*, as a clear exploration of what might constitute a Utopia. Second, I have chosen Wolfe Tone's *Sandwich Islands Memorandum* as an example of an interweaving of both republican and colonial utopianism in the 1790s. His plan for a military colony on the recently discovered remote Sandwich Islands (Hawaii) in some ways resembled James Burgh's Harringtonian-styled Utopia of the Cessares (1764). I conclude that both Berkeley's and Wolfe Tone's disparate and differing utopian projections predicated on the actual locations of Bermuda and the Sandwich Islands formed a background to the former's subsequent practical philanthropy and the latter's developing republican nationalism back home in the 'very world which is the world of all of us, or not at all', as Wordsworth has it.

In chapter 5, "'To the Limits of the Lunar World': Extraterrestrial Voyages and Utopia', I explore utopianism as expressed through works of satire based on extraterrestrial and lunar Utopias. In the tradition of utopian fiction, the travellers discussed depart from a real place to visit the imagined place, and return home. Such utopian satires provide a strong narrative device and offer in Darko Suvin's sense an estranged space from which to comment upon contemporary society. These utopian projections are often shown to allegorise the conflicts and crises of the society from which the respective authors emerge. This chapter provides a critique of the variegated nature of these extraterrestrial narratives offering results as diverse as a prognosis for the renovation of Ireland, the locating of a utopian commonwealth on the moon, and a comprehensive vision for a Plato's republic recast in the limits of the lunar world.

Chapter 6, 'Dark Caverns: Samuel Madden's Futurism', looks at the historical and political context out of which Madden's innovative *Memoirs of the Twentieth Century* – the first literary Utopia set in the future – emerged as a work of utopian satire focused on an imagined future society allied with the inaugural time-travel Utopia. I aim to locate *Memoirs* within the context of Madden's crucial role in the development of the Dublin Society, and also as a fictive representation of much of his concerns as expressed in his practical and pragmatic utopian documents written in relation to the Dublin Society's survival and future.

Chapter 7, 'Conclusion: Some Vague Utopia', looks at the legacy of eighteenth-century Irish utopianism and the way in which it coalesced in subsequent nineteenth-century and twentieth-century utopian visions. It moves from utopian satire to writings on politics and utilitarianism, to the nascent cooperative movement and to utopian communal experiments scattered throughout the country.

Overall, I consider eighteenth-century Irish utopianism through its diverse manifestations in literature, in memoranda and proposals, and in notions of improvement with important links to a wider intellectual and cultural network in Britain, Europe and beyond. Irish utopianism is multifaceted, from the imagined mythic, textual and cartographic provenance of Hy Brasil to manifestations of the Celtic Otherworld and the utopic quality of Tír na nÓg, and to the Dublin Society and its imperative to improve, to practical philanthropy, and to the literary representations of utopian satire and futurism. It is a utopianism that is variously colonial and anti-colonial. It encompasses the writings of well-known and lesser-known Irish writers juxtaposed with the literary and scholarly milieu of Irish speakers at the beginning of the eighteenth century, and their network for disseminating literature and manuscripts throughout the country allied to the utopian ethos of Irish-language scholarship in Dublin. I argue that utopianism in the eighteenth century moves between colonial and anti-colonial viewpoints, from dialogue to satire, from *aisling* to polemic, from visions of a golden age to an imagined Eden far away, between remembrance and futurism, and to discourses of improvement, self-reliance and patriot-ism. The emerging utopianism of the eighteenth century coalesced around both reflections on the past and visions of the future. The 'backward look' (as Frank O'Connor called it in his book of the same name) remained a feature of Irish literature for an extended period. Some writers mourned the passing of a golden age. Meanwhile, others looked forward with clear visions based on societal improvement and on cultural and political progress. This book concludes that the trajectory of the utopian propensity in eighteenth-century Ireland sustained an impressive body of literature and thought, and that prac-tical visions of improvement were firmly in place. Indeed, it must develop further our understanding of the contribution of utopianism to the formation of an identifiably modern society in Ireland.

Defining Utopia

Our understanding of 'Utopia' cannot be reduced to the origins of the word coined by Thomas More in 1516 as the name of the imaginary country he described in his book. It was written in Latin and published as *Libellus vere aureus nec minus salutaris quam festivus de optimo reip[ublicae] statu, deq[ue] noua Insula Vtopia (Concerning the Best State of a Commonwealth and the New Island of Utopia. A truly golden handbook no less beneficial than entertaining)*, and is now known as *Utopia*. The word is based on the Greek *topos*, meaning place or where, and *U* from the prefix 'ou', meaning no or not. More's own use of the word he inaugurated gave rise to definitional difficulties because it was itself from the outset playful. In 'Six Lines on the Island of Utopia', More wrote:

> The ancients called me Utopia or Nowhere because of my isolation. At present, however, I am a rival of Plato's republic, perhaps even a victor over it. The reason is that what he has delineated in words I alone

have exhibited in man and resources and laws of surpassing excellence. Deservedly ought I to be called by the name of Eutopia or Happy Land.[38]

Therefore, the word 'Utopia', which means no place or nowhere, has come to refer to a non-existent good place. 'Utopia' entered other European languages as soon as the book was published in German in 1524, Italian in 1548 and French in 1550. As More was against its translation into English, it was not translated until 1551 by its first English translator Ralph Robynson. In *Utopia*, More's fictitious character Raphael Hythloday (Hythlodaeus in More's Latin) reports on the newly discovered island commonwealth of Utopia somewhere off the coast of South America. The imaginary, ideally ordered island state was set somewhere in the New World – that is, someplace in that corner of the world then being opened up to colonial trade and conquest. As regards the contemporary impact of *Utopia*, the English poet and biographer William Winstanley (*c.* 1628–98) writes in his *Lives of the Most Famous Poets* (1687) about those who sought to set out and find More's island of Utopia:

> It being the idea of a compleat commonwealth in an imaginary island and that so lively counterfeited, that many at the reading thereof, mistook it for a real Truth: insomuch that many great learned men, as *Budeus*, and *Johannes Paludanus*, upon a fervent zeal, wished that some excellent divines might be sent thither to preach Christ's Gospel: yea, there were here amongst us at home, sundry good Men and learned Divines, very desirous to undertake the Voyage, to bring the people to the Faith of Christ.[39]

Here, then, in its early interpretation, Utopia represented a place, a faraway but possibly real land. Yet in the 500 years since More created the word 'Utopia', one would think that there would be general agreement on its meaning. This is not the case, and we should not expect that a single definition will suit all times and places. While More coined the word, the idea already had a long and complex history. Utopias have been uncovered that were written well before More. As the use of the word developed and expanded, new words were created to describe different types of Utopias, such as 'dystopia', meaning bad place, which as far as I know was first used by Henry Lewis Younge (b. 1694) in his *Utopia: or, Apollo's golden days*, printed in Dublin in 1747. The word Utopia inaugurated a genre of literature, and the writers who wrote within that genre experimented and pushed the boundaries, and in so doing expanded the parameters of the genre and the meaning of the word. For example, Jonathan Swift's 1726 *Travels Into Several Remote Nations of the World* (familiarly known as *Gulliver's Travels*) clearly belongs to the genre but also looks very different from More's *Utopia*. As a result, the word Gulliveriana was created to describe this subgenre. Moreover, around the same time that Swift was writing, Daniel Defoe published *The Life and Strange Surprizing Adventures of Robinson Crusoe, of York, Mariner* (1719), now known as *Robinson Crusoe*. *Robinson Crusoe* gave rise to a large subgenre, the Robinsonade, which is often utopian and most often includes a group of people being shipwrecked, the best known being *The Swiss Family Robinson* (1812–13) by the Swiss writer Johann David Wyss. Subsequently, in 1872 Samuel Butler published *Erewhon*, which also belongs in the genre while very different from More's *Utopia*. The word Erewhonian was invented to describe this subgenre. While More's word came to describe a literary genre of utopian literature, it also developed into a way of thinking that Lyman Tower Sargent calls utopianism. As he observes:

> Utopianism refers to the dreams and nightmares that concern the ways in which groups of people arrange their lives and which usually envision a radically different society from the one in which the dreamers live. And utopianism, unlike much social theory, focuses on everyday life as well as matters concerned with economic, political, and social questions.[40]

Utopia and utopianism are often conflated. For example, descriptions of ideal cities or what might be called architectural Utopias have long been correctly considered as part of utopianism, but generally they may not have been considered as part of the literary genre. As with most topics, there are definitional challenges, and one point of confusion arises from the failure to make the distinction between utopianism as a general category and Utopia as a literary genre. In his seminal introductory essay in the field of utopian studies, 'The Three Faces of Utopianism Revisited',[41] Sargent has also proffered a noteworthy description of Utopia. It is the

> story of the men and women who dreamed of a better life for all of us and of those who tried to create that better life. It is also the story of those who had differing dreams and conflicts among them. And it is the story of the fainthearted who were afraid to dream … and feared the dreams of others.[42]

Sargent describes utopianism as 'social dreaming', which includes 'the dreams and nightmares that concern the ways in which groups of people arrange their lives and which usually envision a radically different society than the one in which the dreamers live'.[43] Sargent's use of the term 'social dreaming' is widely accepted as a broad general statement of the phenomenon of utopianism. In this respect, social dreaming may be understood as being comprehensive enough to reflect the expanse of utopian thinking and focused enough to avoid rendering the term meaningless. Within these broad categories, Sargent has identified what he calls 'the three faces of utopianism' – that is, the three principal directions of utopianism: the literary Utopia, utopian practice – which includes utopian communities, utopian experiments or practical Utopias, now generally called intentional communities – and utopian social theory. As Sargent puts it, there are specific definitions of the categories of utopian literature: Utopia, eutopia, dystopia, utopian satire, anti-Utopia, critical Utopia, critical dystopia, flawed Utopia, and intentional community. Sargent's most recent definitions are as follows:

> Utopia: a non-existent society described in considerable detail and normally located in time and space. In standard usage, Utopia is used both as defined here and as an equivalent for eutopia.
>
> Eutopia or positive Utopia: a non-existent society described in considerable detail and normally located in a time and space that the author intended a contemporaneous reader to view as considerably better than the society in which that reader lived.
>
> Dystopia, or negative Utopia: a non-existent society described in considerable detail and normally located in a time and space that the author intended a contemporaneous reader to view as considerably worse than the society in which that reader lived.
>
> Utopian satire: a non-existent society described in considerable detail and normally located in a time and space that the author intended a contemporaneous reader to view as a criticism of utopianism or of some particular eutopia.
>
> Anti-Utopia: a non-existent society described in considerable detail and normally located in a time and space that the author intended a contemporaneous reader to view as a criticism of utopianism or of some particular eutopia.
>
> Critical Utopia: a non-existent society described in considerable detail and normally located in a time and space that the author intended

a contemporaneous reader to view as better than contemporary society but with difficult problems that the described society may or may not be able to solve. This perspective takes a critical view of the utopian genre.

Critical dystopia: a non-existent society described in considerable detail and normally located in a time and space that the author intended a contemporaneous reader to view as worse than contemporary society but which normally includes at least one eutopian enclave or holds out hope that the dystopia can be overcome and replaced with a eutopia.

Flawed Utopia: works that present what appears to be a good society until the reader learns of some flaw that raises questions about the basis for its claim to be a good society, or which even turns it into a dystopia. The flawed Utopia tends to invade territory occupied by the dystopia, the anti-Utopia and the critical Utopia and dystopia. The flawed Utopia is a subtype that can exist within any of these subgenres.

Intentional community: a group of five or more adults and their children, if any, who come from more than one nuclear family and who have chosen to live together to enhance their shared values or for some other mutually agreed upon purpose. The term appears to have been first used in the 1940s.

While over twenty words or phrases have been used to characterise intentional communities, such as utopian community, utopian experiment, practical Utopia, alternative society and experimental community, it is Sargent's position that intentional community is the best of these terms because, as he puts it, 'it specifies the fewest preconditions and has no political or other prescriptive content'.[44] Furthermore, Timothy Miller's definition of intentional community includes the following:

1. The group in question must be gathered on the basis of some kind of purpose or vision, and see itself as set apart from mainstream society to some degree. Intentional communities are not simply group living situations; they are group living situations that have specific purposes and offer alternatives to societal business as usual …

2. The group must live together on property that has some kind of clear physical commonality to it …

3. The group must have some kind of financial or material sharing, some kind of economic commonality …
4. The group must have a membership of at least five adults, not all of whom are related by blood or marriage, who have chosen voluntarily to join in common cause.[45]

Philip Gove in his annotated bibliography *The Imaginary Voyage in Prose Fiction* provides an overview of a series of articles by James T. Presley from the 1870s that attempted to answer a question on 'information about works similar to More's *Utopia*'.[46] Over a four-year period, Presley produced a list of ninety-seven, as well as an introductory classification system, which I quote in full:

1. 'Utopias' proper; works which describe an ideal state of society, according to the notions which the author may entertain of what political and social conditions it is probable or desirable that the human race should hereafter attain to.
2. Those which satirize, under feigned names, the manners, customs, pursuits, and follies of the age or nation in which the writer lives.
3. Those which pretend to give a somewhat reasonable account of the possible or probable future state of society or course of historical events, either near at hand or in remote ages.
4. Those which, merely for the sake of amusement, or sometimes for the purpose of travestying the wonderful adventures related by actual travellers in remote regions, profess to recount travels or adventures in imaginary countries or inaccessible worlds, in which generally the most extravagant fancy runs riot.[47]

While Presley's categorisation emphasises the broad range of utopian works, the early twentieth-century scholar of utopian studies Joyce Oramel Hertzler defined Utopias by identifying a 'distinctive characteristic' of More's Utopia, saying, 'More depicted a perfect, and perhaps unrealizable, society, located in nowhere, purged of the shortcomings, the wastes, and the confusion of our time and living in perfect adjustment, full of happiness and contentment.'[48] Hertzler's *The History of Utopian Thought*, published in 1923, was one of the first studies to use the term in its title. J. Max Patrick also based his definition on More, noting that

a utopia conforms to certain basic features of More's Libellus, which gave the genre its name. A utopia should describe in a variety of aspects and with some consistency an imaginary state or society which is regarded as better, in some respects at least, than the one in which its author lives. He does not ordinarily claim that the fictitious society and its people are perfect in all respects and that he is propounding a total ideal or model to strive toward or imitate; most utopias are presented not as models of unrealistic perfection but as alternatives to the familiar, as norms by which to judge existing societies, as exercises in extrapolation to discover the social and other implications of realizing certain theories, principles and projects.[49]

Both Hertzler's and Patrick's definitions differ in one significant way: Hertzler's Utopias are perfect and Patrick's are not. At this point, we are faced with a challenge over the nature of Utopia. Patrick is correct and Hertzler is mistaken: More's Utopia does not describe a perfect society. In English, 'perfect' means complete beyond practical or theoretical improvement, entirely without any flaws, defects or shortcomings. More's Utopia does not fit that definition. Indeed, it is arguable that More, as a good Christian, could not imagine a 'perfect' society; the base and sinful nature of humanity would preclude that. There are very few Utopias in the corpus that could to some extent be described as 'perfect', and most of those present some version of Heaven. That said, most Utopias are located in time and space so as to provide verisimilitude. For example, More's *Utopia* and the early post-More Utopias were located in faraway, unknown, undiscovered countries. Later Utopias were located in the future or were located on the moon or on distant planets.

The flaw in the ostensibly perfect has deep roots in utopianism. Aristophanes (*c.* 450–*c.* 388 BC) presents the argument in his play *Ecclesiazusæ* (391 BC; translated as 'Assembly Women' or 'Women in Parliament'), where a group of women take over the legislative assembly in Athens and put in place a form of communistic society. Their programme fails not because it is bad but because Athenians are not capable of the required altruism. Aristophanes had a similar theme in *Plutus* (388 BC), where the blind god of wealth is given sight, after which he redistributes wealth to the deserving. However, it rapidly fails and is redistributed again inequitably. Given the centrality of Christianity in the Western utopian tradition, it is not surprising that the desire to achieve perfection in this life is often presented as failure. Medieval Christianity, generally reflecting the position of St Augustine (AD 354–430), contends that life in this world is predicated on the Fall and sin. Consequently, the possibility of major social improvement was limited, and much medieval utopianism was openly heretical.[50] No Christian could believe that perfection in this life was attainable before the Second Coming or the millennium. Writers and thinkers continued to develop and portray utopian imagery, but it had to be located *elsewhere*, such as in the rediscovered Garden of Eden, the legends of Atlantis, the Islands of the Blest, Hy Brasil or St Brendan's Isle.

The earliest modern example of a flawed Utopia by an Irish writer is Oliver Goldsmith's (1728–74) *Asem the Man-hater: or vindication of the wisdom of providence in the moral government of the world. An Eastern tale* (1759). The subterranean world, the eutopia, full of rational people and without vice, seems dull to Asem, and he chooses to return to his native land to build a better life there rather than remain in eutopia, which reveals its flaws to him. J.C. Davis in his classic study *Utopia and the Ideal Society* (1981) defines Utopia as one of five subcategories of the ideal society. As he puts it:

> These types of ideal society are not in practice mutually exclusive, although their premises make them logically inconsistent one with another. The four alternatives to utopia will be called, for convenience, the Land of Cockaygne, arcadia, the perfect moral commonwealth and the millennium. The first two, Cockaygne and arcadia, solve the collective problem by envisaging a drastic change in the supply of sat-isfactions. They differ markedly, however, in their attitude to human appetites.[51]

While the distinction that Davis makes works for the period he reviews (1516–1700), it is often harder to apply them to later Utopias, particularly those of the twentieth and twenty-first centuries. However, Davis offers a succinct appraisal of More's aim in *Utopia* that adroitly connects More with subsequent writers:

> Like so many of the poets, novelists and satirists who came after him, More seems to be saying that we need fiction to see reality afresh: in particular, we need utopian fiction to see the reality of our own society and the costs of putting it right. Inevitably, for a humanist like More, such a project draws on the Platonic 'best state' exercise just as, for its inverse, it draws on the Socratic image of the cave.[52]

Jacqueline Dutton refers to the evolution of Western scholarship as a prelude to changing rules determining the shape of Utopia: 'from a literary genre, it has become a paradigm that can be applied to a wide variety of disciplines and endeavours, including architecture, music, visual arts, politics, philosophy, sociology and even psychology'.[53] Sargent's inclusive reading of utopianism as 'social dreaming' provides a broad general statement of the phenomenon of utopianism that may encompass a wide range of utopian expressions – the spirit of Utopia (Ernst Bloch), the desire for Utopia (Ruth Levitas), critical Utopias and critical dystopias (Tom Moylan), and utopianism (Krishan Kumar). In *The Concept of Utopia*, Ruth Levitas argues that 'utopia is about how we would live and what kind of a world we would live in if we could do just that … utopia is then not just a dream to be enjoyed, but a *vision* to be pursued'.[54] While Sargent encapsulates the visionary, yet contested, quality of utopianism, Levitas highlights the element of agency. She argues that Utopia's function is not solely to express desire but, rather, to enable 'people to work towards an understanding of what is necessary for human fulfilment, a broadening, deepening and raising of aspirations in terms quite different from those of their everyday life'.[55]

Further, in *Marxism and Form*, Fredric Jameson argues that the utopian propensity has become an increasingly self-aware process of knowing and intervening in the world. The utopian process begins with a 'stubborn negation of all that is' and moves to maintain 'the possibility of a world qualitatively distinct' from the one in which we live.[56] Thus, the utopian process is always concerned with humanity's movement towards a horizon, rather than its actual arrival at a predetermined place set by a utopian agenda. Indeed, Jameson regards Utopia as a process: it does not deliver a new reality but rather the imaginative means to envisage new social possibilities. And so, Utopia may prefigure a not yet known or lived reality; utopianism is positive only if it keeps open the possibility of future change. He stresses that most attempts to imagine Utopia reveal its own possibility of existing in the world as it is. He argues that 'utopias have something to do with failure, and tell us more about our limits and weaknesses than they do about perfect societies', but he also stresses the importance of continuing the attempt.[57]

Levitas identifies three aspects of Utopia: content, form and function. These, taken individually or collectively, can combine to provide a definition of Utopia. In the first approach to defining utopian content, the focus is on what constitutes the 'good society'. As a general definition, this is beset with difficulties due to the diversity of opinions about what constitutes a desirable state and how it is to be attained and maintained. The second way of defining Utopia in terms of form centres on Utopia as a literary genre – particularly as prose narrative, which More's *Utopia* inaugurated. The primary feature of this genre is its analysis of the good society, often through the trope of a fictional journey to another place or time, with the narrative being composed like a tour. The visitor is thus guided around the places of the new society before returning home to tell what he or she has observed and learned. The visitor's experiences may also be woven through a utopian narrative to reveal aspects of the society's laws, social relations and organisation. However, defining Utopia solely as a literary form is too restrictive, for as Tom Moylan argues, 'it does not account for the entire range of utopian manifestations'.[58] While content and form are of undoubted significance in our understanding, function represents for Levitas the best basis for an adequate definition. The focus here is on what Utopia is for and how it works for particular purposes. Levitas' discussion centres on whether Utopia enables or negates social change, and how it does this. Utopias might be seen as ideals that lead change in a particular way, or they may be viewed as fantastical, escapist or compensatory, drawing attention away from the negative state of existing social or political conditions. As Levitas posits, neither content, form or function can in themselves provide an adequately stable means for defining Utopia, as they vary. While each has important elements, individually they are limited and unable to account for the complexity of utopian thought and changes in its historical and geographical manifestations.

Levitas, drawing on a term used by commentators on William Morris, identifies 'the education of desire' as the central issue that defines Utopia.[59] Thus, desire moves beyond the limitations of facets of the present, seeking spaces and worlds that are qualitatively different from what already exists. Such desire can take many different forms, and have differing content and functions. Rather than searching for a sole definition based on one of these categories, a more inclusive approach harnesses them and recognises how they may change and interconnect. Within this framework, Levitas offers a definition of Utopia that 'recognises the common factor of the expression of desire. Utopia is the expression of the desire for a better way of being.'[60] Fátima Vieira finds that 'utopia is a programme for change and for a gradual betterment of the present';[61] in this way it functions as a means towards 'political, economic, social, moral and pedagogical reorientation'.[62] Meanwhile, Marie Louise Berneri views the word Utopia as 'synonymous with a happy, desirable form of society. Utopia, in this respect, represents mankind's dream of happiness, its secret longing for the Golden Age, or, as others saw it, for its lost paradise.'[63] In his essay 'Remembering the Future', Vincent Geoghegan uses the term 'utopianism' in a broader sense to describe 'the human need and capacity to create a desirable environment; a conscious and unconscious rearranging of reality, usually involving an imagined future'.[64]

'In the strictest sense of the word, utopia came into being at the beginning of the sixteenth century'; thus Roland Schaer begins his introductory essay in *Utopia: the search for the ideal society in the Western world*.[65] While Schaer emphasises the history of Utopia as beginning with More, Sargent has presented Utopia in a broader sense, and traces the presence of utopianism throughout history. So More had set a pattern for subsequent utopian narratives in presenting it as a report from a traveller, Raphael Hythloday (who had just returned from the island of King Utopus), who functions as the intermediary between the reader's familiar world and the new realm of possibilities offered by the dawning of the global world. As an adviser to his king, More was, not unlike his contemporary in Florence, Niccolò Machiavelli (1469–1527), one of a generation of thinkers who effectively were creating modern political theory. More, concerned about the injustices of his day, opened up political analysis by way of the popular literary form of the travel narrative reporting on the nature of society in those imagined other worlds across the seas. Thus, More imbues travel writing with a political purpose. Although influenced by Plato's *Republic*, More's use of the framing device of the travel narrative allowed him to speculate on utopian alternatives that resonated with the imagined community of England, and by portraying the work as a 'simple' fantasy, a fictive narrative, he was protected (at least for a while) from censure by the Crown.

More's Utopians are 'shrouded in ambiguity', which nearly 500 years of analysis and interpretation has failed to dispel.[66] Ambiguity is central to More's text, as much criticism has recognised. So Swift's likening of his own Houyhnhnms and Yahoos in *Gulliver's Travels* to those Utopians of More is essentially an ironic aside, as Chlöe Houston maintains, 'to remind us that ambiguity and irony have always been a feature of the utopian mode of discourse'.[67] Moreover, many Utopias are, as Sargent points out,

> like a photograph or a glimpse of a functioning society at a moment in time containing what the author perceives to be better and designed to break through the barriers of the present and encourage people to want change and work for it.[68]

The utopian mode of discourse found in the literary Utopia has been addressed by, among others, Darko Suvin and Kenneth M. Roemer. They provide definitional frameworks on one of Sargent's 'three faces', the literary Utopia. For Suvin:

> Utopia is the verbal construction of a particular quasi-human community where sociopolitical institutions, norms, and individual relationships are organised according to a more perfect principle than in the author's community, this construction being based on estrangement arising out of an alternative historical hypothesis.[69]

Sometimes, then, the literary Utopia offers an 'alternative location radically different in respect of socio-political conditions from the author's historical environment'.[70] For Suvin, 'utopias are verbal artifacts before they are anything else'.[71] Even so, Moylan points out that, as a *literary* artefact, 'it is not a static picture of perfection but rather a dynamic representation of human relations in motion, not perfect but better than what can be found in the author's world'.[72] From Suvin's perspective, the focus of Utopia lies in encouraging new ways of thinking about human society or to inspire those who are oppressed to resist. Suvin has called this form of thinking 'estrangement' (as it comes from the Russian formalist Viktor Shklovsky and the German Marxist Bertolt Brecht), and he draws on Brecht's description to advance his point: 'A representation which estranges is one which allows us to recognize its subject, but at the same time makes it seem unfamiliar.'[73] Suvin's work on literary form presented estrangement as a fundamental aspect of both science fiction and Utopia, and he highlighted the bond between these two literary forms. For him, science fiction is 'a literary genre whose necessary and sufficient conditions are the presence and interaction of estrangement and cognition and whose main formal device is an imaginative framework alternative to the author's empirical involvement'.[74] As Lucy Sargisson remarks with respect to the term more generally, 'estrangement' contains a number of cognate terms, each related to distance and difference:

> The modern word 'estrangement' combines the old French *estranger* (modern equivalent: *étranger*) and the Latin *extraneare*. Etymologically, then, estrangement evokes the stranger and the extraneous, the unknown and the outside.[75]

Within utopian studies, estrangement is used according to Suvin's definition.

At a most basic level, Utopias need a certain estrangement. Fictional Utopias, for example, are set apart and distanced from the present. As Geoghegan writes:

> The classical utopia anticipates and criticises. Its alternative fundamentally interrogates the present, piercing through existing societies' defensive mechanism – common sense realism, positivism, and scientism. Its unabashed and flagrant otherness gives it a power which is lacking in other analytical devices. By playing fast and loose with time and space, logic and morality, and by thinking the unthinkable, a utopia asks the most awkward, most embarrassing questions.[76]

Here, then, is estrangement. From its no-place, the '*ou*' of Utopia, Utopia recounts a story. Distanced from reality, the utopian visions thus imagined are potent because they are estranged. Roemer defines the literary Utopia as:

> A fairly detailed narrative description of an imaginary culture – a fiction that invites readers to experience vicariously an alternative reality that critiques theirs by opening intellectual and emotional spaces that encourage readers to perceive the realities and potentialities of their cultures in new ways. If the author and/or readers perceive the imaginary culture as being significantly better than their 'present' reality, then the work is a literary eutopia (or more commonly, a utopia); is significantly worse, it is a dystopia.[77]

Again, by way of definition and contextualisation, Northrop Frye views the Utopia as a '*speculative* myth; it is designed to contain or provide a vision for one's social ideas'.[78] As Frye observes, 'the utopian writer looks at his own society first and tries to see what, for his purposes, its significant elements are. The utopia itself shows what society would be like if those elements were fully developed.'[79] Frank and Fritzie Manuel have noted that 'every utopia, rooted as it is in time and place, is bound to reproduce the stage scenery of its particular world as well as its preoccupation with contemporary social problems'.[80] However, as Sargent argues:

> Since writers of utopias keep inventing new forms for the presentation of their ideas, any definition must have somewhat porous boundaries, and contemporary utopias do not all look like what we previously

called a utopia. In particular, they are more complex, less certain of their proposals, and intended for flawed humanity.[81]

And Barbara Goodwin observes:

> Defining Utopias is difficult in the best of circumstances. The field is politically charged and contested: liberals, conservatives, socialists, and utopians of all stripes propound definitions to fit their agenda; scholars approach utopias from different academic disciplines as well as political perspectives; and utopias have changed (in form, content, and function) in response to an ever-changing world.[82]

All of these definitions bring us back to the tendency to conflate Utopia and utopianism. To what extent does a work have to resemble More's *Utopia* to be considered a Utopia? What is the essence of a Utopia? To me, there are three central aspects of a literary Utopia, all of which must be there. First, the society described must not exist; second, the author must in some way evaluate that society; third, the literary Utopia should encourage and activate new ways of thinking about the author's own society. Utopias as a literary genre are multifaceted, and the shape of the literary Utopia as a paradigm can be applied to a wide variety of disciplines. In other words, Utopias are fluid and many are inescapably political. As J.C. Davis and Miquel A. Ramiro Avilés put it:

> They begin with a sense of unease or dissatisfaction with existing political, economic, social, legal and welfare arrangements and a need to imagine a political order that can maintain a radically improved society. This means they must deal with issues of partisan advantage and conflict. They must re-order the relationships between minorities and the majority and between the weak and the strong.[83]

Though this book aspires to provide a broadly comprehensive overview of the emergence and existence of utopianism in eighteenth-century Ireland, the picture it paints is essentially connected to these definitions and arguments.

CHAPTER 2

Utopian Geographies

My wistful eyes can see, looming, floating in the Sapphire
empyrean, that green Hy Brasil of my dreams and memories ...
John Mitchel, *Jail Journal*[1]

My visions, like
frozen and famished ships,
Break from the ice of winters long,
And spy far off on the ocean's rim
The peaks of I Bhreasail purple and dim!
Daniel Corkery, *I Bhreasail: a book of lyrics*[2]

Utopia in the form of a desire for a better future has been a marked feature of early Irish literature, with its Celtic Otherworld and Christian Heaven. This utopian anticipation can be understood as the production of hopeful visions of a better society. Such hopeful visions are articulated through texts and social practices. They can take many forms. In the Irish context, mostly, although not exclusively, they are presented through the literary realm of the utopian novel and poetry; in the political realm through songs, manifestos, speeches and through eighteenth-century improving societies; and in the lived tradition of nineteenth-century communal enterprises and the early twentieth-century development of the national cooperative movement. It is not surprising that such a utopian propensity exists in a variety of forms and milieux. Thus, architecture, songs, visual images, proclamations, speeches and policies exist alongside the many instances of lived utopianism, from religious and secular communities to political movements. It has also been a consistent aspect of Irish-language literature, most notably poetry, since the seventeenth century, when the Gaelic order collapsed under the weight of the Tudor conquest. This collapse marked the growing ascendancy of English power and the loss of Irish sovereignty, with its related political, cultural and linguistic implications. The sermon, the political pamphlet, the speech from the dock, the manifesto, the rhetorical denunciation: these are among the literary modes of the lived utopian culture in context.

Utopian longing, while evident in much Irish seventeenth-century poetry, reaches its apex in the development of a new genre in the literature, the *aisling*, or vision poetry, of the eighteenth century. The word *aisling* means vision; and as Daniel Corkery argues in *The Hidden Ireland*, 'the vision the poet always sees is the spirit of Ireland as a majestic and radiant maiden'.[3] Before the *aisling* became recognised as a distinct genre, there were vision poems in the Irish language, and in many of them the self-same spirit of Ireland appears and utters her distress and her hopes. The use of the word in its newer technical sense may date from Aodhagán Ó Rathaille (*c.* 1675–1729) (and exemplified in his poem, simply titled 'An Aisling'), who first makes the vision the *spéirbhean* (literally, sky-woman) bewail the exile of the Pretender: it was Ó Rathaille who connected the *aisling* type of poem with the Jacobite cause. In the *aisling*, the poet's emotion is represented by displacement. The poet falls asleep and a beautiful maiden, the *spéirbhean*, usually identified directly or indirectly as Ireland, appears to him and tells of her suffering and the major changes that have taken place in her fortunes. She will be cured with the return and restoration of her lover, identified as the Stuart king.

The eighteenth-century political *aisling* is a recasting of a motif that has a long history in Irish literature. Traditionally, in early Gaelic society the Irish chieftains are portrayed as being the spouses of their land, and the spirit of the kingdom is invariably female. With the demise of the native Irish nobility in the seventeenth century, the plight of Ireland became personified in the womenfolk: the wives, mothers and sisters who were left behind. The sorrow of these individual women awaiting the return of their husbands and lovers became fused in the emergent eighteenth-century *aisling*, where a sorrowful Ireland looks abroad for the return of her rightful leaders whilst suffering greatly at the hands of strangers who were controlling her country in their absence. The awaited Irish rulers were generally those of the native stock who had departed at the beginning of the seventeenth century. Following on from this, the poetry ends in despair, paralleling the attendant dislocation and dispossession suffered by the poets and their patrons, or promises a return to the former state, which will be restored on the return of the prince. As Joseph McMinn has noted, the *aisling* is 'an unusual combination of the political, the religious and the erotic', which includes 'religious allegory, in the form of a miraculous apparition of female beauty, and directs the longing towards the political hope of the Pretender's restoration'.[4] The utopian impulse in this poetry manifests itself, in Breandán Ó Buachalla's formulation, as a form of millennialism:

> The prophetic message foretold the return of the natural order: the rightful king on his throne, the native aristocracy restored to their ancestral lands, the Catholic Church re-established, the rehabilitation of the native intelligentsia. But the restoration of the rightful king was not a goal in itself, it was the mechanism by which more universal changes would be brought about and from which would flow the realisation of the millennial dream ... In Irish political literature, as in other cultures, millennialism constituted the main structure of meaning through which the contemporary events were linked to an exalted image of an ideal world; it provided a set of images in which people could express both individual and collective needs.[5]

Ó Buachalla's succinct connection of the exalted image of an ideal world provides a store of images for both individual and collective modes of expression. It connects to the utopian propensity of the *aisling* tradition, and the utopianism manifested through this tradition harkens towards such an ideal world. Such individual and collective needs occur and recur in *aislingí*, centred on nostalgia, on remembrance. Nostalgia – from the Greek *algos* (meaning suffering) and *nostos* (home) – as originally defined and diagnosed in the seventeenth century, was a highly distinctive expression of longing: a painful desire to return home.[6] Nostalgia came to define the sad mood originating from the desire to return to one's native land. Such longing was certain to find its way into seventeenth and eighteenth-century Irish-language poetry given the dislocations occasioned by colonialism, for 'going home' for Gaelic poets and their patrons, having been dispossessed and dislocated, would mean an ending of the processes of colonialism. Even so, while the *aisling* was the primary genre of Irish Jacobite verse, it could also be an aesthetic object in itself, not merely the means to an assumed end. This, perhaps, is captured by Sean O'Faolain in his account of a visit to Killarney in 1940. He combined the link between the 'real' landscape and the stimulus it provides to the individual imagination receptive to composing an *aisling*. As he phrases it, in the early morning light

Killarney reveals itself in a form of transfiguration, and it was most often at such an hour of early morning that the old poets suffered the dreams, apparitions, or ecstasies which formed an entire separate class of Gaelic poetry, known as *Aislingé*, or, *Visions*, poems whose theme is always the same.[7]

Writing on the *aisling* tradition, Corkery observes that the *aislingí* were the popular songs of the period, so they were part of the oral tradition. While in Kerry, about two miles from Dingle during the summer of 1915, he records:

I heard an old illiterate woman break suddenly into one of them, changing, however, not without a twinkle in her eye, a word here, a name there, to make the poem fit in with the fortunes of the Great War in its early phase.[8]

And so, Corkery captures the pliable mode of the *aisling*. As a distinct part of the oral tradition, it may be subverted and recast, as in Corkery's anecdote, as a commentary on the emerging dystopian narrative then unfolding through the First World War. In many respects, the *aisling*, the journey to Hy Brasil (also O'Brazeel, O-Brazile or Hy-Brazil), a Celtic Elysium with its medieval origins in St Brendan's immram *Navigatio Brendani* and the inspirational quality of the Celtic Otherworld as expressed in the mythology of Tír na nÓg (The Land of Youth), are central to an understanding of the Irish eighteenth-century utopian imagining.[9] Perhaps the best-known example of the latter is the Irish-language poem *Laoi Oisín ar Tír na nÓg* [*The Lay of Oisín in the Land of Youth*] composed by Micheál Coimín (*c*. 1688–1760) (his surname anglicised as Comyn or Cummin), an Anglo-Irish Protestant landowner and a native of County Clare. It is called *Laoi Oisín* partly because Oisín is the hero of the story and partly because he is also presented as the narrator. It is written in the language of one of the better-educated Munster poets of the middle of the eighteenth century, who drew on the older legend and traditions the story embodied. It became so associated with the poet that it is sometimes known as 'Comyn's Lay'. The date of the poem may be given approximately as 1750.[10] It is likely that Coimín would have been familiar with the utopian visions of the classical writers of Greek and Roman mythology and the many permutations of the Elysian Fields and the Islands of the Blest.[11]

For more than a hundred years this poem existed only in manuscript, copies of which would have passed from hand to hand, and in this way and also by widespread oral transmission it spread to the neighbouring counties of Kerry, Galway and Mayo, to all the western counties of Ireland, and even, it is generally thought, to western Scotland. The poem was not printed until 1859 due to the difficulties in getting work in the Irish language published. It was first published for the Irish Ossianic Society, with an introduction by Brian O'Looney. Other versions were published down through the years. Coimín's poem was ultimately the major textual source of Yeats' 'The Wanderings of Oisín', a long, dramatic lyric in three parts, which was published in 1889. However, during the course of the hundred years of its unprinted existence, circulated in manuscripts and by oral recitation, the poem could not fail to be altered, added to and adjusted. Some of the versions known orally in the counties of Galway and Mayo, for instance, differ greatly from the first printed edition.

The story in outline is this. One day, Finn and his Fenians are hunting around Loch Lein, one of the lakes of Killarney. The beautiful landscape is described (as translated from Irish):

> It was a summer's morn and a mist hung o'er
> The winding shore of sweet Loch Lein,
> Where fragrant trees perfume the breeze
> And birds e'er please with a joyous strain.[12]

In a moment of transfiguration reminiscent of O'Faolain's words on Killarney quoted above, a beautiful maiden – Niamh – suddenly appears, astride a white steed and coming apparently from the sea:

> Her milk-white steed was of worth untold
> Nor bridle of gold did the charger lack –
> A saddle all covered with purple and gold
> Lay bright to behold on the steed's proud back.[13]

She speaks to Finn, and tells him that she has travelled from the Land of Youth. She has heard of the fame of his son Oisín, and declares her love for him, and wants him to go with her to Tír na nÓg, and in a clearly utopian mode, Niamh recounts the delights of the distant Land of Youth. It is a place of abundance, filled with music and undreamt-of stores of gold, and where endless life, beauty and strength abound. It is the

Delightful land beyond all dreams!
Beyond what seems to thee most fair –
Rich fruits abound the bright year round
And flowers are found of hues most rare.[14]

Oisín consents to go to Tír na nÓg, and their journey begins. In lines that
bring to mind John Winthrop's (1588–1649) statement that the Puritans came
to the New World to build a 'citty upon a hill', Oisín on his own journey to a
'new world' recounts that 'we saw in our path strange sights, Cities on heights
and castles fair' (ll. 193–4).[15] Upon reaching the Land of Youth, Oisín finds an
ideal place, where he lives for a long time until he yearns to visit Erin again.
Niamh consents to let him go, warning him not to dismount from his horse
when he returns to Erin, as he will never be able to come back to the Land
of Youth. Oisín, upon returning to Erin, is amazed to find that he has been
away for three hundred years, and he is grieved to find that his father Finn
and the Fenians are no more. He resolves to return to the Land of Youth. In
an attempt to help some workmen move a stone and perhaps to show his
great strength, he is thrown from his horse, and after falling to the ground
becomes a blind, old man and mortal once more. He is fated never to see the
Land of Youth again.

In its representation of the Celtic Otherworld, there is both a utopian
and a Christian element. It is an eighteenth-century description of the old
Irish Elysium, known by diverse names, the oldest of which appears to have
been Magh Meall (Pleasant Plain), another being Tír na mBeo (Land of the
Living). In the nineteenth century this Irish Elysium became a theme for songs
and poems. In the Celtic Otherworld, Tír na nÓg represented the distant
ideal land of the ever-young. While Hy Brasil became a Celtic version of the
Atlantis myth, it was also depicted as an earthly paradise of eternal happiness.
In particular, redolent of Utopia, Tír na nÓg and Hy Brasil are frequently
seen as imaginative projections of a new place or state. Like More's island,
this place is sealed off from the present, lying in another space and time as the
embodiment of a social and political ideal. Thus, the ambiguity of the word
is maintained as it refers to a better place that is nowhere or is elusive in the
present-known world.

As a genre of utopian imaging of the Celtic Otherworld, the transforming
voyage to, and topos of, Hy Brasil occurs and recurs in Irish utopianism. Swift
would most likely have adapted the tradition of Hy Brasil in his *Gulliver's
Travels* (1726), as it is in the tradition of imaginary travel and shipwreck. In

his earlier work *A Tale of a Tub* (1704), Swift writes of a 'great' philosopher of 'O.Brazile' who had devised a nostrum to assist the composition in one small portable volume of a universal system 'of all Things that are to be Known, or Believed, or Imagined, or Practised in Life'.[16] It is not surprising that almost everyone is familiar with the legend of Atlantis, the paradise that was said to have been overwhelmed by the sea during a violent seismic disturbance. Although Mediterranean in origin, the legend of Atlantis has similar themes in Celtic folklore. The most famous of these is Hy Brasil, a physical embodiment of the Celtic Otherworld.

Belief in Hy Brasil lay deep in the popular culture of people along the Irish coast. It existed as a terra incognita. It was generally thought of as a submarine island or a phantom island shrouded in fog. But once every seven years the veil of fog would lift, and an enchanted sunken island with mountains, verdant pastures filled with sheep, and gleaming cities would all rise to become visible. It became variously Tír fé Thoinn (The Submarine Country), Má Meala (Plain of Honey) and Tír na mBuadha (Land of Talents). It became, as Thomas J. Westropp (1860–1922) writes, quoting lines written by Sir David Wilson in his *The Lost Atlantis* (1892), 'an imaginary island of Brazil that flitted about the maps of the fourteenth and fifteenth centuries with ever-varying site and proportion, till it vanished'. It was not a reef or a shoal but a mist or mirage 'sprung from the sea without root'.[17] Moreover, Walter B. Scaife, writing in 1890 on Brasil as a geographical appellation, recounts:

> This name seems to have something of the will-o'-the-wisp character; for on various maps it may be seen designating a great Antarctic continent, extending to the South Pole, or a small island near the arctic circle; or it may be as far west as the southern part of South America or as far east as the vicinity of the coast of Ireland.[18]

Following on from this, Scaife notes that the form of the name 'is almost as various as the positions in which it is found'.[19] He lists thirteen variations: Brasilia, Bresilia, Prislia, Prisilli, Brasielie, Brazili, Brasil, Brassil, Brazil, Brazill, Brazile, Presillg and Brasi.[20] Because of the many different locations in which Hy Brasil (Brasil Island) appears and the many variations of its name, it is relevant to try and uncover their varying locations. These Brasil Islands seem to lie in four different parts of the Atlantic. The most southerly of these is in the Azores, roughly in latitude 37°N. There is one located west of Brittany, one west of Ireland, and one east of Newfoundland.[21] My focus is on the

Irish Brasil Island as it is the basis of the literary references and writings of Richard Head, Manus O'Donnel and others who are at the centre of this study. Even so, two questions remain as to why the medieval geographers and mapmakers placed an island off the west coast of Ireland where there is none, and why they gave it this name. While mapping out new territories, geographers and makers of nautical charts called 'portolan charts' sought to achieve as much accuracy as possible. The portolan charts were mainly based on coastal features such as headlands, bays, river mouths, ports and adjacent islands. The focus was on cartographic accuracy as the charts were to be put to practical use. Where possible, the charts included aspects of older maps based on first-hand observation and on information from returning mariners and seafarers. As the circles of world trade and cultural exchange began to expand northwards to include northern Europe and the British islands, the need for portolan charts expanded. However, for Ireland – lying on the margins of the ancient world and unconquered by the Romans – older maps did not exist. There is no map of Ireland known from earlier than 1489.[22] Because the west was both unknown and an area of mystery, both geography and lore aligned. The interweaving of the practical mapping of real places and the mapping of imaginary places grew apace. As Barbara Freitag puts it:

> Thus, beside actual discoveries we also find islands of a mythical nature in the Atlantic: the *Elysian Fields*, the *Isles of the Blest*, the *Fortunate Islands*, *Thule*, *Ogygia*, the *Garden of the Hesperides*, *Atlantis* are some of the names given to them. It would appear that the basis for a firm belief in islands lying to the west and north of Europe was bequeathed to the Mediterranean mapmakers by these ancient tales and fables.[23]

Jason Pearl speaks of a 'utopian geography' that is 'an imaginative projection undergirded by actual – though vague spatial coordinates'.[24] And so those early cartographers and geographers opened up a distinctly utopian imaginary. They contributed a new space (a *novum*) to the imaginative landscape that assisted the creation of the very earliest literary references to Hy Brasil. Ptolemy, the Greek astronomer of the second century, provided the earliest geographical data for Ireland. He believed that the seas were full of islands, and he is reputed to have assigned 25,000 of them to the Atlantic Ocean.[25] From the fourteenth century Hy Brasil appears on several European maps. So far as we know, it first appeared on a map attributed to Angellinus Dalorto of Genoa, made in the year 1325. It appears as a disc of land of considerable girth set in the Atlantic Ocean in the latitude of southern Ireland. It disappeared from cartographic records in 1865. Interestingly, Freitag suggests that our understanding of the existence of Hy Brasil could benefit from pursuing a different line of enquiry. We could consider the possibility that in the not-too-distant past there *was* an island there: Hy Brasil/Brasil Island. It did exist, but has since sunk beneath the surface of the waves.[26] Over the centuries, many gentlemen have been recorded as spending their family fortunes in pursuit of the phantom island. Hence in the early fifteenth century Sir Thomas Arundell of Filley, 'having injured his fortune by a wild adventure in attempting to discover an imaginary island called Old Brazil, on the coast of America, sold his manor and barton, and removed to the parish of Sithney'.[27] While Arundell sought his imaginary island off the coast of America, Sir Richard Buckley of Anglesey is reported to have fruitlessly undertaken the discovery of the island 'not far from the North West part of Ireland and by then called O'Brazile' 'by twice manning out a vessel of his own, from Beaumaris'.[28]

Westropp recounts Roderic O'Flaherty's (1629–1718) story of one Morough Ley, who in August 1668 was at Irrosainhagh, to the north of Galway bay. He was carried off by two strangers to O Brasil for two days, and then returned to Seapoint, near Galway, hoodwinked. He had been given a medical book that was not to be opened for seven years. After the seven years had passed, he opened the book and realised that he had the ability to treat many different kinds of human ailments even though he had not received any medical training.[29] W.G. Wood-Martin, writing in *Traces of the Elder Faiths of Ireland*, also mentions the medical treatise:

> A curious MS on medical subjects in the Royal Irish Academy, traditionally believed to have been originally obtained by a native of Connemara, transported by supernatural means to the enchanted isle of Hy Brasil, where he received full instructions with regard to all diseases, their treatment and cure, and was presented, on leaving, with the MS to guide him in his medical practice.[30]

Westropp says that he had personally seen the island three times, the last sighting having occurred during the summer of 1872:

> It was a clear evening, with a fine golden sunset, when, just as the sun went down, a dark island suddenly appeared far out to sea, but not on the horizon. It had two hills, one wooded; between these, from a low

plain, rose towers and curls of smoke. My mother, brother, Ralph Hugh
Westropp, and several friends saw it at the same time; one person cried
that he could see New York![31]

Westropp is extremely credulous about the actual existence of Hy Brasil, and
also of Morough Ley's account of his visit to it, which in many ways seems the
antithesis of the trope of Hy Brasil as an imaginary projection. As viewed by
W.G. Wood-Martin, there was a place somewhere in the Western [Atlantic]
Ocean that was called by many different names: it was 'one of the Elysiums
of the Primitive Ireland, as well as of classic writers'.[32] This Elysium appears
to have corresponded in Wood-Martin's opinion to 'the Land of the Saints
of early Irish Christianity, where the souls of the blessed await the Day of
Judgement'.[33] Within the traditions of pagan peoples, the departing point
from this world and ingress to the next lay to the west. In the mythological
legend of Condla Rua, the hero sets out in a pearl-encrusted currach and
travels on the immense ocean until he disappears in the glow of the great white
sun on its journey westward to the Islands of the Blest. One of the earliest
literary references to Hy Brasil is in a work by the English playwright James
Shirley. He moved to Dublin from London in 1636, leaving a city where
plague had forced the theatres to close. His friend John Ogilby had already
decamped to Dublin, and a new theatre – the first public theatre in Ireland
– had just opened in Werburgh Street (the opening of a theatre in Dublin
may have been seen by Shirley as an opportunity to find an audience). Shirley
penned three plays for the theatre during his time in Dublin. However, life
did not go as well as he had expected. Although his plays were successful, the
audiences were smaller than he had hoped for. He returned to London in
1640, before the Werburgh Street theatre was closed down and the company
of actors dispersed as a result of the rising of 1641. Two years after his move
to Dublin, Shirley ruefully remarked that he had still not found the city or
its inhabitants – those witty theatre-going ladies and gentlemen he had heard
tell of in London. This is the focus of Shirley's writing in the prologue he
composed for Thomas Middleton's play *No Wit, No Help Like a Woman's*:

> IIe tell you what a Poet sayes, two yeare
> He has liv'd in *Dublin*, yet he knows not where
> To finde the city: he observ'd each gate,
> It could not run through them, they are too strait:
> When he did live in England, he heard say,

> That here were men lov'd wit, and a good play;
> That here were Gentlemen, and Lords; a few
> Were bold to say, there were some Ladies too:
> This he beleev'd, and though they are not found
> Above, who knows what may be under ground:
> But they doe not appeare, and missing these,
> He says he'll not believe your chronicles
> Hereafter, nor the maps, since all this while
> *Dublin's* invisible, and not *Brasile*.[34]

In the last two lines, Shirley seems to suggest that in striving to find Dublin he was unsuccessful. Dublin is a will-o'-the-wisp to a very real Brasile. Subsequently, a book entitled *Poor Robin's Vision* was published anonymously in 1677. It is now generally attributed to William Winstanley, whose nom de plume was Poor Robin. In this book Hy Brasil is portrayed as a fool's paradise. The author comments that 'many are brought into a Fools Paradice [*sic*], by gladly believing there is no such place at all; or that it stands upon fairy-ground, or is that Inchanted Island, the imaginary O Brazeel'.[35]

In 1663, just five years before Morough Ley's account, Richard Head (*c.* 1637–86) began his eclectic literary contributions both to utopian drama and to the lore of Hy Brasil. While little is known about Head's life, William Winstanley in his *Lives of the Most Famous English Poets* (1687) and Head's own narrator Meriton Latroon in his picaresque narrative *The English Rogue* (1665) provide some details. Winstanley recounts that Head was born in Ireland, the son of an English-born Church of Ireland clergyman. His father was killed in the rebellion of 1641, whereupon both William and his mother moved to England. He spent some time in the University of Oxford, where it is thought his father had formerly been a student. According to Calhoun Winton in his essay 'Richard Head and Origins of the Picaresque in England', Head's father may have been an Oxonian, as there was a John Head, BA of New Inn Hall registered in 1628.[36] An inveterate gambler, Head fell into financial difficulties and became an apprentice to a Latin bookseller in London, attaining a good proficiency in that trade. After marrying, he returned to Ireland, where he composed his drama *Hic et Ubique: or, the humours of Dublin*. Winstanley records that it was 'a noted comedy; and which gained him a general esteem for the worth thereof'.[37] Winstanley also notes that Head dedicated *Hic et Ubique* to the then Duke of Monmouth in the hope of his becoming his patron and supporter. When this did not happen, Head returned to London and took a house in Queen's-Head Alley, near Pater-Noster Row. He continued his trade as a bookseller, but his money reportedly 'went out by handfuls, as it came in piece by piece'.[38] He took up his pen again and wrote *The English Rogue*. Indeed, Head had much of the rogue in him, and his putative narrator Meriton Latroon gives details of his own life that mirror Head's. Latroon states that he was born in Ireland of English parents, and that four years after his birth the rebellion began, so unexpectedly 'that we were forced to flee in the night; the light of our flaming houses, reckes of hay, and stacks of corn, guided us out of the town, and our fears soon conveyed us to the mountains'.[39]

While Latroon's and Head's autobiographical details converge on these points, any further reading of extensive resemblances between Head and his fictive creation Latroon can be rightly viewed as conjecture. Winstanley provides us with the only extant account of a meeting with Head. He records that he met Head after the first part of *The English Rogue* was published. They met 'at Three Cup Tavern in Holborn, drinking over a glass of Rhenish'.[40] Moreover, Winstanley notes that in the midst of such sociability, he composed a verse that reads as a paean to Head's *English Rogue*:

> What Gusman, Buscon, Francion, Rablais writ,
> I once applauded for most excellent Wit;
> But reading thee, and thy rich Fancies shore,
> I now condemn what I admir'd before.
> Henceforth translations pack away, be gone,
> No Rogue so well-writ as the English one.[41]

Winstanley's verse links Head's work from its first appearance with the European picaresque tradition, and foregrounds the complex interactions between contemporaneous picaresque fictions. Subsequently, Head's three texts on Hy Brasil came to foreground the complex interactions and interpretations around that phantom island and its chroniclers.

Head's comedy *Hic et Ubique: or, the humours of Dublin* was privately performed in 1663.[42] *Hic et Ubique* presents Dublin as a utopian space for English émigrés, a neutral space, superior to London. However, Head satirises this English fantasy with reminders of 'present' actual Dublin – what Christopher Wheatley terms 'a crowded landscape peopled with inconvenient relics of a messy history who decline to be written out of the story'.[43] And so the émigrés are required to adapt and begin the tenuous movement from 'nationless utopia toward an Irish identity'.[44] Phantastick, one of the English immigrants in Dublin in *Hic et Ubique*, tries to impress Mrs Hopewell:

> I liv'd in *Utopia* three months, where no English Man before durst
> venture, the Dukes only daughter taking notice of my super-excellent
> qualifications, as likewise the exact simetrical [*sic*] proportion of my
> body, fell so deeply in love with me, that I was necessitated to satisfie
> her desires, to save her life. And to save mine (the *Duke* being informed
> of what was done) there being no shipping in the harbour, I was fain
> to put to sea in a Wash-bowl, and the only sayl I had, was the fore part
> of my shirt.[45]

The fantasy is multilayered, but the core illusion is Phantastick's attractiveness
to women. Hic et Ubique (the name of a character) chastises Phantastick's
sailing outfit with a typical double entendre: 'A yard I grant him. But what did
a do for want of a mast[?]'[46] Thus, the utopian fantasy is denigrated as unattainable because of impotence, which Wheatley argues 'figuratively suggests
the inability of utopian dreamers to achieve completion'.[47] Yet in Dublin,
at least in the beginning, Phantastick lives in Utopia. Questioned about
this by another character, Contriver, he responds: 'The Duke of *Utopia* lives
not merrier than us; we eat, drink, and sleep, without the least care; for our
hearts are so continually oil'd by good liquor, that they are antidoted against
sorrow.'[48] Elsewhere, Head portrays London itself as a financially impoverished
dystopia in comparison to the perceived utopian space of Dublin:

Phantastick	First then, Houses and Shops are so dear in *London*, that some Shopkeepers are forc'd to sell their wares in the Country.
Hic	I believe so, and their wearing-cloaths too.
Phantastick	The Mercers and Booksellers are deeply in law about the fee-simple of *Ludgate*, O 'tis disputable which shall carry it. As for Newgate that's to be let.[49]

Head, as we have noted, was a gambler, and having become bankrupt moved
to Dublin. Essentially, he is satirising the English adventurers who think
Dublin is likely to be better than London, despite the realisation of the very
real 'present' Dublin. Utopia, if not discovered, can be created. The character
Contriver is a projector, a speculator who views Ireland as fertile ground for
get-rich-quick schemes:

The bogs lie near the Mountains, which will afford me earth enough to dam'em up: but first IIe lay a foundation of hurdles, such as *Dublin* is built on, to support the Masse of Earth. So it shall be; tis as clear as a Mathematical Demonstration. The benefit that will redound hereby, will be triple. First a vast quantity of unprofitable Acres made arable, next a discovery (it may be) of gold and silver Mines, which the barrennesse of the Mountains demonstrate: and lastly metamorphosing a mountainous into a Champian Countrey [*sic*]. Here's the worst on't, I shall loose [*sic*] my name by't. The King will confer on me little lesse than the Title of Duke of *Mountain*, Earl of *Monah*, or Lord *Drein-Bog*.[50]

Thus, Contriver's improvements require the erasure of the known landscape, creating a renovated Ireland. His entirely fictitious paper scheme leads to his being conferred with ridiculous titles. While Ireland is an unlikely place to achieve wealth, the mythically utopian space is replete with the opposing forces of Catholic and Protestant, settler and native, of the feudal and the mercantile, which serve to problematise the utopian space. In a movement from the emerging, less than utopian space of Dublin, Contriver expands his utopian projection: 'This very day did I find in an old Map, *O Brazeel* with its height.'[51] Such commentary anticipates Head's subsequent satirising of English adventurers who in their search for the unattainable O Brazeel instead reach Montecapernia, the 'mountain of goats' which represents Ireland in his *The Western Wonder: or, O Brazeel* (1674).[52] Head and his companions set off for the utopic island visible off the west coast of England. Head is in this account searching for an island revealed to him in a dream, which, in a style prefiguring the later genre of the *aisling* or vision poem, occurs when he

> fell asleep in a Summers afternoon, and dream'd I saw an Eagle unnaturally great, soaring in the Air; whilst I was wondring at his greatness, he immediately stoopt, and took me up within his talons, and flew away with me with incredible celerity over mountains and valleys, and at length brought me to the sea-side: where having rested a little while, he took me up again, and carried me to an island; and having set me down, vanished.[53]

He finds himself in a place of abundance full of 'all the delicates Nature is capable to produce, which are too many here to enumerate. The verdant Fields, and pleasant Groves, were not to be parallel'd; but no sign where any

Corn was sown: whatever grew, came up spontaneously without the labour of the hands.'[54] Having seen this 'paradise',[55] his guide tells him that the isle 'was under the power of the Prince of the Air, and had been so for many years; but the time is near at hand and it shall be so no longer'.[56] Head is filled with wonder, and as his guide vanishes, the former eagle returns to him and once more scoops him up in his talons. He brings him back to his habitation, and then Head awakes. He ponders on his dream and decides it must be O Brazeel he had seen and he was its discoverer. He informs a friend of his experience, and he agrees to provide a vessel of some thirty tons so that they can set out together to find the island of O Brazeel.

They set sail on 9 October 1672. At sea for days, their ship springs a leak and they take to a lifeboat, and on a dismal night wander the sea until they see a light towards which they row. They are rescued by the crew of a larger ship, which quickly becomes shipwrecked on Montecapernia. Head recounts it is divided into two parts, South and North, and 'there is so great a difference in the manners and language of both places; the South understanding the North, for the most part, as little as the English do the Cornish'.[57] Though the natives are pleasant, 'it is a thousand pities the People are so sloathful [*sic*], being given to no manner of Industry, Husbandry, or any other useful improvement'.[58] Religion is also addressed, and the lack of it, or at least of Protestantism, causes Head to see this as the root of the natives' vices. As he phrases it, 'Many notorious Vices are among them, which they look upon to be things of another complexion; and this I believe proceeds from their ignorance in Religion.'[59] It is, as Wheatley has noted, the presence of Irish Catholics in the landscape that distinguished the real from the utopian, the real Montecapernia from the utopic and ultimately unattainable Hy Brasil. Head's disenchantment with the inhabitants of Montecapernia ultimately evokes a colonial register: in seeking the island of Hy Brasil and finding Montecapernia, he shows that the phantasmal island is reflected solely through the purview of his own colonial gaze. The presence of the Irish distinguishes Montecapernia from O Brazeel, the real from the utopic. As Michael Griffin argues, 'The difference between Montecapernia and O Brazeel is essentially the difference between Ireland real and Ireland ideal, as Head sees it.'[60]

The subtitle of Head's *O-Brazile, or the Inchanted Island* (1675) is, interestingly, *A perfect relation of the late discovery and wonderful dis-inchantment of an island on the north of Ireland: with an account of the riches and commodities thereof communicated by a letter from London-Derry, to a friend in London.* William Hamilton of Londonderry relates how, in 1674, a Captain John

Nisbet of Killybegs, County Donegal had filled several vessels with butter, tallow and hides, and sailed to France. On the return trip his vessels were laden with French wines. When near the coast of Ireland, just as the sun was rising, he happened upon the coast of a phantom island filled with cattle and horses. They explored the island, and with night approaching they built a fire to ward off the cold, and this action drew out the inhabitants. They had been shut up in a castle through the diabolical and demonic powers of a great necromancer who had cursed the island. But the spell of enchantment had been broken by the fire, so they were free from imprisonment, and the island would forever be more visible. Captain Nisbet and his crew sailed back to Killybegs with gold and silver that they were given to spread the news of their remarkable discovery of O'Brazile, an O'Brazile ultimately attained and liberated. In 1724 a pamphlet entitled *The History of the Inchanted-Island of O'Brazile* was published. It proffered an account of a visit to O'Brazile, including a description of the island, its inhabitants, its history and customs. The influence of both Henry Neville's *Isle of Pines* and Richard Head's *O-Brazile* is apparent. Notably, this is the first Hy Brasil publication to have been published in Dublin, not London. The story claims to be an eyewitness account by a mariner by the name of William Hogg on board a ship that sailed from Londonderry, on the north coast of Ireland, to Boston, New England. On the return journey to Ireland in 1717, about twenty leagues off the coast of Galway, the mariners saw a land they had never seen before. After they went ashore, they found themselves on O'Brazile, where they remained for the next seven years.

Meanwhile, the editor of Manus O'Donnel's *A Voyage to O'Brazeel* (1752), a submarine island, asserts that the work is a 'literal translation of an old *Irish* manuscript, which came accidentaly into my hands: I found the story both improving and surprising, and therefore concluded that I would do my country an acceptable Service in translating it.'[61] This is a familiar device in eighteenth-century literature. The idea of an impartial editor translating a late sixteenth or early seventeenth-century Irish-language manuscript adds a semblance of truth or the appearance of access to what could be called the Irish language's secret treasures. As the editor is unable to date the text, he conjectures that it was written sometime during Queen Elizabeth's reign, when 'the Reformation was in its infancy'[62] O'Donnel's voyage is pseudonymously anthologised in the *Ulster Miscellany*, a 386-page anthology of prose, verse and drama published without identifying the editor, authors, publisher or place of publication in 1753.[63] Michael Griffin and Breandán MacSuibhne have noted that the *Miscellany* is a 'mixed political bag of mid-eighteenth-century

Patriotism. The contributors are loyal to the constitution in church and state.'[64] O'Brazeel is depicted as bathed in a miraculous submarine light, with its domed roof of water repelled by oaks that must be kept constantly burning. It is, as the editor notes, a version of Milton's 'cave within the Mouth of God'[65] from Book 6 of *Paradise Lost*, 'where light and darkness in perpetual round/Lodge and dislodge by turns, which makes through Heaven/Grateful Vicissitude, like day and night'.[66]

The O'Donnels' adventures in O'Brazeel began one morning during the reign of Elizabeth. Bryan O'Donnel, owner of a considerable farm at Cloughaneely in north-west County Donegal, went for a walk by the seashore. When he did not return, his family sent a servant to look for him. The servant returned having found no trace of him. They believed that he had fallen into the sea, while some local lore concluded that he had been carried away by the fairies. A month after his father's disappearance, Manus O'Donnel was walking by the sea and was 'surprised to see my father coming towards me with a cheerful countenance'.[67] They walked together until they came to a boat at anchor. His father said they would go out to sea as he had something to show him. He asked Manus to fetch fire, and Manus ran to a cabin and got some burnt turf, which he brought to the boat. They rowed out to sea, and Bryan said he would sink the boat. He bored a hole in the bottom of the boat and the water came rushing in. Then he kindled the oak stick, which burned like a candle. Although the boat was sinking, no water came in over the sides. Instead, it stood like a wall on each side, and formed an arch over their heads like a vault. They went deeper and came to a place of magnificent light. When they reached an appropriate depth, Bryan began to sail the boat with the stick. When he held it at the head of the boat, the water fled from it and receded towards the stern, and so pushed the boat into the vacuum ahead of it. Soon they reached an open sea, although they were still under water, which arched over the submarine sea like a canopy. Then, in the distance, Manus saw an island, the island of O'Brazeel. On reaching the 'most delicious country',[68] they came ashore and walked to a farmer's house. The farmer greeted them, and treated them to two glasses of excellent liquor and a genteel dinner. Bryan explained that Manus was his son and that he himself was the stranger who had been at the governor's house the previous month. Bryan explained that the governor had allowed him to bring his son to the island, and the farmer then accompanied them to the governor's house, where they were greeted with a warm welcome. Manus thought that he was in 'fairyland, and nothing but inchantments round me'.[69]

The governor arrived and told them the story of the island: how it came to be a submarine island and how they could repel water from the sinking island by burning oak. In the evening the governor detailed the laws, religion and governance of the island. As the governor spoke about religion, he said to the O'Donnels, 'You saw our public worship, it is pure and simple.'[70] Bryan O'Donnel replied, 'I think you stripped religion too bare; it looked naked wanting those ornaments and dress which all Christians use.'[71] The governor responded that they had not stripped it but preserved it as they had found it. He noted, 'The Church came out of the hand of Christ and his apostles, as our first parents did out of the hands of their creator naked and innocent.'[72] The governor stated that they had no use for dress or ornament, and that they are very careful in religious matters to guard against anything that can lead to superstition or idolatry. They do not use these things unless they see a possibility of their doing good, which he said – as a direct comment to the Catholic O'Donnels – 'is not the case of these vestments, signs and ceremonies which are used amongst you'.[73] After some more discussion, the governor gave them a document, *A Summary of the Christian Faith*, which they were allowed to take with them when they left. They wanted to stay, but the governor insisted that they go to where they could do most good. Upon leaving, Bryan O'Donnel said to the governor that 'he and the rest of the inhabitants of O'Brazeel, should always claim his love and gratitude'.[74] They left, and returning home by the same way they came, they soon reached the Irish shore. Upon his return to Ireland, Manus O'Donnel noted: 'I thought our case like that of Adam and Eve when they were forced to leave their paradise. However, I took up this firm resolution, that I would always strive to come up to the same perfection and virtue that was so visible among these excellent people.'[75] In O'Brazeel, the Catholic O'Donnels uncover a submarine Protestant colony, and in so doing reveal their anti-colonial stance, a stance also maintained by Manus O'Donnel from the beginning, where he noted 'we have too many instances of the cruel barbarity of conquerors in our times, who have laid waste whole countries, destroying the bodies of the inhabitants'.[76]

As Sargent argues, utopianism was an important part of the process of colonisation.[77] As depicted, O'Brazeel is a Protestant settler colony, and in a link with Sargent's analysis is an example of the situation he describes in which 'most settlers wanted to improve their own lives and some had a specific utopian vision in mind'.[78] As such, O'Brazeel, as depicted in *A Voyage*, is a place of plenitude that has been bestowed upon the inhabitants because of their pure and simple faith. The island's origin myth began when the apostle

Matthew was preaching among the Britons and Irish. His companion was Joseph, surnamed Justus. When they were in the county of Donegal, they crossed over to the island of O'Brazeel, which, as the governor mentioned, 'at that time lay off the western coast of that county about seven or eight leagues, as may be yet seen in some of your old maps of Ireland'.[79] When Matthew left the island of O'Brazeel, Justus remained behind to be teacher and pastor to the people. And as he said, 'by this man's preaching and practice, the whole island were so firmly rooted and grounded in the love of God and virtue, that their lives and properties were nothing in comparison to their hopes of a happy futurity'.[80] The island became known as the island of saints. At that time the island was very poor and many of the inhabitants were 'obliged to go over into *Ireland* for work and the necessities of life'.[81] As a result, they became tainted with the vices of the mainland, and so began to 'fall off from that purity and strictness of life, which they had hitherto preserved pure and unsullied'.[82] Such corruption was destroying the island, so the heads of the families decided to pray publicly to the Almighty three times a week 'that he sink their island, and themselves into the ocean, rather than suffer their virtue to be defaced with the corruption of the Irish vices'.[83]

One day, as they came out of church where they had been praying, they saw a man on horseback coming towards them. He carried with him a large wallet or bag containing a great quantity of acorns. He told them that their wish would be granted if they could ensure that they would first divide the lands of the island equally among the families, and the mountain in the middle of the island would be held in common by all and would be known as Mount Horeb. All this was to be done within eight days, during which several of the inhabitants, tainted by sin, left the island due to their lack of faith. On the eighth day the horseman returned and the acorns had grown into large stately oaks. He asked them to cut down as many of the oaks as would kindle four large fires on the side of Mount Horeb above the woods, at equal distance. Fires were also to be kindled in their homes of the same timber. It was revealed that the island would not be fixed to the solid earth but would float on the surface of the water like a heavy log of timber. He asked them to dig a deep hole of a considerable breadth in the bottom of a pond. They did this until they pierced through to the sea underneath, and as water rushed through, the island began to sink.

As the island descended, the water, instead of running in upon the land, formed a glorious vault, or arch, over their heads, and the island sank to its present depth. It was underwater and cut off from the vices and luxury of the terrestrial world. The soil of the island, which had been unsuited to self-sufficiency, was transformed into a better quality and was to be blessed and receive all the beauty of the primitive world. At this point the horseman dissolved into a diffusive light, then this light came to perpetually adorn the 'happy island'.[84] According to Griffin and MacSuibhne, this outcome 'accords to a utopian trope of millennial deliverance'.[85] The light of the prophet that still graces the island is, according to O'Brazeel's governor, 'like that which accompanied the Israelites in the wilderness; it illuminates us, but is obscure darkness to others'.[86]

The land thus blessed, the people must remain industrious in order to maintain the providential gift. Each couple was obliged to provide for their own retirement after their eldest child inherited the land at the age of thirty, thereby assuring continuity. No man may marry before he is thirty years of age, or any woman before she reaches twenty-five. In a family, only one sibling is allowed to possess land, and another gets a portion; this relates merely to the two eldest children, who are therefore to be called proprietors, having a fortune either in land or money, although the land always goes to the male child if the two eldest are of different sexes. Only a certain class, either land-owning or moneyed, may marry. All others, belonging to a class known as 'younkers', are sent to become tradesmen, seamen, monks, teachers or public servants.

A Voyage's primary concern is the prospect of people of different religions living together in one state. The O'Donnels are reluctant to leave, and Manus O'Donnel's opening words in *A Voyage* shows that their journey to the Christian paradise of the saints – a paradise that had been almost lost but was regained – evoked a desire to ensure that it was protected from unwanted colonisation, as in his opening lines: 'tho' I am going to give the world an account of a most delicious country, and a happy people, it is not with a view of stirring up any enterprising prince or general to go and conquer it'.[87] According to Donald S. Johnson, O'Brazeel was 'the garden of the Hesperides, west of Ireland, where the sadness of life could be escaped'.[88] Johnson also judges it the site where 'Christian writers created from this pagan island a land of truth for those of the Faith', and to them O'Brazeel was variously a Land of the Promise of the Blessed, an earthly paradise or a faraway Eden.[89] In the context of *A Voyage*, it is possible that it is the result of early patriot attempts to configure the connections between the Catholic/natives and Protestant/settlers through the narrative of Gaelic history and literature. While Richard Head's O'Brazeel works are political rather than religious allegories, and are culturally and politically Anglocentric, *A Voyage* adheres to the Gaelic narratives of O'Brazeel.

In 1752, in Newport, Rhode Island, an eight-page chapbook was published entitled *Old Ireland's Misery at an End. Or, the English Empire in the Brazils restored.* The same work was also published that year in Boston, Massachusetts. It tells how three fishermen – Thomas White, John Brown and William Cunningham – met an enchanted lady in the shape of a mermaid on 5 June 1752 on a sandbank in the harbour of Lougres on the west coast of Donegal. The story recounts how White, Brown and Cunningham had been sailing in a small fishing boat when they saw the mermaid in a distressed state. When they asked her the reason for her sadness, she answered that it was not them that she wanted, but the minister of the parish, a Revd John Smith. She said that she would give him a full account of her misery and of her place of abode. The fishermen went ashore and called to the minister's house. When he heard their account, he mounted his horse and accompanied them to the seashore, where they saw the mermaid sitting on a sea bank. The minister asked what is was that she wanted. She said that she was the only daughter of the Prince of Lebennon (Lebanon), in earlier times Pliston (Palestine) or the Holy Land, and a member of the half tribe of Monnasses (also rendered Mannasseh). The Holy Land had been hidden from all people because of her own tribe's wickedness 730 years earlier (AD 822). A quarter of the tribe had been turned into mermaids, and another part was located 'in the Brazils covered in the Sea by the Hand of the Lord',[90] but for seven hours in every seven years, she recounted, the island is without water. However, all will be changed in twenty months' time: a north wind will rise that will clear the island of water permanently, and 'then we will all return to the Land of Jerusalem, and no water will ever cover the island any more, and People out of most parts of the Earth will inhabit it, which will cause great War between the Christian Kings and Princes'.[91] After giving this account, the mermaid gave details of an enchanted kingdom so often seen by mariners off the Irish coast, 'lying in 47 degrees 13 min. North Latitude'.[92] She described its climate, soil, fountains, groves, orchards and castles, but particularly the 'famous city of *South Castle*, which for beauty far surpasses any City in Europe or the known World' and the 'Palace of Phoebus, 300 Miles farther North from South Castle, whose glorious Appearance exceeds all other Palaces'.[93] The mermaid then made some prophecies: there would be some bloody battles and contests about the election of kings, but the *English* Crown would prevail: 'the New Ireland' would be subject to an English government and 'old Ireland' would be relieved from all taxes and duties, and 'all those People that have of late gone to *America*, will return and live in the famous and plentiful Country. And they will come from the farthest part of the World, and the World will be united into one Religion and serve one God.'[94] John Smith, the minister, here intervened and asked her if the castles and cities would stand as they had before, after the cataclysm associated with the re-emergence of the island in January 1754. She replied that they would still stand and that they would be inhabited by Christians. She also prophesised that on 15 August – apparently meaning August 1752 – several parts of the island would be visible from the shore and people would run from all parts to see it, but a great gust of wind would suddenly smother it and it would not be seen again until 'the Day that it shall be recovered, and shall no more disappear'. She then gave a description of a most horrid, bloody, tyrannical war that is coming among the Christian Kings and Princes. It would be so cruel that men would lament to see so many thousands die. The last tumult and rebellion in Scotland and in some parts of England – the Jacobite rising in support of Bonny Prince Charlie – had not 'wrought fruits of Repentance'; the Almighty would send plagues to punish the disobedient and multitudes would be found dead in the streets.[95] And 'there shall be Wars and Rumours of Wars in all Parts of the World, both by Land and Sea'.[96] As she uttered these last words, there was a 'terrible Noise of Thunder',[97] which she said was a signal for her to return. As she skimmed gently along the surface of the water, she repeated the following lines:

> An inchanted Isle lies close to the *Irish* shore,
> Whose poor inhabitants always sigh and roar,
> In these strange Countries that's seldom seen,
> With thirty-eight Cities which have been,
> Never as yet discovered, but unknown,
> To other Nations, have laid hid alone;
> Not found by foreign sword nor foreign trade,
> Tho' many ships across their Voyage have made,
> But unacquainted live 'till God shall please,
> To manifest his Secrets and show us these;
> When 25 moons are spent it will be found,
> Which surely will enrich the British Crown.
> Many for want of Faith disbelieve these Lines,
> But they'll not doubt when they profit find.[98]

In literary terms, *Old Ireland's Misery* holds less standing than *A Voyage*. Both the Rhode Island and Boston publications were of a mere eight pages and contained many typographical errors. However, there is an interesting interconnection between *A Voyage* and *Old Ireland's Misery*: they are both set in roughly the same geographical location and use the trope of Hy Brasil to achieve albeit different outcomes. *A Voyage* is predicated on colonialism and religion, while *Old Ireland's Misery* aligns Hy Brasil (the Brazils) with the spectre of impending war that will lead to the elimination of residual Jacobite disobedience, after which a brighter world will be revealed. It is thought that the author of *Old Ireland's Misery* was Revd James MacSparran (1693–1757). He was born in Dungiven, County Derry, and after emigrating to America became rector of St Paul's church, near the village of Wickford in Rhode Island. The link to MacSparran as the most likely author of *Old Ireland's Misery* can be made through reference to his 1753 publication *America Dissected*. According to Kerby Miller, writing in *History Ireland*, it is 'considered the first Irish emigrant's guidebook', and MacSparran may have written it to discourage further emigration from Ireland to America.[99] Essentially, it is a cautionary tale exhorting would-be emigrants to remain in their native country. On the title page, MacSparran promised to expose 'the intemperance of the climates ... destructive to human bodies', the 'badness of money; [the] danger from enemies; but, above all, the danger to the souls of the poor people that remove thither, from the multifarious wicked and pestilent heresies that prevail in those parts'. It is unlikely that *America Dissected* discouraged potential emigrants, for, as Miller points out, 'the very conditions that MacSparran condemned in the colonies – their social fluidity and the weakness of royal and ecclesiastical authority – were more likely to attract rather than to repel the dissenters who comprised the great majority of contemporary migrants'.[100]

Set in context, *America Dissected* could be seen as part of MacSparran's many efforts to enlist Irish patronage to help him gain a prominent ecclesiastical position in Ireland, which would allow him to return to his native land. This did not happen, but the theme of *Old Ireland's Misery* does dovetail with *America Dissected* in this respect: the would-be emigrants who refrain from going to America would find themselves in the new Ireland free of taxes and duties. As revealed in *Old Ireland's Misery*, imminent political and military battles will be won by the English Crown, and as MacSparran's title implies, the 'English Empire' will be restored in the Brazils, in the very place where remnants of the mermaid's tribe had been cast. In its entirety it augurs an end to previously troubled connections between Ireland and England. The new

Ireland, while subject to the English Crown, would have certain legislative autonomy, and returning emigrants would find a utopian colony, a mappable space distinct from, yet intersected with, England.

In conclusion, the narratives of Richard Head stand at the interface between late seventeenth and early eighteenth-century utopian writings. He blends picaresque-style travel narrative, imaginative elements, colonial aspirations, stock themes and Irish folklore. In his *Hic et Ubique*, a dramatic comedy, the utopic space of Dublin as envisioned by the English émigrés is in marked contrast to the perceived dystopian space of London. This utopic scene allows the contrasting mores of native and settler, Catholic and Protestant, feudal and mercantile to be played out and allegorised. As Wheatley puts it, 'utopic space allows a vantage point from which neither the traditional interpretation of Ireland as colonised victim, nor the revisionist view of Ireland as simple reflection of the larger European aristocratic society, is excluded; rather, the interplay between the positions is dramatized'.[101] Ultimately, the utopic space of Dublin does not exist: the only utopic space remains the private stage on which it was performed. It was acted privately, not in the realm of a public theatre, licensed by Charles II, but in a private room, ultimately serving to highlight the gaps in the present reality between England and Ireland, and the myriad factors that clutter the would-be Utopia. Head's O'Brazeel texts are political, and they are both culturally and politically Anglocentric. In *The Western Wonder*, he comments on Irish Catholicism, but his views are from a colonial perspective, and are suffused with an uncritical exposition of colonisation. Head's utopianism is indicative of a utopianism of the coloniser. In transplanting Sargent's views on colonisation to seventeenth-century Ireland, Head's O'Brazeel texts could be viewed as literary companions to the process of colonisation.

While Manus O'Donnel's *A Voyage* is closer to the Gaelic narratives of Hy Brazil, both the editor and the O'Donnels affect an anti-colonial stance. O'Brazeel was a paradise that had almost become lost due to the corrupt vices learnt in Ireland, but it was saved, and became if not a paradise lost then for a short time a paradise in abeyance and found again. It is a Protestant colony, but one that its Catholic visitors want to see protected from potential conquerors and preserved as a paradise, an imaginary model of benign social practice. *Old Ireland's Misery* conjoins Ireland and the Brazils. Only after tumult and war is a transformed utopic space attained and ultimately contained with the wider empire. Meanwhile *Laoi Oisín ar Tír na nÓg* represents in a traditional style the fabled Celtic Elysium, as opposed to the other modes of literary composition practised by Coimín's contemporaries, such as *aislingí*, satires, burlesques or occasional poems on contemporary political or local events. And so in a traditional style he evokes the inspirational qualities that converge around 'elsewheres' as evocations of Irish literary utopian expression. *A Dialogue*, discussed in chapter 1, demonstrates the many improving visions of Prior and the Dublin Society, and emphasises the need for practical utopianism against the background of the distressed state of contemporaneous Ireland. *A Dialogue* and *A Voyage*, both published in 1753, combine fundamental aspects of eighteenth-century utopian imagining: first, the discourse of improvement, and, second, the imaginary projection of the voyage to, and the topos of, Hy Brasil as a locus for addressing emergent history in colonial Ireland. All of the works discussed in this chapter were created between 1641 and 1760 – a period during which, as Toby Barnard writes in *The Kingdom of Ireland, 1641–1760*,

> Commentators looked for and found different Irelands: a kingdom, a province, a collection of provinces, congeries of settlements of varying vintages, a near and ancient colony. Depending on the perspective of the viewer, it was portrayed as an unexploited El Dorado, grim Golgotha where the bleached bones of settlers, soldiers and natives attested to the repeated efforts to establish stable English communities, or an Eden forfeited by the transgressions of the occupants. Apprehensions and aspirations were projected into the landscape, so that contradictory descriptions resulted. These Irelands were not all imagined.[102]

Here, then, Barnard foregrounds the disparate and ambiguous perspectives on Ireland, and the themes and threads of eighteenth-century Irish utopianism pivot on the interplay between these 'different Irelands'.

CHAPTER 3

Improving Visions:
The Early Philosophical Societies
and the Dublin Society

Whether, as others have supposed an Atlantis or Utopia, we also may not
suppose an Hyberborean island inhabited by reasonable creatures?
George Berkeley, *The Querist*[1]

George Berkeley, in a clearly utopian mode, asks 'whether, as others have supposed an Atlantis or Utopia, we also may not suppose an Hyberborean island inhabited by reasonable creatures?' His question encapsulates the utopian trajectory of his work. It was posed in *The Querist* (edited by Samuel Madden and first published in 1735), in which Berkeley, in the role of an observer, asked a series of questions on the paradoxes of Irish political, social and economic life.[2] Commenting on Berkeley and *The Querist*, Richard Warburton, one of the founders of the Dublin Society, said 'it is well worth attending to by the Irish nation. He is indeed a great man, and the only visionary that I ever knew that was.'[3] *The Querist* emerged from the same impulse as Berkeley's *Proposal* some ten years earlier for a college to be located in the New World and his plan for 'the City of Bermuda, Metropolis of the Summer Islands'. It was an impulse predicated on a desire for a better life, the improvement of society, and social and economic well-being. Berkeley's utopian impulse moves from his early efforts at improvement in Ireland to the New World, and comes to rest in *The Querist*, as he again aims to improve his own society back home.

Berkeley came to attribute to his Bermuda project all the ennobling characteristics of the earthly paradise as it had been traditionally imagined since

Greco-Roman antiquity. His early intellectual life gives an insight into his latent and later utopianism, a utopianism manifest most notably in his participation in the early Dublin societies. It is interesting to note how Berkeley's practical philanthropy and politics coexist with the philosophical dreams of More and Bacon and with his own vision of Ireland's future and his utopian project set in the New World. Tracking Berkeley's utopianism from Ireland to the New World and back again thus begins in the early years of his life.

Early life and intellectual background

Ireland's most famous philosopher was born in (or near) the town of Kilkenny on 12 March 1685. His early years were spent at Dysart Castle, overlooking the River Nore, near Thomastown, County Kilkenny. Little is known of the early life of his parents; his father was of English descent, from Staffordshire. George Berkeley saw himself as Irish, or what we would now call Anglo-Irish. In 1696 he was enrolled in the Duke of Ormond-founded grammar school, Kilkenny College, then called the Eton of Ireland. It was formerly the school of Jonathan Swift and William Congreve (1670–1729). Berkeley's entry is recorded in the Kilkenny school register: 'George Berkley, Gent: Aged 11 years. Entered the Second Class, July 17: 1696'.[4] In the same year Thomas Prior also became a pupil of the college. Although Prior was some years Berkeley's senior, a friendship developed between the two boys that was destined to last a lifetime. Berkeley remained a pupil for four years; but here, too, we have little information, although we may assume that he showed early signs of ability since he was entered in the second class. We learn from Prior's biographer Desmond Clarke that the boys were taught classics, Hebrew, poetry and oratory.[5] Discipline appears to have been very strict and school rules harshly enforced. Berkeley's youthful promise is noted in one recorded incident from this period. During July 1699 he and some friends explored the nearby cave of Dunmore, and he later wrote a detailed account of the visit and read it in the chapel of Trinity College, Dublin on 11 January 1705. In this essay, while describing the 'formidable darkness that fills the hollows of this capacious cavern',[6] he refers to crystallisation and petrifaction, and to the theories of René Descartes (1596–1650) and John Woodward (1645–1728). The cave of Dunmore has been described by many travellers, but Berkeley's description seems to have been written earlier than any other. The essay can be read as an example of Berkeley's latent utopianism. Herein, he draws on the memory of his visit six years earlier, giving a description of the drops of clear water: 'the noise of these falling drops being made somewhat augmented by the echo of the cave, seem to make an agreeable harmony amidst so profound a silence'.[7] His vivid description of the cave of Dunmore recalled from memory does not at first appear to evoke any element of utopianism. However, midway through the essay he imbibes the utopian, as he notes:

> in short, here you may see whatever you can possibly imagine, whether men, beasts, fishes, fruits, or anything else. Now, though as much be confidently reported and believed of our cave, yet, to speak ingeniously 'tis more than I could find to be true: but, on the contrary, am mightily tempted to think all that curious imagery is chiefly owing to the strength of the imagination; for like as we see the clouds so far comply with the fancy of a child, as to represent to him trees, horses, men, or whatever else he's pleased to think on, so 'tis no difficult matter for men of a strong imagination to fancy the petrified water stamped with the impressions of their own Brain, when in reality it may as well be supposed to resemble one thing as another.[8]

In referring to the strength of the imagination – the dreams or nightmares which foreshadow Berkeley's interpretation and description of the subterranean world of the cave – a utopian spirit emerges. It comes to reside in the liminal and imaginative landscape, as the melancholy vault becomes the metaphorical space out of which the utopian or the dystopian may emerge.[9]

Berkeley's utopianism emerged more fully as his academic life continued. At age fifteen, on 21 March 1700, he was matriculated at Trinity College, Dublin. His official contact with the college lasted until 1724, when he was appointed dean of Londonderry. It was between 1707 and 1713 that his connection with Trinity was at its closest and most productive. The title pages of his three most influential books – published in 1709, 1710 and 1713 – describe him as 'George Berkeley, M.A. Fellow of Trinity College, Dublin'. The provost for nearly all this time was the celebrated Peter Browne, later bishop of Cork and the author of two works much talked of in their day, *The Procedure, Extent, and Limits of the Human Understanding* (1728) and *Divine Analogy* (1733). Berkeley took his BA in 1704. He then remained in the college and seems to have been a member of at least two college societies.

Berkeley's minor mathematical works, *Arithmetica* and *Miscellanea*

Mathematica, are from this period. The latter, published in Latin in 1707, includes his *De Ludo Algebraico*, which sets out his idea for an algebraic board game. Through these mathematical publications, Berkeley may have hoped to strengthen his chances of obtaining a college fellowship. His opportunity came in 1706, when a vacancy arose. Berkeley, as Joseph Stock, his early biographer, records, then 'sustained with honour the very trying examination, which the candidates for that preferment are by statutes required to undergo' and was admitted to fellowship on 9 June 1707.[10]

From 1706 to 1709 Berkeley was working on his immaterialist philosophy, for which he is best known. He coined the term 'subjective idealism' to emphasise his view that matter did not exist, for he regarded it as unknowable. It is arguable that his immaterialist philosophy provided the conceptual framework for the utopian character of his Bermuda project. We can see this work in two private notebooks, which have been preserved and are held by the British Library. They were first published in 1871 by A.C. Fraser, who called them Berkeley's *Commonplace Book of Occasional Metaphysical Thoughts*. They have been re-edited about four times, and are now generally called the *Philosophical Commentaries*. The two notebooks comprise 900 entries or notes, many in the form of questions or pithy sentences, sometimes of an enigmatic nature. The *Commentaries* range over nearly every topic of the three philosophical classics that Berkeley published between 1709 and 1713, although there is much in the *Commentaries* that Berkeley never published. The *Commentaries* allow us to see the influences on Berkeley's thinking. This is relevant in Berkeley's case since his three early works contain few references to the writings of other philosophers. However, it is evident from them that he was inspired by the work of John Locke (1632–1704) and Nicholas Malebranche (1638–1715). Locke's *Essay Concerning Human Understanding* (1690) had, as J.V. Luce has established, been put on the course at Trinity College very soon after its publication in 1690.[11] More than any other book, 'the Philosopher's Bible', as it is sometimes called, assumed the role of authority in matters philosophical. As David Berman puts it, 'without Locke's *Essay* there would hardly have been a Berkeley, Brown, Hutcheson, or Burke; at least, they could not have been the philosophers we know them to be'.[12]

Berkeley's philosophical horizon was not confined to contemporary writers of the seventeenth and early eighteenth centuries. He was also responding to ancient writers, drawing inspiration from Plato, Aristotle and other classic philosophers. While Locke and Malebranche seem to be influences on Berkeley's thought, it is important to see his work in both an international and indigenous context. The international context would include the work of Plato (whom Berkeley is supposed to have called his favourite author), Aristotle and Isaac Newton (1642–1727). The indigenous context includes the local Irish influences on Berkeley's thought: William Molyneux (1656–98), Robert Molesworth (1656–1725) and John Toland (1670–1722).

Berkeley's adjustment in his self-identification has been noted by Thomas Duddy: 'while a student at Trinity College he referred to the Irish as "natives", which indicates that he did not identify with them and did not see himself as Irish in any sense that might confuse him with his unreconstructed neighbours'.[13] But a few years later, in his philosophical notebooks, Berkeley was using phrases such as 'we Irish' and 'we Irish men'. Duddy argues that Berkeley uses these phrases 'as a way of emphatically dissociating himself from the "English" philosophy of Locke'.[14] As Berkeley puts it, 'there are men who say … the wall is not white, the fire is not hot, etc. We Irishmen cannot attain to these truths.'[15] Denis Donoghue has suggested that to Berkeley 'We Irish' 'meant, I think, those men, upper-class Protestants, who had no power and only whatever prestige accrued to them from their talents in philosophy, divinity, law, and natural science'. He notes that such men – 'Molyneux, Archbishop King, Swift, and Berkeley himself – were often provoked into sentiments that could be mistaken for those of modern nationalism'.[16] The 'mistake' may, according to Duddy, have to do with 'the fact that the sentiments in question are *moral* sentiments, and are duly expressed in the language of entitlement, rights, and justice'.[17] Tellingly, Berkeley, in making a case for his own class, as Donoghue argues, is implicitly making a case for all, including the Catholic peasantry.

After Berkeley received his coveted fellowship, he published a short paper, 'Of Infinities', which he read in what appears to have been his philosophical debut to the Dublin Philosophical Society on 19 November 1707. Two months later, on 11 January 1708, he delivered a sermon (his first extant) in the College Chapel on the afterlife. In February 1709 he was made a deacon. In the following year he was ordained. Berkeley was now established in his college career, as a lecturer in Greek, Hebrew and divinity. He was preparing for the publication of his first two major books, *An Essay Towards a New Theory of Vision* (1709) and *A Treatise Concerning the Principles of Human Knowledge* (1710). Neither book, and particularly not the *Principles*, was well received. Berkeley's friend Sir John Percival (1683–1748) wrote to him from London in August 1710:

I did but name the subject matter of your book [the *Principles*] to some ingenious friends of mine and they immediately treated it with ridicule, at the same time refusing to read it … A physician of my acquaintance undertook to describe your person, and argued you must needs be mad, and that you ought to take remedies. A Bishop pitied you that a desire and vanity of starting something new should put you on such an undertaking.[18]

Berkeley's *Passive Obedience* (1712) contains his primary views on moral and political philosophy. His next project was a rewriting of his immaterialist position. He believed that his *Principles* had been rejected partly because of style and presentation, and so he recast the work in the *Three Dialogues Between Hylas and Philonous* (1713). While the *Three Dialogues* are more elegant and accessible, and can almost be read as pure literature, they must give way to the *Principles* as the authoritative statement of his philosophy. The *Principles*, as we have it, is only the first part of a work that was to include at least one and at one time two other parts. Even in the second edition of the *Principles* (1734), the last authorised by Berkeley, 'Part I' is still displayed in the text. Concerning the second part, Berkeley told a correspondent in 1729 that he had 'made considerable progress in it; but the manuscript was lost about fourteen years ago, during my travels in Italy, and I have never had the leisure since to do so disagreeable a thing as writing twice on the same subject'.[19]

Berkeleys' career falls into three phases, each marked by a utopian cause or motivation. In the first phase (1709–13), he developed his immaterialist philosophy, which he hoped would reform philosophy and lead humanity to a radically theistic or spiritualistic view of the world. This phase of philosophical idealism began while he was still a student, and concluded with the publication of the *Three Dialogues* in 1713, when he was twenty-eight years old. The second phase spans the years from 1713 to 1735, the year in which the first part of *The Querist* was published. This phase, the middle period – which includes the time span of his utopian Bermuda project – saw Berkeley in, among other places, London, Oxford, Dublin, Paris, Turin, Naples, Rome, Florence, Boston and Newport, Rhode Island. This was by far the most active period of his life, when he met many of the leading figures of his day and arguably made his most overtly utopian contribution. The third and final phase spans the years 1735 to 1753, his middle and old age, when, among other things, as bishop of Cloyne in east County Cork he promoted a medicine called tar water that he believed would cure or alleviate all physical ailments; this was a phase of medical idealism.

The Dublin Society and its antecedents

In many ways, Berkeley and his ideas epitomise the overall utopian idealist trend in eighteenth-century Irish philosophy. He was joined in this by others, such as Thomas Molyneux and Thomas Prior, during what David Berman calls Ireland's 'one golden age of philosophy'.[20] The context for this utopian trend emerged first in the late seventeenth century through the founding of two philosophical societies in Trinity College, Dublin. It was from this communal approach to the advancement of knowledge that the Dublin philosophical societies were launched between the years 1683 and 1707. The tradition was 'philosophical' in the broad sense of the term as it was understood at that time. The project took the form of meetings once a week for the communication and discussion of papers. This intellectual initiative was continued with the Dublin Society, founded at a meeting in Trinity College on 25 June 1731. This tradition stemmed from Francis Bacon (1561–1626), author of the utopian work *New Atlantis* (1627), which stated his grand design for recalibrating science with utility as its main aim, evoking the ideal of the new union of science and Christianity. The Baconian method called for the systematic collection of data by observation and experiment. The progress of knowledge was a cooperative enterprise in which a range of information could be gathered and discussed by like-minded people with a view to promoting humanity's domination over nature. Knowledge, in short, could be power.

This institutional and intellectual process first began in England, before taking root in Ireland. The Royal Society of London had its beginnings in the English Civil War, which engulfed much of Britain during the mid-seventeenth century. In 1640, two years before the onset of the Civil War, several individuals calling themselves 'natural philosophers' began holding regular meetings in private homes and taverns. These meetings continued in an irregular fashion during the troubled Civil War period, and often centred on Gresham College, in London, to which many of them were connected. By 1658 life under Cromwell's Commonwealth had compelled the natural philosophers to suspend their meetings. Events began to move swiftly in 1660, with the end of the Commonwealth and the restoration of the Stuart monarchs. Meetings resumed, a Society of Philosophers was founded, and in December 1660 it obtained the patronage of King Charles II. Among the first fellows of the society were Christopher Wren, John Wallis, Robert Boyle and Robert Hooke.

The years immediately following 1660 were fruitful. The society in London found formal accommodations at Gresham College, began a library, and in 1665 published its first volume of *Philosophical Transactions*. The Royal Society itself had antecedents in an Oxford Society founded in 1651 and also in London's Gresham College, which dated back to 1596. The founders of the society were conscious of their obligation to the early Continental academies, those scientific societies in Europe which existed long before the foundation of the Royal Society. One of the earliest had been the Accademi dei Lincei, established in Rome in 1601. Perhaps the most important and influential, however, was the Academia del Cimento, which flourished in Florence between 1657 and 1667. In France, too, there had been several scientific groups. From the first entry in the *Journal Book of the Society*, dated 28 November 1660, it is clear that the debt to those early European scientific academies was acknowledged by society members. It was hoped that some way could be found to hold regular meetings in order to debate subjects similar to the manner in other countries, where there were voluntary associations of men in academies for the advancement of all aspects of learning. Of course, despite these wider linkages, the society advanced independently and obtained its second charter from Charles II in April 1663, when it first adopted the title of The Royal Society of London for Improving Natural Knowledge. The English society was unlike some of those on the Continent – which were frequently subsidised by wealthy partrons – in that it was obliged to provide its own finance. The aims of the society, as expressed by Robert Hooke, were:

> To improve the knowledge of naturall things, and all useful arts, manu-factures, mechanick practises, engines, and inventions by experiments (not meddling with divinity …) … To examine all systems, theories, principles, hypotheses, elements, histories, and experiments … prac-tised by any considerable authors ancient or modern. In order to the compiling of a complete system of solid philosophy for explicating all phenomena produced by nature or art.[21]

In this development, we can see the spirit of the new science focused in a capital city and working along with a minority group in the university to produce an important institutional advance. The pattern was to be the same in Ireland, but the formal emergence of an organised Dublin society was delayed upwards of twenty years. The time lag was hardly surprising. Ireland was much poorer and less well organised than England, and the country had suffered very severe disturbance during the Cromwellian period. After the Restoration, though, Dublin began to experience a period of rapid growth, with the city population trebling from about 20,000 to 60,000 during the reign of Charles II.

In 1683 Dublin-born William Molyneux became, in his own words, 'the first promoter' of the Dublin Philosophical Society. Its genesis, however, can be traced to an earlier development: in 1678 Moses Pitt, a London bookseller, launched an ambitious project for an English atlas that he hoped would match the great Dutch atlases of Jansson and Blaeu. The project – to be a complete work of eleven volumes, with all maps and written descriptions of all the countries then known – was submitted to the Royal Society. The scheme was approved, and a committee of seven fellows, headed by Sir Christopher Wren, was appointed to supervise it. The committee was later replaced by a board of directors, of which Hooke was the most active figure, and finally Hooke acted as sole supervisor. Molyneux became one of the original subscribers – one of the few from Ireland – and in 1682 he undertook to gather the Irish material for the atlas. Molyneux wrote to John Flamsteed, the Astronomer Royal, whom he had already visited at the Greenwich Observatory. He asked for the longitude of London and other places, for, as quoted by his biographer J.G. Simms,

> I must let my worthy friend understand that I am set upon writing the descriptive part of Ireland for the atlas and design to give it to Mr Pitt; for the maps I hope to procure those of Sir William's Petty's survey, but his charts want both longitudes and latitudes, which I intend to put to them before they be re-engraved.[22]

Pitt was presumably satisfied with Molyneux's aptitude for the work. A list of sixteen queries was drawn up. They covered a wide variety of subjects: the soil and its products – animal, vegetable and mineral – rivers and lakes, population, towns, trade, history and any curiosities of art or nature or antiquity. The queries were printed up in a leaflet made available through a Dublin bookseller, and may have been sent to a selection of would-be contributors. The answers were to be sent to Molyneux's address in Dublin, and it was stated that some gentlemen in Dublin would meet weekly to examine any material submitted by Molyneux. The meetings were held in Trinity College, and a leading part was taken by then provost Narcissus Marsh, who was himself a subscriber to the English atlas. In May 1682 Marsh wrote to Archbishop Michael Boyle of Armagh, who noted that, as quoted by Theodore Hoppen, 'we are now (a club of us who meet every week in the college) upon the design of giving an account of Ireland to be printed in the new atlas'.[23] Among those Molyneux approached for information were his brother-in-law, Sir William Domville, who gave him a description of Queen's County (Laois), and his cousin, Nicholas Dowdall, who gave an account of County Longford. Molyneux did not confine his inquiries to his own Protestant community but sought out representatives of the other Irish tradition. One of his correspondents was Roderic O'Flaherty (1629–1718), who had studied both classical and bardic learning, and whose family estate in County Galway had been confiscated after Cromwell's victory. O'Flaherty produced a substantial account of west Connacht, which many years later was published under the title *A Chorographical Description of West or h-Iar Connaught, Written A.D. 1684*. In this work, O'Flaherty writes with enthusiasm of his native region, praising its climate and its wealth of natural resources. As mentioned above in chapter 2, O'Flaherty also provides a link to Morough Ley's unexpected voyage to Hy Brasil.

Molyneux drew on accounts gathered from all his correspondents to draft the description of Ireland for the atlas. However, his work was in vain, as the English atlas was brought to a sudden halt after the publication of four volumes covering the northern part of continental Europe. Moses Pitt was arrested for debt in London, and the scheme collapsed with only four of the eleven projected volumes having been published. At this point, Molyneux burned all that he had written. However, he kept the correspondence he had received, hoping that some day the projected atlas would be continued. Molyneux's correspondence with O'Flaherty and his descriptions of west Connacht led to a lasting friendship and to the development in Molyneux of an interest in early Irish history. Molyneux was later to assist in getting O'Flaherty's magnum opus *Ogygia* printed. As Molyneux wrote to his brother:

> I have in my hands and do suddenly intend to send them over the first part of the *Ogygia*. I think, indeed, 'tis not contemptible, and that is enough to be said of anything relating to the profound antiquities of our country, concerning which little has yet been said that would not raise scorn in a reader.[24]

Molyneux, as a student of law in London after he left Trinity in 1675, mentions how already as an undergraduate in Trinity College he had spent most of his time reading the *Philosophical Transactions* of the Royal Society, and the works of Descartes, Bacon and Gassendi. It is therefore hardly surprising that as a young Baconian he would engage in the atlas project with his enthusiasm for natural philosophy. After the ending of the project, Molyneux wrote:

> In the October of 1683 I began to busy myself in forming a society in this city, agreeable to the design of the Royal Society in London. I should not be so vain as to arrogate this to myself, were there not many of the gentlemen at present [1694] listed in that society, who can testify for me, that I was the first promoter of it, and can witness how diligent I was therein. The first I applied to ... was ... Dr St George Ashe, who presently approved of the undertaking, and assisted heartily in the first efforts we made in the work. I first brought together about half a dozen, that met weekly in a private room in a coffee-house ... merely to discourse of philosophy, mathematicks, and other polite literature, as things arose *obiter*, without any settled rules or forms. But our company increasing, we were invited by the Rev. Dr. Huntington, then Provost of the College, to meet in his lodgings; and there we began to form ourselves in January 1684, and took on us the name of the Dublin Society.[25]

Thus, it was while working on collecting material for the atlas that Molyneux began to focus on forming a society in Dublin similar to that of the Royal Society in London. It seems probable that the general work on the atlas, and in particular the weekly meetings to consider progress, suggested to him that this would be a suitable opportunity to establish such a society. He was encouraged by a cordial letter from Dr Plot, secretary of both the Royal Society and the Oxford Society, assuring him that both societies would welcome the establishment of a similar society in Dublin. Molyneux referred to his new society as a Conventio Philosophica, that is, a Philosophical Assembly, employing 'philosophical' to cover the pursuit of knowledge in general. But the assembly soon began to place special emphasis on the new science that it was primarily designed to further. The society engaged in correspondence, particularly with the Royal Society of London. In January 1684 it was recommended that the group be officially known as The Dublin Society for the Improving of Naturall

Knowledge, Mathematicks and Mechanicks. The work of the society went busily ahead, with no less than 159 papers produced in its first period from 1684 to 1687. Considerable attention was devoted to medical topics, and a wide range of scientific problems was investigated. On the technological side, papers were read on topics such as land transport, navigation and ballistics.

The range of the society's interests may be judged from the following examples. In January 1686 George Ashe gave an account of a new solid fuel he had invented, one consisting of a mixture of clay and coal dust. A paper by Narcissus Marsh on acoustics was notable for its coinage of the term 'microphone', which here appears for the first time in scientific literature. In May 1684 a long discussion took place on problems connected with keeping a diary of the weather. Molyneux studied the tides in Dublin Bay, and was in correspondence with the Astronomer Royal in England about the times of high water. He provided a vivid description of his fleet of ships in little models of about one and a half to two feet long. Surveying the operations of the society, it is probable that, as Irvin Ehrenpreis puts it, 'we shall discover a remarkable range of subjects foreshadowing episodes or images in Swift's writing: astronomical researches which anticipate Laputa ... a toy fleet like the one Gulliver would steal from Blefuscu'.[26] As Gulliver in Blefuscu says:

> The *Blefuscudians*, who had not the least Imagination of what I intended, were at first confounded with Astonishment. They had seen me cut the Cables, and thought my Design was only to let the Ships run adrift, or fall foul on each other: but when they perceived the whole Fleet moving in Order, and saw me pulling at the End, they set up such a scream of Grief and Despair, that it is almost impossible to describe or conceive.[27]

Gulliver returns with the fleet to Lilliput, and after three weeks ambassadors from Blefuscu arrive in Lilliput to sue for peace.

All of this varied activity was interrupted in April 1687, the month of James II's Declaration of Indulgence (or the Declaration for the Liberty of Conscience), comprised of two proclamations granting broad religious freedom in England and suspending penal laws enforcing conformity to the Church of England. It allowed persons to worship in their own homes or chapels. The declaration was greatly opposed by Anglicans in England and their Episcopalian counterparts in Scotland because it did not appear to guarantee that the Anglican Church would remain the Established Church. The

Declaration of Indulgence was voided when James II was deposed during the Glorious Revolution of 1688–89.

The rising tension that resulted from the Declaration of Indulgence put an end to further meetings, and the society went into abeyance during the events that culminated in the Battle of the Boyne in July 1690. However, when peace was restored the society was revived, with its second lease of life commencing in a meeting on 26 April 1693. The society had become well known and respected in Dublin, and managed to attract two archbishops, five bishops, a dean, the provost of Trinity College and five fellows of that institution, as well as three peers, the son of an earl, a baronet, four knights, seven physicians and three judges. Forty-nine people had joined by the end of 1693. Also on the roll of members was Bartholemew Van Homrigh, lord mayor of Dublin in 1697 and father of an even more famous daughter, Swift's 'Vanessa'. As Hoppen states, 'his membership is perhaps evidence of a growing interest in the Society's affairs among Dublin's mercantile class'.[28] The society was soon writing to renew its links with the Royal Society, and making ambitious plans for compiling a natural history of Ireland. Nineteen papers survive from this second phase, four of them dealing with the Giant's Causeway. The society was still functioning in April 1697, four years after its revival, but its regular meetings seem to have lapsed by the summer of that year.

The third Dublin Society, or the third phase of the Dublin Society's activity, was closely connected with the enterprising Trinity undergraduate Samuel Molyneux (1689–1728), son of William, who entered the college in 1705. He was a close friend of George Berkeley, who gave him private tuition and later corresponded with him on philosophical matters. Berkeley's early *Miscellanea Mathematica* (1707) is dedicated to him. Molyneux decided to revive the society his father had founded. Some of the papers contributed show the practical interests of the society. Thomas Molyneux wrote on coal mining in Ireland, and Berkeley contributed two papers. The third Dublin Society lasted less than a year. Meetings had ceased by August 1708, and Samuel Molyneux left Ireland for good the following year. We know that Berkeley was involved in the operation of two philosophical societies in Trinity in the year before the revival of the Dublin Society in 1706. Largely, members met each week to discuss some part of the new philosophy; at this time Berkeley's philosophical preoccupations would have covered Descartes and Locke.

Through the Dublin philosophical societies a framework was built that forms part of the prehistory of the Dublin Society. This led to the emergence of an important link between the interest in science and improvement on the one hand, and Irish independence on the other. In this linkage we can locate the basis for the general utopian vision of eighteenth-century Ireland. In the year of his death, 1698, William Molyneux published a book that caused a stir: *The Case of Ireland's Being Bound by Acts of Parliament in England, Stated.* Grounding his thesis in natural justice, Molyneux made a strong case for the complete independence of an Irish parliament. He was familiar with the damage inflicted on the Irish economy in general, and on the wool trade in particular, by British legislation. In effect, Molyneux raised the idea of home rule, and was the first to do so.

On 25 June 1731, fourteen men met in the rooms of the Philosophical Society in Trinity College and unanimously agreed to form a society to be called the Dublin Society for Improving Husbandry, Manufactures and Other Useful Arts; the word 'Sciences' was added to the title at a subsequent meeting in July 1731. The fourteen men present were Judge Ward, Sir Thomas Molyneux, Thomas Upton, Dr Stephens (who chaired the first meeting), John Pratt, Richard Warburton, Revd Dr Whitecomb, Arthur Dobbs, Dr Magnaten, Dr John Madden, Dr Lehunte, Mr Walton, Thomas Prior and William Maple. The second meeting of the founders was held a week later under the chairmanship of Thomas Prior, who was requested to draw up the rules for the regulation of the society. The founders of the society were of Anglo-Irish stock, second and third generation, Irish-born. The gathering of the founding members had a strong Trinity College flavour. Of the fourteen names, nine (and possibly ten) were Trinity graduates, and two, Revd John Madden and John Whitcomb, were fellows.

Judge Michael Ward, a member of the Irish parliament for County Down, was one of the group of parliamentarians whom Primate Boulter described as being 'on the Irish side'.[29] Sir Thomas Molyneux, a brother of William, was a professor of physics, a scientist, a Fellow of the Royal Society and a friend of Boyle, Newton, Dryden, Evelyn and Locke. Arthur Dobbs, while a member of the Irish parliament, was successful in carrying through an Act for planting trees and enclosing wasteland. He advocated an improved system of land tenure, and favoured a relaxation of the penal laws against Catholics and Dissenters. Later in his life, Dobbs was active in promoting the search for the Northwest Passage, and in 1764 was appointed governor of North Carolina, where he died in 1765. William Stephens was a physicist and physician attached to the Royal Hospital in Kilmainham as well as Mercer's and Steevens' hospitals, and was the author of a number of botanical books. Lehunte was also a doctor, with some large estates in Wexford and was recognised for his charitable and philanthropic enterprises. He was also a Member of Parliament. A fourth member of the Irish parliament was Richard Warburton, a landowner noted for his interest in tree planting and land improvement. Pratt, Walton and Upton were also large landowners, and Thomas Upton was a Member of Parliament. Alexander Magnaten (or MacNaghten) was a well-known Dublin physician who gave a considerable amount of his time and fortune to alleviating distress among the impoverished of the city.

Two clergymen of the Established Church were among the founders: Revd John Madden (brother of Samuel Madden), vicar of St Ann's and later dean of Kilmore, and John Whitecomb (or Whetcomb), a Fellow of Trinity College, bishop of Clonfert, then of Down and Connor, and later still archbishop of Cashel. The two most dedicated founders of the society were Thomas Prior and William Maple. Prior is generally recognised as the prime mover in the society, and was its most active promoter. Prior was a lawyer and a landowner and a friend of Berkeley, Swift and Lord Chesterfield. He was active in the founding of the Lying-in Hospital, and was a founder member of the Physico-Historical Society. His writings included *A List of Absentees of Ireland ... with Observations on the Present Trade and Conditions of that Kingdom*, which was published in 1729 and is one of the most important pamphlets of the period. It was widely criticised and considered subversive in its content. In it, Prior was critical of the absentee landlords, not only publishing their names and incomes but demanding a tax on all incomes moved abroad. It was a courageous step to write and publish it as it pilloried his own class and many of his friends, and exposed the negatives in the economic, political and religious circumstances in Ireland. Charles Ford, a friend of Swift's, objected strongly to the pamphlet and to being mentioned in Prior's *List* as among those 'who live constantly abroad and are seldom or never seen in Ireland'.[30] The *List of Absentees* ran through many editions and was continually brought up to date; an enlarged edition was published by Faulkner in 1783, thirty-two years after Prior's death. In a foreword to the 1732 edition of the work, he renewed his appeal for a tax on absentees. Prior in his *List* calculated that a sum of more than £600,000 was sent out of the country annually, a sum that should have been usefully invested at home, since an impoverished country could not afford such a loss of resources. In *A List of Absentees*, Prior was not merely engaged in pamphleteering, he was engaging in practical experiments similar to those he set out in his pamphlet. For example, he tells us:

We have of late been put into a method of tanning hides with the

help of Tormentil Roots instead of Bark, and have had some successful Experiments therein; and if upon farther and compleat Trials in
all Sorts of Leather, this practice shall be found to succeed; 'tis hop'd,
it may come into general use, and thereby save yearly above £16,000
which we pay for foreign bark, and enable us to export our Hides fully
tann'd, and thereby enlarge the value of our exports.[31]

The experiments in tanning were undertaken by Prior's friend, William Maple,
and their results were put to practical use by the Dublin Society. Maple,
after Prior, was the most tireless supporter of the Dublin Society: he acted as
registrar from its foundation until his death in 1762. By September 1731 a
committee consisting of Prior, Whitecomb, Pratt, Stephens and Dobbs had
drawn up a plan of projects distributed throughout the country. It is evident
from the earliest records of the society that its main priority was to increase
the amount of land under tillage by reclaiming boggy and marsh ground, and
to encourage the planting of forests and hops and fruits. On 18 December
1731 the 'Rules for the Regulation of the Dublin Society' were adopted to
enable the society to carry out its aims and objectives. The rules provided for
the election of new members after the first hundred people had subscribed
to the objectives of the society, and also made provision for the election of a
president, a vice-president, two secretaries, a treasurer, a curator and a registrar,
as well as a standing committee of twenty-one members.

By the end of the second year of the society's existence, progress had been
made on furthering its aims. A number of papers on drainage, the cultivation
of hops, the improvement of flax growing, direction for planting and growing
clover, rye grass, manuring, the cultivation of broccoli, saffron, and a dissertation on dyeing were written into the minute books. In order to provide
a practical approach to the subject of planting, improving the quality of soil
and carrying out experiments, a plot of land was leased in the neighbour-
hood of Ballybough, County Dublin. The dissemination of information to
the public was improved in December 1736 when it was decided to publish
a paper each week in the *Dublin Newsletter* on some aspect of husbandry
or other useful arts. It soon became known as the Dublin Society's 'weekly
observations'. In the first few months of its existence, it was agreed that Jethro
Tull's (1674–1741) *Horse-Hoeing Husbandry* should be printed for distribution in Ireland. Tull's work had had a major effect on English agriculture
with the development of a seed drill that sowed in rows. With its compelling
combination of theory and practice, his publication was the first in its field

to advocate a mechanical alternative to traditional methods of tillage. The first Dublin printing appeared in 1731 as a 'specimen', or summary version, under the title *The New Horse-houghing Husbandry*. Aaron Rhames, who was appointed first printer to the society, printed the work, and 2,000 copies of it were distributed throughout the country. The society maintained its keen interest in agriculture. *A New Method of Draining Marshy and Boggy Lands* was the first paper read and discussed at a meeting of the Dublin Society, in September 1731.

Over the years, Prior and his associates in the Dublin Society also aimed to encourage the industrial life of the country as well as modern methods in agriculture. This tendency was powerfully advanced with the publication of Berkeley's *The Querist*. Prior and Berkeley were but two of many public-spirited individuals who looked to the Dublin Society for help and guidance in the economic rehabilitation of the country. Commenting on this, A.A. Luce in *The Life of George Berkeley* writes: 'He and Prior and Madden, and later Chesterfield had wide and lofty aims; they fostered the fine arts, as well as the useful arts and crafts; they encouraged agriculture and manufacture in many branches ... they encouraged the palpable spirit of invention and improvement'.[32]

Although the society had attained a measure of importance and was exerting an influence on public opinion, its work was hampered by a lack of funds. It was at this stage that Dr Samuel Madden, a Church of Ireland clergyman, landowner and author of the 1733 utopian work *Memoirs of the Twentieth Century*, became the first patron of the society. Some years earlier, Madden had started a scheme of premiums for students at Trinity College. In 1738 he published his *Reflections and Resolutions Proper for the Gentlemen of Ireland*, a work that mirrored many of the aims and objectives of the Dublin Society. He was aware of its work and was a member by 1733. Prior describes him as 'worthy and as useful a member of his country as I know in it'.[33] He was aware of the financial situation of the society when he wrote his *Letter to the Dublin Society, on the Improving Their Fund*, which was published anonymously in 1739. To augment the funds of the society, Madden suggested an appeal should be made to wealthy men, and if a sum of £500 could be raised or guaranteed, he would personally contribute an annuity of £130. He also suggested that the society establish an experimental garden, encourage new manufactures and aim to procure a royal charter. In making his offer of an annual annuity, Madden suggested that when the necessary monies had been raised or guaranteed, the fund should be allocated in premiums as follows:

£30 for practical experiments in agriculture and gardening, £50 for the best invention in any of the liberal or manual arts, £25 for the best picture, and £25 for the best statue produced in Ireland. He also suggested that he would use his influence to raise more funds, and was able to report in 1740 that subscriptions received by him for promoting arts and manufactures amounted to almost £900 per annum.

With such a sum available to it, the Dublin Society in 1740 published an advertisement promoting the fact that a system of awarding premiums was being initiated 'to promote such useful arts and manufactures as have not hitherto been introduced, or have not yet been brought to perfection in this kingdom', and that the society intended 'to encourage by premiums, annual contributions, or other methods, any persons who are well skilled in such arts and manufactures, and will carry them on in the best and most skilful manner'.[34] In order to achieve this, the society requested that

> gentlemen and others who are conversant with husbandry, trade, or manufactures, and wish well of their country, will favour them with their company and advice, that they may be better able to judge what improvements are proper to be encouraged, what encouragements are convenient and in what manner they may best be applied for the benefit of the country.[35]

A special committee was appointed to attend at Parliament House every Thursday to meet with those willing to give their ideas and to offer suggestions as to where the premiums may be best distributed.

The first premiums were adjudged in January 1741, when a number of claimants presented their entries. These included artificial leather, spinning cotton, twilled stockings, earthenware, stonework, sculptures, engines for scutching flax and a surveying instrument. By 1745 premiums were awarded for a wide variety of agricultural and manufacturing ventures as well as for paintings and sculptures. In the area of manufactures, encouragement was given to brewing, linen, lace and papermaking. With regard to agriculture, premiums were offered for a wide variety of projects, especially for afforestation, tillage and land reclamation. The benefits of this approach were acknowledged by Lord Chesterfield in a letter to Thomas Prior in 1747:

> They [the members] have done more good to Ireland with regard to arts and industry, than all the laws that could have been formed; for

unfortunately there is a perverseness in our natures which prompts us to resist authority, though otherwise inclined enough to do the thing if left to our own choice. Invitation, example and fashion with some premiums attending them, are, I am convinced, the only methods of bringing people in Ireland to do what they ought to do – and that is the plan of your society.[36]

The success of the scheme can be gauged from the fact that the list of premiums offered in 1746 occupies four or five written pages but that by 1766 the list takes up twenty-six pages in the minute book and covers a variety of projects, including land and mountain reclamation, the draining of land, afforestation, cereal and crop production, beekeeping, fisheries, livestock breeding, and the manufacture of iron, steel, wool combs, stockings, gloves, bone lace, felt hats and wheel carriages. In all, more than £3,000 had been offered in premiums, a substantial increase from that initially suggested by Madden. In 1790 the Irish parliament made an annual grant of £5,000 to the society, £300 of which was to be used for the provision and maintenance of a botanic garden. This allowed the society to fulfil its aim of uniting science with agriculture and husbandry, and to promote education in science by the founding of the Botanic Gardens in Glasnevin, Dublin.

A strong utopian precedent and tradition was therefore built up through these early Dublin philosophical societies, both inside and outside the walls of Trinity College. As J.V. Luce argues, a key feature of these early philosophical societies is not simply their formal organisation but their motivation:

> I refer to the growing concept of Ireland as a historic nation quite distinct from England, though owing allegiance to the British Crown. Such a nation, it was felt, was entitled to its own autonomous Parliament through which its leading citizens would be able to protect and further its interests.[37]

I would argue this motivation forms the intellectual background to what was to evolve into Berkeley's Bermuda project, providing him with the possibility of realising an autonomous region in Bermuda distinct from, if not wholly independent of, the British Crown. The early Dublin philosophical societies and the Dublin (subsequently, Royal Dublin) Society and later the Royal Irish Academy clearly represent a utopian propensity in late seventeenth-century and early eighteenth-century Ireland. The societies offered an emergent space, a forum in which innovative ideas and speculations could be discussed and implemented. Through it all was a concern for the improvement of Irish society. This did not occur in isolation but was part of a wider trend that existed in continuous relation to the entire society. The members of these societies were aware of contemporary work in science and of what was happening in the Royal Society in England, and were engaged with current thinking.

The palpable spirit of invention and improvement, while cognisant of international trends and writings, was, I believe, an indigenous Irish utopian trend. It had at its core the remit of *improvement*, of bettering society, of experimentation, of advance. The Polish philosopher Leszek Kolakowski (1927–2009), writing of the range of the word Utopia, notes how a word that

> emerged as an artificially concocted proper name has acquired, in the last two centuries, a sense so extended that it refers not only to a literary genre but to a way of thinking, to a mentality, to a philosophical attitude, and is being employed in depicting cultural phenomena going back into antiquity.[38]

Kolakowski, in noting the extension in the range of meanings of Utopia, has captured the essence of what the early societies, culminating in the founding of the Dublin Society, comprised: a way of thinking, a mentality, a philosophical attitude that coalesced around practical and visionary patriotism, liberalism and nationalism, and which aimed for the ultimate transformation of everyday life. In retrospect we can view this new direction as a utopian propensity presented by those who may never have thought of themselves as utopists. The early societies and the Dublin Society epitomise Raymond Williams' notion of a 'structure of feeling' that comes to characterise the lived experience, or the quality of life, of a particular time and place. Williams chose the term 'feeling' to emphasise, as he put it, 'a distinction from more formal concepts of "world-view" or "ideology"'.[39] 'Structure' relates to elements of consciousness and relationships in a living, ongoing and interconnected continuity, elements that can be viewed as a 'structure': 'as a set, with specific internal relations, at once interlocking and in tension'.[40] A 'structure of feeling' as the lived culture of a particular historical moment thus suggests a common set of perceptions and values shared by a particular generation.

The utopianism of the Dublin societies, and the generation of people surrounding them, can be seen as an emergent 'structure of feeling', as these intellectual societies were committed to notions of improvement, with important links to a wide intellectual stratum flourishing in Britain and Europe. It was a patriotic structure of feeling, emerging in the Swiftian culture of Dublin in the 1720s and 1730s. In subsequent years, as Griffin puts it, 'Swift's savage indignation gave way, ultimately, to a more romantic form of patriotism: more credulous perhaps, but with a unifying potential reflecting the general will of an emerging public sphere'.[41] This patriotic structure of feeling coalesced around the emerging public sphere, and, by the later century, included an Irish republicanism that was influenced by France, America and England juxtaposed with aspects of Gaelic culture. As we have noted, the utopian radicalism of the Society of United Irishmen's *Northern Star* newspaper (launched on 2 January 1792), with its many references to James Harrington's republican Utopia *The Commonwealth of Oceana* as a paradigm, is an example of that confluence of the national and the international. However, in advance of such late eighteenth-century and early nineteenth-century utopian radicalism, figures such as Berkeley, Prior and John Percival sought to galvanise a sense of identity and nationhood, or, as Hone and Rossi put it:

> Berkeley indeed seems to have conceived himself and his young friends as the leaders of a nation about to be reconstructed. This nation would have its philosopher in the author of the *New Principle* [Berkeley], its economist in Prior, its arbiter of taste and manners in Sir John Percival.[42]

Of course, the nation to be reconstructed had to be forged out of the context of colonialism, and the emerging utopianism of Berkeley and others can only be understood in its eighteenth-century colonial context.

CHAPTER 4

George Berkeley's New World Utopia and the Pacific Utopia in the Writings of Theobald Wolfe Tone

There shall be sung another golden age,
The rise of empire and of arts,
The good and great inspiring epic rage,
The wisest heads and noblest hearts.

George Berkeley, 'On America'[1]

Verily the land is a good land. It was here, amongst these
very cedars, that noster George Berkeley desired to establish a
Missionary College.

John Mitchel, *Jail Journal*[2]

A fter Berkeley left Ireland in early 1713, he arrived in London and soon became acquainted with the literary elite, meeting Irish-born Richard Steele (1672–1729), the editor of *The Tatler;* Joseph Addison (1672–1719), co-founder with Steele of *The Spectator* (published 1711–12); Alexander Pope (1688–1744); and John Arbuthnot (1667–1735). Berkeley's introduction to these men was through his writings, though he may have been introduced to others by Swift, with whom he had become friendly in Ireland. The two men had a great deal in common: they attended the same school and university, and they were both Anglican clergymen and writers. Swift, then at the height of his political powers, gave Berkeley more substantial assistance. In his 'Journal to Stella' on 12 April 1713 Swift writes:

> I went to Court to-day on purpose to present Mr. Berkeley, one of
> your Fellows of Dublin College to Lord Berkeley of Stratton. That Mr
> Berkeley is a very ingenious man, and a great philosopher, and I have
> mentioned him to all the ministers, and have given them some of his
> writings; and I will favour him as much as I can.[3]

In calling Berkeley a 'great philosopher', Swift had in mind a moral quality,
the love of wisdom, raising Berkeley above the level of self-seeking humanity.
Berkeley came to London partly with the intention of publishing his *Three
Dialogues*, which he did in May 1713, by which time he was involved in
another literary enterprise. Following the demise of *The Tatler*, Steele had
started a new periodical, the *Guardian*, for which he enlisted Berkeley's
assistance. Steele was, like Swift, an important shaper of public opinion in
England. In the first collected edition, published in 1714, Steele states that
'Mr. Berkeley of Trinity College in Dublin has embellished [the work] with
many excellent arguments in honour of religion and virtue'.[4]

Berkeley discussed many topics in his *Guardian* essays, among them the
afterlife, education and religion, including the Christian idea of God. By
all accounts he was the third-biggest contributor, Steele and Addison being
the first and second. In October 1713 he left for Sicily as chaplain to Lord
Peterborough. His appointment had been brought about by Swift, and it
lasted about ten months. This developed Berkeley's taste for travel. After a
few months in France, where he may have met Malebranche, he travelled
to Italy. He returned from the Continent to London in late 1714, during
uncertain times. The death of Queen Anne had plunged Britain into political uncertainty, and it was not clear if an attempt would be made to bring
back the exiled Stuart pretender, or whether the Act of Succession would
be maintained. The Tory leader, Henry St John (1678–1751), with whom
Berkeley was acquainted, was conspiring with the Stuarts. However, at this
stage Berkeley had little or no sympathy for the Jacobites, issuing a vigorous
pamphlet, *Advice to the Tories Who Have Taken the Oath* (1715), in which he
called upon the Tories to honour the Oath of Allegiance to King George I.

In 1716 Berkeley hoped for a position in St Paul's church on North King
Street in Dublin, but the preferment did not materialise. He then left on
his second Continental tour, travelling as tutor to St George Ashe (1698–
1721), son of the Church of Ireland cleric St George Ashe (1658–1718).
This tour was more extensive than the first, lasting four years, during which
time he gained a wide appreciation of the arts, particularly architecture – an

interest that would be illustrated by, among other things, his plan for the City of Bermuda and the house he would have built in Rhode Island. Was it a coincidence that Berkeley chose to call his projected college 'St Paul's' – to compensate for his failure to secure the Irish St Paul's with the far more ambitious St Paul's, Bermuda? By 1724 he had obtained the deanery of Derry, but by then he had turned his life towards Bermuda.

The Bermuda project (1722–31)

In 1721 Berkeley published *An Essay Towards Preventing the Ruine of Great Britain*, a tract on the moral, social and religious corruption of Britain. Berkeley attacks the freethinkers, and the tone of his essay was explained by the 'miseries the nation was plunged into by the fatal South Sea scheme in 1720'. He was downcast as a result of the social corruption brought to light after the failure of the South Sea Company in its gigantic speculations connected with British trade in South America. Some Englishmen had just come through a roller-coaster journey of speculation known as the South Sea Bubble, and its bursting left both reputations and fortunes depleted. This gigantic fraud was accompanied by many lesser ones. The financial crash also left England with social instability, as private gain and wealth had ranked ahead of the public good, and was a symptom of larger social discontent. Berkeley noted:

> We have long been preparing for some great catastrophe. Vice and villainy have by degrees grown reputable among us; our infidels have passed for fine gentlemen, and our venal traitors for men of sense, who knew the world. We have made a jest of public spirit, and cancelled all respect for whatever our laws and religion repute sacred. The old English modesty is quite worn off, and instead of blushing for our crimes we are ashamed only of piety and virtue. In short, other nations have been wicked, but we are the first who have been wicked upon principle.[5]

As Hone and Rossi observe, 'it became a fashion in London to descant upon the corruption of Europe: polite society professed to desire nothing better than to escape from its complex frivolities to the virtues of the simple life'.[6] As a counterpoint to this, Alexander Fraser avers that 'America filled the imagination of one to whose vision was disclosed a spiritually prosperous future for mankind amidst new surroundings'.[7] As an alternative site for this new direction in society, Bermuda offered the best option for Berkeley's proposed college, and at this juncture it was favoured by an interesting stroke of good fortune. 'Mrs Hester van Omry', he writes to Percival on 4 June 1723,

> a lady to whom I was a perfect stranger, having never in the whole course of my life to my knowledge, exchanged one single word with her, died on Sunday night. Yesterday her will was opened, by which it appears that I am constituted executor the advantages whereof is computed by those who understand her affairs to be worth three thousand pounds, and if a suit she had depending be carried, it will be considerably more.[8]

The will, which had originally been in favour of Swift, had been altered on 1 May 1723, and in it she divided her property between Berkeley and Robert Marshall of Clonmel. John Percival congratulated Berkeley on his good fortune in a letter dated 30 June 1723, but cautioned him to secure the protection and encouragement of the government in funding his Bermuda project. In addition to the legacy, which he called a 'providential event', Berkeley's career prospects improved.[9]

Having returned to Ireland in 1721, Berkeley had sought the position of dean of Dromore, with the right of appointment claimed by Dr Lambert, the bishop of Dromore. The result was a prolonged legal case in which he was unsuccessful. Rumours of a probable vacancy in the deanery of Derry seemed to offer a more favourable chance of success than that of Dromore. After three years he secured the deanery, 'the best Deanery in this kingdom', Percival exulted, and 'said to be worth £1,500 p.a.'.[10] The legacy and the deanery alike could have provided the philosopher-dean with the basis for a future that was orderly, rational, cultivated and calm. Yet they were clearly not seen as a means for enriching himself. At this point in the history of the world, and in the decline of Great Britain, a quiet deanery represented for him not so much a position as a port of embarkation. For Berkeley, a royal charter and private subscriptions remained to be secured to facilitate and promote his Bermuda project.

The actual utopian moment of travel started when he set out for London in September 1724. He was undoubtedly emboldened by a letter of commendation dated 3 September 1724 that Swift, then in Dublin, had written to Lord Carteret (1690–1763), who had been appointed to succeed the Duke of

Grafton as lord lieutenant of Ireland. Berkeley's first biographer, Joseph Stock, includes this letter in his *Works of George Berkeley*. As he puts it, the letter 'deserves a place here, both because it contains a number of particulars of our Author's life, and is besides a proof, as well of the friendly temper of the writer, as of his politeness and address'.[11] As Stock observes, the letter gives an account of Berkeley's life while illuminating Swift's willingness to garner support for him. However, it also reveals the utopian aspect of Berkeley's proposed project.

In the letter's first paragraph, Swift gives a concise summary of Berkeley's life, his philosophy, and his positive influence on others, such as Dr George Smalridge (1663–1719) of Lichfield (a contemporary of Joseph Addison and a well-known figure in London in Queen Anne's day). He then describes Berkeley's travels through Europe and his success in becoming dean of Derry:

> There is a gentleman of this kingdom just gone for England. It is Dr George Berkeley, Dean of Derry, the best preferment among us, being worth £1,000 a year. He was a Fellow of the University here; and going to England very young, about thirteen years ago, he became the founder of a sect called the *Immaterialist*, by the force of a very curious book upon that subject. Dr Smalridge and many other eminent persons were his proselytes. Dr Berkeley spent above seven years in travelling over most parts of Europe, but chiefly through every corner of Italy, Sicily, and other islands. When he came back to England he found so many friends that he was effectually recommended to the Duke of Grafton, by whom he was lately made Dean of Derry.[12]

In the second paragraph of the letter, Swift refers to Berkeley's Bermuda project: 'I am now to mention his errand. He is an absolute philosopher with regard to money, titles, and power; and for three years past has been struck with a notion of founding a University at Bermudas, by a Charter from the Crown.' Swift continues: 'He shewed me a little tract, which he designs to publish; and there your Excellency will see his whole scheme of life academico-philosophical, of a College founded for Indian scholars and missionaries.' Swift asserts that he had attempted to dissuade Berkeley from his scheme: 'I discouraged him by the coldness of Courts and ministers, who will interpret all this as impossible and a vision.' He then asks Lord Carteret

> either to use such persuasions as will keep one of the first men in the Kingdom for learning and virtue quiet at home, or assist him by your

credit to compass his romantic design; which, however, is very noble and generous, and directly proper for a great person of your excellent education to encourage.[13]

Tellingly, Swift, while supporting Berkeley as an eminent person, does not overtly support or dismiss his 'romantic design'. He is aware that it may appear quixotic, impossible, a vision – the typical range of negative responses to a utopian scheme. The 'scheme of life academio-philosophical' is presented by Swift as Berkeley's singular (utopian) vision. He therefore provides a letter of commendation for Berkeley whilst withholding his own thoughts on the Bermuda project. For several reasons, Berkeley seems to have lost hope in the Old World and was looking towards America. His reflections on the corrupted state of society in the Old World, as evidenced by the South Sea Bubble, had caused him to turn with eagerness to a more unsullied world of men and affairs that he believed to exist across the seas. Moreover, as Carole Fabricant argues, 'Berkeley's life included mental and physical interactions with other islands as well – England, Ischia, Bermuda, Aquidneck – all of which reveal the idealizing tendencies of Berkeley's imagination and play a role in his quest to recreate Eden out of the shards of a fallen world.'[14]

It was in the early months of 1722 that he formulated his plan for a missionary and arts college in Bermuda, to recast Eden out of those shards of the fallen world. The plan was to be a part of his life for the next ten years. We first learn of the project from his letter to John Percival of 4 March 1723, which reads:

> It is now about ten months since I have determined with myself to spend the residue of my days in the island of Bermuda; where I trust in Providence I may be the mean instrument of great good to mankind. Your Lordship is not to be told that the reformation of manners among the English in our Western Plantations, and the propagation of the gospel among the American savages, are two points of high moment. The natural way of doing this is by founding a College or Seminary in some convenient part of the West Indies, where the English youth of our Plantations may be educated in such sort as to supply the churches with pastors of good morals and good learning – a thing (God knows) much wanted.[15]

This letter, which predates Swift's to Lord Carteret by six months, contains the kernel of Berkeley's utopian vision. First, he notes that it is about ten months since he had decided to spend the remainder of his days in Bermuda. He identifies his desire to be 'the mean instrument of great good to mankind'. He acknowledges that Percival will already be aware that the propagation of the gospel among the American 'savages' and the reformation of behaviours among the English in the New World are points of concern. Through his proposed founding of a college or seminary, society would be improved, as English youth would be educated in morals and religious affairs to supply the churches with pastors. In addition,

> In the same Seminary a number of young American savages may be also educated till they have taken the degree of Master of Arts. And being by that time well instructed in the Christian religion, practical mathematics, and other liberal arts and sciences, and early imbued with public-spirited principles and inclinations, they may become the fittest instruments for spreading religion, morality, and civil life among their countrymen, who can entertain no suspicion or jealousy of men of their own blood and language, as they might do of English missionaries, who can never be so well qualified for that work. Some attempts have been made towards a college in the West, but to little purpose, chiefly I conceive for want of a proper situation wherein to place such college or Seminary, as also for want of a sufficient number of able men well qualified with divine and human learning, as well as with zeal to prosecute such an undertaking. As to the first, I do think the small group of Bermuda Islands the fittest spot for a college on the following accounts.[16]

Furthermore, in the seminary, American natives could be instructed in the Christian religion and in the liberal arts and sciences, and then could spread their learning among their own people.

Berkeley lays out his vision and names the proposed location for the implementation of it. He highlights his need for support and for men of zeal to be part of the undertaking. His vision moves from the personal to the pragmatic. His Utopia is based on the remote geography of Bermuda, but needs the beneficence of others to become real. In the same letter Berkeley recounts why he chose Bermuda: it was nearly equidistant from all the other American colonies, and had trade with them all. As with many utopian settings, Bermuda provided an abundance of the necessary provisions of life.

It was secure from attack and its people were characterised by their simplicity of manners. Then, too, there was the benign climate of Bermuda:

> the summer refreshed with constant, cool breezes, the winters as mild as our May, the sky as light and blue as a sapphire, the ever green pastures, the earth eternally crowned with fruits and flowers. The woods of cedars, palmettos, myrtles, oranges, etc., always fresh and blooming. The beautiful situations and prospects of hills, vales, promontories, rocks, lakes and sinuses of the sea. The great variety, plenty and perfection of fish, fowl, vegetables of all kinds, and (which is in no other of our Western Islands) the most excellent butter, beaf, veal, pork and mutton.[17]

He states that

> half a dozen of the most agreeable and ingenious men of our college are with me in this project. And since I came hither I have got together about a dozen Englishmen of quality and gentlemen, who intend to retire to these islands to build villas and plant gardens, and to enjoy health of body and peace of mind.[18]

Berkeley concludes that the gentlemen who would accompany him on this journey may find, in fact, 'whatsoever the most poetical imagination can figure to itself in the golden age, or the Elysian fields'.[19] In a subsequent letter from Daniel Dering in Dublin to his cousin John Percival, dated 5 March 1723, after he had also received a letter from Berkeley on his Bermuda plan, he writes how Berkeley had spoken of 'restoring the golden age in that corner of the world'.[20] And in a letter dated 6 February 1724, Percival, writing to his brother Philip on Berkeley's plan, said that he knew 'not why in time that little spot may not become the Athens of the world, since the persons who intend to go are men every way qualified to raise learning to as high a pitch as we know it was in that of Greece'.[21]

In his correspondence around this period – the early days of his Bermuda project – Berkeley uses language that is clearly utopian. This tone is also echoed by the Percival brothers and Dering in their letters to Berkeley and in their correspondence between themselves. In his allusion to the golden age, Berkeley is connecting with the utopian dimension of the classic myths, most notably the creation myths of the golden age and the earthly paradise. As Sargent observes, 'such myths from ancient Greece and Rome, Sumer,

and early Judaism were central to the development of western utopianism'.[22]
The most famous depiction of a golden age is that of the Greek poet Hesiod
(*c.* 700 BC), who wrote of a golden race that dwelt in Olympus: 'all good
things were theirs, for the fruitful earth unstintingly bore unforced her plenty,
and they, amid their store enjoyed their landed ease which nothing stirred
loved by the gods and rich in many of herd'.[23] The main themes keeping the
memory of a happy portion of the earth alive are, as Jean Delumeau argues,
'the Golden Age, the Elysian Fields, and the Happy Isles, the three being
sometimes combined, sometimes kept separate'.[24] The version of the golden
age that passed down into the Middle Ages was that of the Roman author
Ovid (43 BC–*c.* AD 17). Hesiod had focused on abundance, a joyful life and
an easeful death, while Ovid wrote of freedom from law courts and absence
of war. He notes in *Metamorphoses*:

> In the beginning was the Golden Age, when men of their own accord,
> without threat of punishment, without laws, maintained good faith
> and did what was right. There were no penalties to be afraid of, no
> bronze tablets were erected, carrying threats of legal action, no crowd
> of wrong-doers, anxious for mercy, trembled before the face of their
> judge: indeed, there were no Judges.[25]

Berkeley, in alluding to the myths of a golden age, forms a clear thread of
connection from those traditions, before More's *Utopia*, to the future. The
Bermuda project would thus restore a golden age in 'a region whose idyllic bliss
had sung, and from which Christian civilisation might radiate over the Utopia
of a New World with its magnificent possibilities in the future history of the
human race',[26] but, to be sure, this would be a future Utopia. This Utopia, hewn
from the golden age of the past, in a flight from the present, corrupted Western
world consequently becomes both an alternative space and a promised land.

Until 1728, four years after the date of Swift's letter, Berkeley lived in
London, negotiating and otherwise promoting his Bermuda enterprise. The
project captured the imagination of diverse figures. Berkeley spoke before a
sceptical audience at the Scriblerus Club, and Hone and Rossi recount that
when he spoke about his project, 'the company were struck dumb and after a
pause, simultaneously rose and asked leave to accompany him to the plantations'.[27] In Dublin, a few irreverent sceptics, unimpressed by the promise of
healthy climes and sapphire-blue skies, found the whole idea mad and chi-
merical. Even before any public announcement had been made on the project,

Dublin wits, having heard of the dean's intent, found a target for ridicule. As Edwin S. Gaustad relates late in 1723, a young girl was sent around to Berkeley's rooms in Dublin to present him with some verse: 'The Humble Petition of a Beautiful Young Lady: to the Reverend Doctor B-rky-y':

> Dear Doctor, here comes a Young Virgin untainted
> To your Shrine at Bermudas to be Married and Sainted;
> I am Young, I am Soft, I am Blooming and Tender,
> Of all that I have I make you a Surrender;
> My innocence led by the Voice of your Fame
> To your Person and Virtue must put in its Claim:
> And now I behold you I truly believe,
> That you'r [*sic*] like Adam as I am like Eve:
> Before the dire Serpent their Virtue betray'd,
> And taught them to Fly from the Sun, to the Shade:
> But you, as in you a new Race has begun,
> Are Teaching to Fly from the Shade to the Sun;
> For you in Great Goodness your Friends are Persuading
> To go, and to live, and to be wise in your Eden.
> Oh! Let me go with you, Oh! Pity my Youth,
> Oh! Take me from hence let me not loose [*sic*] my Truth;
> Sure you that have Virtue so much in your mind,
> Can't think to leave me who am Virtue behind,
> If you'll make me your Wife, Sir, in Time you may fill a
> Whole Town with your Children and likewise your Villa;
> I famous for Breeding, you Famous for knowledge,
> I'll Found a whole Nation, you'll Found a whole Colledge [*sic*];
> When many long Ages in Joys we have Spent,
> Our Souls we'll resign with utmost content:
> And gently we'll Sink between Cypress and Yew,
> You lying by me, and I lying by you.[28]

This broadside parodies Berkeley's proposed plan for a college in Bermuda. It succinctly juxtaposes the presence of the untainted young maiden with Berkeley's own vision of Bermuda: pure and untainted, free of the corrupted practices of the Old World. The maiden representing Eve, and Berkeley portrayed as Adam, are presented as potential cohorts, a resultant union of their intellectual and physical fecundity poised to propagate the New World.

Berkeley's *Proposal*

The 'little tract' referred to by Swift was first published in London in 1724 under the title *A Proposal for the Better Supplying of Churches in Our Foreign Plantations, and for Converting the Savage Americans to Christianity.*[29] Berkeley's *Proposal* outlines his vision for a college in Bermuda and how it was to be funded and founded. He acknowledged that several representatives of the Church had not been found wanting in propagating the gospel in foreign parts. They had combined into societies for that very purpose, most notably the Society for the Propagation of the Gospel in Foreign Parts founded in 1701 by Thomas Bray. In the opening paragraph, Berkeley argues:

> It is nevertheless acknowledged that there is at this day but little sense of religion, and a most notorious corruption of manners, in the English Colonies settled on the Continent of America, and the islands. It is also acknowledged that the gospel hath hitherto made but a very inconsiderate progress among the neighbouring Americans, who will continue in much the same ignorance and barbarism in which we found them above a hundred years ago.[30]

Berkeley thought it convenient that a constant supply of worthy clergymen should be available, first, for the project, and, second, for propagating Christianity among the 'savages'. Hitherto, the clergy sent over to America had proved 'very meanly qualified both in learning and morals for the discharge of their office'.[31] In this project Berkeley seems to be propagating his own spiritual Utopia fashioned from the failings in the current situation. His proposed college or seminary is to be based in Bermuda, the island 'once thought to be enchanted and [to] hold special magic powers'.[32]

As envisaged, the college would achieve two ends. First, that the youth of the English plantations might be fitted for the ministry; 'men of merit would be then glad to fill the churches of their native country, which are now a drain for the dregs and refuse of ours'.[33] The second objective was that 'the children of "savage" Americans, brought up in such a Seminary and well instructed in religion and learning, should make the ablest and best missionaries for spreading the gospel among their countrymen'.[34] The young students of the college would be educated thoroughly in religion and morality, and also in 'a good tincture of other learning; particularly of eloquence, history, and practical mathematics; to which it may not be improper to add some skill in physic'.[35] Having publicly presented his idea for the college in Bermuda with its aims and goals, Berkeley makes his appeal for a Charter for the college:

> If his Majesty would graciously please to grant a Charter for a College
> to be erected in a proper place for these uses, it is hoped a fund may
> be soon raised, by the contribution of well-disposed persons, sufficient
> for building and endowing the same.

A postscript to the edition of the *Proposal* published in 1725 noted that the charter had been granted, and that Berkeley was to be president of the college, aided by nine fellows. The three fellows named in the charter are William Thompson, Jonathan Rogers and James King of Trinity College, Dublin. In the *Proposal*, Berkeley gives his reasons for choosing Bermuda as the location for his college: the island was equidistant from most of the main colonies; it had a good climate and a rocky coastline that would protect the college from pirates; and, although there was a good supply of essential provisions since the island produced no enriching commodity, the teachers of St Paul's would not be tempted to become traders. Finally, the present inhabitants were presented as contented and innocent, free from avarice and luxury.

Success was rapid for Berkeley's promotional efforts at government level after he arrived in London in 1724. Hone and Rossi note that a patent was passed for erecting a college on the island of Bermuda for 'the propaganda of the Gospel among the Indians and other Heathens on the continent of America, and constituting Dr Berkeley, Dean of Londonderry, principal of the said college'.[36] It is possible that the real reason Berkeley's plan found acceptance in London, even among politicians, was perhaps the need to create a utopian counterweight to Jesuit propaganda in the New World and also to prepare the ground for a successful expansion of English rule, since the broadening of empire was something Berkeley himself had promised. Since the *Proposal*, unlike Berkeley's initial letter to Percival, was a public document, it included an appeal – or, to be sure, several appeals – to nationalist pride, to phobias about Roman Catholicism, and to prospective financial contributors. In the spirit of Richard Hakluyt (*c.*1552–1616) a century and a half earlier, Berkeley declared that the fate of the empire might rest upon the encouragement of this design, for if colonies should fall under the influence of other nations, Britain's wealth and 'so considerable a branch of his Majesty's revenue'[37] would also fall. Likewise, following Hakluyt and Samuel Purchas (1575–1626), Berkeley reminded his readers that 'the Protestant religion hath of late years considerably lost ground, and America seems the likeliest place wherein to make up for what hath been lost in Europe'.[38] If the correct method – that is, that described in the *Proposal* – be not taken, then Spain in the south and France in the north 'may one day spread the religion of Rome, and with it the usual hatred to Protestants, throughout all the savage nations of America'.[39]

Berkeley made it clear that 'the honour of the crown, nation and church of England' depended on the success of his Bermuda project.[40] If achieved, Berkeley argued, his project would 'cast no small lustre on his majesty's reign, and derive a blessing from heaven on his administration, and those who live under the influence thereof'.[41] Here, then, Berkeley associates the colonial enterprise with his utopian Bermuda project. If successful, it will benefit the Crown, the nation and the Church of England. Berkeley, in envisioning his utopian seminary within the macrocosm of the colonial, is an exemplar of the nexus of colonialism and utopianism. However, permission to establish his college was not enough; he also needed financial support if it was to become a reality. Berkeley opened a public subscription, which reached £3,400, with John Percival contributing £200 and Robert Walpole the same amount. In May 1726 the House of Commons asked George I to grant funding for the Bermuda college, to be derived from the sale of St Christopher Island, which had been ceded to Britain by the Peace of Utrecht (1713–14). The sum agreed for the college was £20,000. Berkeley writes to Percival from London on 17 May 1726:

> Your Lordship hath every way been so good a friend to St Paul's College in Bermuda, that I think it my duty to acquaint you with the success which hath of late attended it, the Commons of Great Britain having last Wednesday voted an address to His Majesty that he would be pleased to make such grant out of lands of St. Christopher's for the endowment thereof as to him shall seem proper. The point was carried in a full house with but two negatives, and those pronounced in so low a voice as shewed that the persons who gave them were ashamed of what they were doing.[42]

By this time, Berkeley had had the response necessary for his *Proposal*, a utopian document, to become a reality in the establishment of his college. This pragmatic Utopia complemented Berkeley's poetic representation of the New World as Utopia in 'On America; or the Muse's Refuge: A Prophecy in Six Verses'.

'Westward the course of empire ...'

The influence of the 'New World' as more than a geographical fact was to become one of the driving metaphors of the Western literary imagination, supplying a rich vein of poems, plays, songs and fiction. Berkeley's poetic representation of the New World as Utopia is found in 'On America; or the Muse's Refuge: A Prophecy in Six Verses'. His lines appear at once both as a poem and a prophecy. It is unclear as to when the verses were composed. Berkeley, writing from London, enclosed them in a letter to Percival dated 10 February 1726. The letter is replete with details about potential benefactors for his Bermuda project, and Berkeley concludes with the following: 'you have annexed a poem wrote by a friend of mine with a view to the [Bermuda] Scheme. Your lordship is desired to shew it to none but of your family, and allow no copy to be taken of it.'[43] Despite disavowal of authorship, it appears that Berkeley is the poem's author, and tellingly it appears it was composed at least two years before he left England for America. One reason for Berkeley's caution regarding copies was that his 'prophecy' regarding America was, of course, not yet realised. When he finally published the poem a quarter of a century later (in his *Miscellany* (1752)), he had, in the intervening years, made several changes. In its final and more familiar form it is as follows:

> The Muse, disgusted at an Age and Clime,
> Barren of every glorious Theme,
> In distant Lands now waits a better Time,
> Producing Subjects worthy Fame:
>
> In happy Climes, where from the genial Sun
> And virgin Earth such Scenes ensue,
> The Force of Art by Nature seems outdone,
> And fancied Beauties by the true:
>
> In happy climes, the Seat of Innocence,
> Where Nature guides and Virtue rules,
> Where Men shall not impose for Truth and Sense,
> The Pedantry of Courts and Schools:
>
> There shall be sung another golden Age,
> The rise of Empire and of Arts,
> The Good and Great inspiring epic Rage,
> The wisest Heads and noblest Hearts.

> Not such as Europe breeds in her decay;
> Such as she bred when fresh and young,
> When heavenly Flame did animate her Clay,
> By future Poets shall be Sung.
>
> Westward the Course of Empire takes its way;
> The four first Acts already past,
> A fifth shall close the Drama with the Day;
> Time's noblest Offspring is the last.[44]

To be sure, accounts of the New World as a desirable place preceded Berkeley's poem. 'Westward, like the Sun', John Dryden had written at the turn of the century, and Edmund Waller, too, had written in 1645 of Bermuda in his poem 'Battle of the Summer Islands':

> So sweet the air, so moderate the clime,
> None sickly lives, or dies before his time.
> Heaven sure has kept this spot of earth uncurst
> To show how all things were created first.[45]

Berkeley twice employed the phrase 'happy climes' in association with Bermuda. It had also long been celebrated by Shakespeare and Marvell. It was used as a trope in the early decades of the eighteenth century, and elicits comparison with Horace's Islands of the Blest.[46] It also connects with the representations of the Fortunate Isles of medieval legend, which St Brendan and his companions found when they, as Weston puts it, 'came unto a water, so clear and bright to see, from Eastward ever springing, Westward it floweth free'.[47] America was new in both senses of the word: new in relation to geological and human time, and new in relationship to European observers. America was still, in John Locke's celebrated phrase, 'in the beginning', and had seemed at first sight to live in the golden age of its own. Or as Carlos Fuentes' twentieth-century phrase puts it, 'America is its own utopia.'[48]

'On America' connects with the established poetic tradition of the New World idyll. Noah Porter, speaking at Yale College on 12 March 1885, on the two hundredth birthday of Berkeley, notes that Berkeley's 'well-known lines, though evincing little poetic genius, are the sober expression of his enthusiastic aspirations and his hopeful faith'.[49] The poem's utopian impulse is manifest as it crosses from the matter of fact and the classical idea of decay

('The Muse, disgusted at an age and clime' representing a decayed Europe, into the world of the imagined where 'in happy climes' 'there shall be sung another golden age') to the golden age of which Ovid spoke, now refashioned and recreated anew. And so the utopian frisson of 'On America' is predicated on what is imagined. Berkeley envisions a New World Utopia suffused with genial sunshine and a bountiful landscape whilst containing the possibility of producing 'the wisest heads and noblest hearts'. This New World idyll is juxtaposed throughout with the representation of a decayed and corrupt Europe, yet a Europe that once was as the New World 'fresh and young'.

Although Berkeley's 'On America' predates the first usage of the word 'dystopia' in 1747, Europe as represented in the poem stands as a dystopia to the New World Utopia. The best of Europe is past. Another golden age can only unfold in the New World, and its unfolding will see 'the rise of empire and of arts'. Unlike the traditions of Utopias from Eden to the *aisling* portrayals of Ireland, this imagined golden age is located in the future, a time of which 'future poets' will write. Significantly, Berkeley's 'On America' represents a key shift from a squandered golden age in Europe to the imagined and future New World Utopia. The 'traveller-philosopher', wrote Joseph-Marie Degerando in 1800, 'now sails to the farthest corners of the Globe, travels, in fact, along the roads of time. He travels in the past. Every step he takes is a century passed. The Islands he reaches are for him the cradle of human society.'[50] Berkeley is such a 'traveller-philosopher'. As prophetic muse, he harkens for Ovid's golden age – seeing it as a refuge – by moving into the past, as Degerando suggests, to awaken the possibility of another golden age in the future. Rexmond C. Cochrane refers to Berkeley's verses as a 'poetic compendium of eighteenth-century ideas'.[51] Moreover, in keeping with the expression of the westward motif, Cochrane demonstrates that Berkeley's verses are notable as 'perhaps no other poem in the Age of Reason included in the brief compass of six quatrains so many of the commonplaces of the prevailing quasi-optimistic intellectual development'.[52] It was in the west, proclaimed in all those ancient visions and prophecies, that it could be said Berkeley saw his personal New Atlantis, or, more felicitously, what Cochrane terms 'that heavenly city of the eighteenth-century rationalists which was to be realised in the not-distant future'.[53]

It is not that anything about Berkeley's verses is especially original in point of language or technique, but they do strike a utopian tuning fork, and immediately a whole orchestra of possibility may have stirred a contemporary reader or listener. In *George Berkeley: idealism and the man*, David Berman has considered much of the content of 'On America', particularly the line 'the four first Acts already past'.[54] He draws on a sermon given by Zachery Pearce (1690–1774), who had been personally involved in gathering subscriptions for the Bermuda project. Pearce refers to Isaiah 49:6, which proclaims 'salvation unto the end of the earth', and argues that this 'prophecy' is to be fulfilled in America. Berman looks at the similarity between Pearce's sermon and Berkeley's poem, and he uses Pearce's sermon as a key to understanding the 'Acts' mentioned in the poem. He suggests, drawing on the biblical source of Pearce's sermon, that the 'Acts' are the different phases in the spread of Christianity. Thus, Christianity 'was published at first in Judaea, from whence it spread to Samaria, and other Parts where the Jews dwelt … till at last … St. Paul, by the Direction of the Holy Spirit, began to apply himself to the Gentiles'.[55] We seem to have here the three acts, and the fourth would be the establishment of Christendom in Europe. The fifth act, then, was to be the general conversion of America, the close of the religious drama. This may not be the only interpretation of Berkeley's enigmatic last stanza, but he gave us little help in his letters of the period, in his publications, or indeed in the letter of 1726 when we first learn of the poem. Berman's interpretation seems apt: Berkeley's *Proposal* of 1724 is a pragmatic utopian document and it is complemented by the visionary 'On America', a poem and a prophecy for the future spread of Christianity's spiritual empire. In the 'located elsewhere' of Bermuda, the dream of the heavenly city of the eighteenth-century philosophers, the idea of progress and the imperative to improve remained to be configured.

Berkeley's American sojourn

In the years 1727–28, Berkeley found himself in a difficult position. The cause of the trouble was the college's double source of prospective revenue. The sum of £5,000 had been privately subscribed – a large sum, but, not supplemented, almost useless without the parliamentary grant. As A.A. Luce puts it:

> had Berkeley been depending solely on private subscriptions or solely on the grant, he would not, I believe, have sailed when he did. His prospective colleagues and his close friends did not want him to go; but some of the subscribers, not understanding the position about the Treasury grant, could see no reason why a start should not be made, and doubts were beginning to be expressed about Berkeley's intentions.

So he set sail for the West to satisfy the subscribers; he left in a 'private manner' to avoid the opposition of his associates in the enterprise.[56]

Writing to Thomas Prior, Berkeley said he would proceed 'privately' to set out for America to lay the foundation for his 'Utopian Seminary', and to await the fulfilment of promises made and hope cherished.[57] Berkeley sailed on the privately commissioned *Lucy* (Captain Cobb, master) from Gravesend in September 1728, bound for Rhode Island. He was accompanied by his wife Anne Forster Berkeley; Miss Handcock, a travelling companion of his wife; Richard Dalton of Lincolnshire, who was to remain in America; John James of Bury St Edmunds, who later succeeded to the baronetcy and returned to England; and John Smibert, an English artist who was to become the first trained portrait painter in America, and who remained there until his death in 1751. Smibert was meant to teach art and architecture at the Bermuda college.

   Why should Berkeley sail for Rhode Island with a view to establishing a college in Bermuda? Part of the answer is that his home preferments were to lapse, in accordance with the terms of the charter, eighteen months after his landing in Bermuda. Thus, if he had gone directly to the island, he would have had to vacate his deanery within a year. It would have been imprudent to take such a risk until it became certain that the promised government grant would be paid. Another part of the answer is that Berkeley all along meant to purchase an estate on the mainland to supply provisions to Bermuda, thus encouraging trade between the island and the American continent. In a letter to Berkeley in April 1729, Henry Newman (1670–1743) adds as a postscript: 'if you should be induced to pitch your stake in New York Government there is an island called Fisher's Island of which Mr. Winthrop is proprietor, who I believe would give you a good tract of land toward encouraging your settlement there'.[58] Leaving England to take up temporary residence in Rhode Island showed, too, that Berkeley was in earnest in his project. At the same time he would be in a convenient location to travel to Bermuda when the funds were received.

   Berkeley and his fellow travellers landed in Virginia early in January 1729 after four months at sea. In a letter to Percival (dated 7 February 1729),[59] he says he was well received, with many honours bestowed on him by the governor, William Gooch, and the principal inhabitants. They had a ten-day stay in Virginia. John James and Richard Dalton chose to make the rest of the journey overland, while Berkeley, his wife, Miss Handcock and John Smibert sailed on up the coast to Newport, their original destination. They finally arrived at Narragansett Bay in Rhode Island on 23 January 1729. Though not a bishop, Berkeley as dean of Derry was the highest-ranking ecclesiastical dignitary to visit up to that point. Apart from his status as an Anglican, Berkeley was something of an international celebrity, as much of his philosophical work would have preceded him. Wilkins Updike, in his *History of the Episcopal Church in Narragansett*, speaks of the friendship between Daniel Updike and Berkeley. Daniel Updike's son Lodowick recalled

> when as a boy, his father used to take him to hear Bishop Berkeley preach at Trinity Church, in Newport, where he pretty constantly officiated during his residence in the colony. Like all really learned men, the Dean was tolerant in religious opinion, which gave him a great and deserved popularity with all denominations. All sects rushed to hear him; even the Quakers, with their broad-brimmed hats, came and stood in the aisles.[60]

This anecdote of Lodowick Updike shows the regard in which Berkeley was held during his years in Rhode Island. A retrospective examination of this narrative shows how Berkeley's visit blended in with a utopian folkloric memory long after his visit had ended. Occasional mention of Berkeley is made in contemporary memoirs of New England life, such as those of the Updikes. His friends are named as including the Honeymans, the Hammonds, the Babcocks, Governor Robinson, the Mumfords and James MacSparran (subsequently, author of *America Dissected* and *Old Ireland's Misery*). Berkeley purchased a farm a few miles outside of Newport; he had the sturdy two-storey house on the land rebuilt and called it Whitehall. In a letter to Bishop Martin Benson of Gloucester, dated 11 April 1729, he declared: 'I do not think I could be so useful in any part of the world as in this place.'[61] In a letter to Thomas Prior (9 March 1730), Berkeley says, 'I live here upon land I have purchased and in a farmhouse I have built in this island. It is fit for cows and sheep and may be of good use for supplying our college in Bermuda.'[62] From this letter it would appear that Berkeley bought land in Rhode Island as an investment in order to supply provisions to Bermuda when the time came.

Berkeley spent nearly three years in America, and at some point began to doubt the wisdom of placing his college in Bermuda, and thought it may have been possible to situate it in America. A.A. Luce suggests that this change of direction came about through Berkeley's friendship with Henry Newman. He is almost forgotten now, but he was the main London agent for the Bermuda project, and most of Berkeley's American business passed through his hands. Before Berkeley sailed from Gravesend to America, Newman had written eight letters to acquaintances in America in which he speaks in general terms of Berkeley's plans, making no mention of Bermuda, though the letters do show that Berkeley was definitely bound for Rhode Island and meant to use it as a base before establishing his college. Newman wrote to Governor Jenks of Rhode Island (1727–32) on 28 August 1728:

> Hon. Sir: Having long since known your character and when you were in London the honour of some acquaintance with you, I take leave to recommend to your patronage and advice the Rev. Dr. Berkeley, Dean of Londonderry, whose zeal for the service of religion and humanity has exercised him so far as to induce him to undertake a voyage to America, in hopes of being instrumental to making the Gospel of Jesus Christ more known than it has been hitherto among the natives of the continent. He hath obtained a patent from our most gracious King for erecting a school or college for such purpose … John James and Richard Dalton, Esq., gents of honour and fortune are so good as to accompany the Dean in his setting out upon this design … They have travelled through the most polite parts of Europe, and if they arrive with you will have the pleasure of communicating their experience to the uncultivated parts of America.[63]

It was through his friendship with Newman that Berkeley learned about the politics and history of New England – for example, of Connecticut and its century-old dispute with Rhode Island. He came to know of Rhode Island, as yet without a college, but, as Luce puts it, 'high in favour with the home authorities, unique among the Plantations for her enlightened principles of civil and religious liberty; of Newport with her beautiful situation and genial climate, at that time a rival to New York in importance'.[64] Indeed, Newman had written to Berkeley shortly after his arrival in Rhode Island:

> I believe you are now satisfied that if you had made a short voyage to America before you had published your proposal you would have very much altered your scheme; but I hope you will have it in your power to rectify your first project in whatever it was amiss, and that your friends here may easily obtain a royal licence for such alterations as may be recommended by you.[65]

Despite Newman's advice, Berkeley did not have the power to rectify his position so as to establish his college in America rather than in Bermuda. After all, the royal charter had been granted for the establishment of a college in Bermuda, and all support and all funding was directed towards that end. Berkeley had hoped that by crossing the Atlantic and securing a possible source of supplies for the college in Bermuda he could convince the Treasury of the feasibility of the project, and have the promised funds released to him. When Berkeley began, as Luce argues, to tentatively solicit for a relocation of the college from Bermuda to Rhode Island, the chances of his getting the grant faded. As Luce observes, 'every argument for Rhode Island was against Bermuda and therefore against the Bermuda grant'.[66]

While in Rhode Island, Berkeley spent the bulk of his time writing his longest book, *Alciphron*, in which he defends Christianity against the freethinkers. By 1731 there was growing criticism about Berkeley's Bermuda project from, among others, Thomas Bray, an Anglican clergyman and briefly commissary to Maryland, and one of the founders in 1699 of the Society for Promoting Christian Knowledge (SPCK) and in 1701 of the Society for the Propagation of the Gospel in Foreign Parts (abbreviated as SPG). Berkeley had joined the SPCK early in 1725 and the SPG upon his return from America. To many of the patrons of Bray's two societies, Berkeley had made his own financial appeal when he set about seeking funding for his Bermuda project. However, Bray's biographer H.P. Thompson notes that his subject came to criticise Berkeley's plan. Bray saw, as Thompson relates, the whole scheme as impractical:

> The Bermudas were by no means the idyllic islands pictured by Berkeley, but rough and impoverished. It would be difficult to persuade Indian lads to go there – they would not even go to the 'Brafferton' hostel specially provided for them at William and Mary College – and if they did, they would be so denationalized that their tribes would not have them back, nor would they wish to return.[67]

All this and more Bray sets out, suggesting instead his own plan to form settlements near the borders with the native Americans, where carpenters, farmers and tailors would show them the crafts of 'civilisation', while clergy and schoolmasters would teach them the Christian faith. Percival, in his *Journal* of 10 March 1731, from which Rand quotes, speaks of a Dr Downs, bishop of Down, who had sent 'an impertinent letter to the Dean requiring him to come home, and calling his scheme idle and simple'.[68] In the winter of 1730–31 the final blow to the Bermuda project came in the form of Sir Robert Walpole's (1676–1745) message relayed through Edmund Gibson (1669–1748), bishop of London, informing Berkeley that the promised grant would never be paid. The details are provided by Stock, Berkeley's biographer:

> After having received various excuses, Bishop Gibson … (in whose diocese all the West Indies are included) applying to Sir Robert Walpole, then at the head of the treasury, was favoured at length with the following answer: 'If you put this question to me', says Sir Robert, 'as a minister, I must and can assure you that the money shall most undoubtedly be paid as soon as suits with public convenience: but if you ask me as a friend, whether Dean Berkeley should continue in America expecting the payment … I advise him by all means to return home to Europe, and to give up his present expectations.'[69]

Berkeley returned to London in October 1731 dejected but not beaten. Indeed, his return signalled a new creative period. The importance of the Bermuda project is reflected in Berkeley's writings of 1732–35, most of which argued against freethinking in religion, as this, Berkeley believed, had undermined his planned college. In a letter dated 10 March 1731, he writes: 'What they foolishly call free thinking seems to me the principal root or source not only of opposition to our College but of most other evils in the age.'[70] Berkeley was to allude to his disappointment in the two title pages of *Alciphron* (present in the 1732 editions), each of which has a vignette (see figures 1 and 2). In the first volume's vignette, Berman argues that 'Berkeley links the abandonment of his project with the abandonment of God. He does this by means of an open, spouting fountain, to the right of which there are three labourers digging a cistern.'[71] The meaning of the vignette becomes clearer from one of the mottoes beneath it, a quotation from Jeremiah 2:13: 'They have forsaken me the Fountain of living waters, and hewed them out cisterns, broken cisterns that can hold no water.' On one level, Berman argues, 'the vignette symbolises the rejection of God and religion by the free-thinkers or, as Berkeley prefers to call them, following Cicero, "minute philosophers", against whom *Alciphron* was written'.[72] This message seems to be reinforced by the vignette's second motto, taken from Cicero's *De Senectute*, section 85: 'But if when dead I shall be without sensation, as some minute philosophers think, then I have no fear that these philosophers, when they are dead, will have the laugh on me.' At another level, the fountain vignette represents the abandonment of Berkeley's

Bermuda project by the English government and by those who had formerly supported it but had ceased to do so. The link between this vignette and a pivotal passage in his 1724 *Proposal* is central:

> to any Man, who considers the divine Power of Religion, the innate Force of Reason and Virtue, and the mighty Effects often wrought by the constant regular Operation even of a weak and small Cause; it will seem natural and reasonable to suppose, that Rivulets perpetually issuing streaming through all Parts of America, must in due time have a great Effect, in purging away the ill manners and Irreligion of our Colonies, as well as the Blindness and Barbarity of the Nations round them: Especially, if the Reservoir be in a clean and private Place, where its Waters, out of the Way of any Thing that may corrupt them, remain clear and pure; otherwise they are more likely to pollute than purify the Places through which they flow.[73]

Here, then, Berkeley identified his proposed college with 'a Fountain, or Reservoir of Learning and Religion'. This identification can also be seen in the 'Bermuda Group' paintings, which have been collated and reproduced in a book entitled *Images of Berkeley* (see figures 3 and 4).[74] The paintings contain in the background 'rivulets ... issuing from a fountain or reservoir', which must stand for Berkeley's project. The vignette and the *Proposal* both convey Berkeley's hope for a spiritual and moral cleansing hewn from a New World Utopia. By 1732 Berkeley's project has been 'absolutely abandoned' not only by Walpole but also by former supporters of the plan, among them Robert Clayton (1695–1758). In a letter dated 2 March 1730, Berkeley speaks of 'this continued delay' that has 'made those persons who engaged with me entirely give up all thoughts of the College ... So that I am absolutely abandoned by every one of them'.[75]

In the second vignette, the seated figure, Berman argues, is that of Robert Walpole; 'by refusing to pay the £20,000 granted by Parliament, he was chiefly responsible for defeating Berkeley's project'.[76] Here again we have two mottoes printed beneath the engraving. The first is from Hosea 12:7: 'The balances of deceit are in his hand'; the second is from Plato's *Cratylus*, section 428d: 'The worst of all deceptions is self-deception.' Thus, the first vignette symbolises the abandonment of Berkeley's project, while the second depicts one of the forces that defeated it, and both identify the freethinkers, the target of *Alciphron*, whose infidelity Berkeley describes as 'an effect of narrowness and prejudice'.[77]

Berkeley's identification of his college with 'a Fountain, or Reservoir of

They have forfaken me the Fountain *of living waters, and hewed them out cifterns, broken cifterns that can hold no water.* Jerem. ii. 13.
Sin mortuus, ut quidam minuti Philofophi cenfent, nihil fentiam, non vereor ne hunc errorem meum mortui Philofophi irridcant.
Cicero.

Figure 1: Vignette from title page of *Alciphron*, vol. 1 (1732)

The Balances of Deceit are in his Hand. Hofea xii. 7.
Τὸ Ϝ̓ξαπατᾶꝛ αὐτὸν ὑφ᾽ αὑτᾶ. πάντων ναλεπώτατον. Plato.

Figure 2: Vignette from title page of *Alciphron*, vol. 2 (1732)

Learning and Religion' can also be seen in the visual legacy of the Bermuda project, notably in two paintings by John Smibert, both known as *The Bermuda Group*. (Smibert succeeded in becoming the first professional portrait painter in America. His detailed group portrait of Berkeley and his entourage is the largest canvas painted in America before 1750.) One of the paintings – the smaller of the two, dated *c.* 1730 – is in the National Gallery in Dublin (figure 3). The second, dated *c.* 1739, is in Yale University Art Gallery (figure 4). While nearly indistinguishable to the casual viewer, there are many obvious though subtle differences between the two paintings. The smaller painting features full-length figures of Berkeley, whose imposing stance, closely aligned to the column behind him, heightens his status as a 'pillar' of the planned religious and educational project in Bermuda. The man seated to the left is probably John Wainwright, Berkeley's friend and patron and, later, baron of the exchequer in Dublin; Wainwright had commissioned Smibert to create this portrait of the expeditionary party. The Transylvanian carpet tablecloth of a medallion and split-leaf border pattern is shown in full. The other individuals portrayed are: Mrs Anne Berkeley and the Berkeleys' first child Henry; Miss Handcock; John James of Bury St Edmunds (standing behind the two women); Richard Dalton of Lincolnshire (behind Wainwright), who was to remain in America; and John Smibert (in the background, retiring and unobtrusive). Smibert had met Berkeley in Italy, probably in 1720. They met again in London, and Berkeley often stayed with him in Covent Garden. He was meant to teach art and architecture at the Bermuda college. It has been argued by David Bjelajac that the painting 'proposes the alchemical power of the arts and letters to transform America's "virgin earth" into Berkeley's "golden age"',[78] with Anne Berkeley's golden-coloured dress and the child's golden hair symbolising a prosperous future. As the only sitter in the portrait born on American soil, Bjelajac contends that the child Henry 'personifies the western fruition of human destiny or "Time's noblest offspring" in the New World'.[79]

There are also subtle differences between both paintings in the use of colour, particularly in the colour of Dalton's coat, in the position of Miss Handcock's hand, and in the finished details. The first painting also contains, in the background, rivulets issuing from a fountain or reservoir, which must surely stand for Berkeley's project. Miss Handcock is pointing at something: her gesture seems symbolic rather than merely naturalistic; her left arm and hand are held seemingly awkwardly, and in pointing to the background she is pointing to the purpose or goal that drew them to America. Thus, the painting depicts the *Proposal*'s extended water image, evoking Berkeley's hope for the spiritual and

Figure 3: *Dean Berkeley and His Entourage – The Bermuda Group* (Dublin)
by John Smibert, *c.* 1730 (oil on canvas, 61 cm x 70 cm).
With permission of the National Gallery of Ireland

moral cleansing of the New World. In the later painting on the larger canvas, Miss Handcock's hand is lowered and seems to have moved away from the image in the background – perhaps an artistic assertion of the failure of their proposed Bermuda project.

The subtle differences between the paintings may relate to the dates they were painted, with the larger canvas, painted *c.* 1739, representative of an unsuccessful Bermuda project, signified by the positioning of Miss Handcock's hand. Scholars view the smaller painting as a sketch that preceded the larger one; they date it from late 1729 (the boy Henry was not born until June 1729) to some time in November 1730.

Beyond all question, Berkeley's 1724 *Proposal* was flawed. The main thrust of the plan, as the lead title made clear, was 'the better supplying of churches in our Foreign Plantations', but stemming from a vision of a New World Utopia, a Christian social order, a learned and virtuous ministry. These were

Figure 4: *The Bermuda Group (Dean Berkeley and His Entourage)* (Yale)
by John Smibert *c*. 1728, reworked 1739 (oil on canvas, 176.5 cm x 236 cm).
With permission of Yale University Art Gallery

the ultimately unattained goals. If the *Bermuda Group* painting of 1730
represents the project as hopeful possibility, two other portraits of Berkeley
encapsulate the project as a distant prospect and in stormy retrospect. In *Dean
Berkeley Pointing* (1730) by John Smibert (figure 5), Berkeley is pointing to a
rocky island that could signify Bermuda, and hence his project. On the island
there appears to be running water, the recurring symbolic motif Berkeley
first introduces in the *Proposal*. In the subsequent portrait of Berkeley dated
May 1733 and by an unknown artist (figure 6), the ship on the stormy sea
is undoubtedly meant to symbolise Berkeley's journey to America and his
Bermuda project; the book that Berkeley holds is entitled *Voyage to the Indies*.
The painting represents the Bermuda project in retrospect both in its date
and aspect, and in the panoply of extant visual images of the Bermuda project
effectively marks its end.

Figure 5: *Dean Berkeley Pointing* by John Smibert, 1730 (oil on canvas, 101.5 cm x 75 cm). With permission of the National Portrait Gallery, London

Figure 6: *Georgius Berkeley*, artist unknown, 1733
(oil on canvas, 124.5 cm x 99 cm).
With permission of the Archbishop of Canterbury
and the Church Commissioners

Berkeley's New World Utopia

In islands men placed their ideal states … to reach felicity one must cross water.
Donald S. Johnson[80]

As Zhang Longxi puts it, 'if at the most basic level, the idea of utopia suggests the vision of an alternative and better society beyond reality, then it already implies some degree of discontent with the *status quo*'.[81] Berkeley's 1724 *Proposal*, a utopian document in the form of an extended speculative essay, harnessed such a vision predicated on the actual location of Bermuda. The intellectual basis of his *Proposal* and his subsequent plan for 'The City of Bermuda Metropolis of the Summer Islands' (figure 7) emerged from strong discontent with the status quo in Europe.[82] The connection between the exploration of the New World and utopian thinking was over two centuries old by the time Berkeley and his supporters hoped to fund and found a college in Bermuda. The *Proposal* as a speculative document includes descriptions of the as yet non-existent intentional community. It is both utopian and pragmatic: utopian in its critique of Europe, and pragmatic in its immediate aims and its need to secure government sanction and funding. Berkeley's Utopia presents a narrative space specifically designed to serve a cultural purpose by offering a retreat from the corrupt past and a vision of the future predicated on the propagation of the gospel in a Christian Utopia in the New World. However, something more than a Christian interest may have inspired Berkeley in his project. Hone and Rossi argue that Swift was incorrect in saying that Berkeley loathed 'power', as they put it, for 'as a youth he had dreamed of becoming the philosopher of a resurgent nation, and had to that end associated himself with the young of his college, like Prior and Madden'.[83]

In Bermuda, in a 'flight from the world', Berkeley could mould and direct a community. He could establish an ideal state, where *his* philosophy, *his* economics, *his* views on architecture would prevail. Berkeley's preparations extended to drawing up a plan for 'The City of Bermuda Metropolis of the Summer Islands'. The plan survived, but, unlike the *Proposal*, it was never presented to Parliament. Out of his classical imagination, Berkeley drew a symmetrical plan of the city. The main street extends into a square with a steeple at its centre, while at the further end a church is skirted by open porticos. Behind the square are two triangular spaces, one containing a theatre, the other an academy of architecture, sculpture and painting. At the edge of the city, the fish and herb markets are connected by the 'walk of death', as the cemetery forms the boundary line of the metropolis, backed by groves of cypress trees. The houses along the main street and on either side of the square have gardens from which doors open out into public parks and groves. The college itself stands on a peninsula, a quarter of a mile from the city. Berkeley's plan was developed, I believe, to stand not only as a symbol of the 'New City of Bermuda' but also to contribute to the creation of an ideal Christian society that would provide all the prerequisites of complete happiness and fulfilment. For Berkeley, the integration of his college in Bermuda into a whole city plan seemed to enable a retreat from Europe, a reconfiguring and relocating of self and society in a New World Utopia.

The connection between Utopia and the city has been traced by Lyman Tower Sargent and by historian and architectural critic Lewis Mumford back to the ancient Greeks, who thought of the ideal state and political community as a city. Plato (*c.* 429–*c.* 347 BC) in his *Republic* projected his ideal commonwealth in the spatial form of an ordered city state. Mumford proposes that these influential visions of the city were not products simply of Hellenic speculation but rather that they reflected earlier ties between Utopia and the city that had been realised in the archetypal ancient cities in Egypt and Mesopotamia. In those societies, according to Mumford, the city actually *was* Utopia; it was the very first Utopia, created by a king acting in the name of a god, and established as a sacred place through the building of a temple and surrounding walls, with an intrinsic relation to the cosmic order. It was this connection between the royal, the religious and the cosmic that clearly differentiates the city from other kinds of settlement. As Mumford puts it, 'the city itself was transmogrified into an ideal form – a glimpse of eternal order, a visible heaven on earth, a seat of life abundant – in other words, utopia'.[84] The dualism of the utopian elements in Berkeley's Bermuda project manifested, first, in the *Proposal*, and, second, in his plan for the City of Bermuda. His city as Utopia existed within the broader narrative of the establishment of an intentional community. Berkeley set out a personal vision of time and space, an imaginative projection of a newly planned city. Like More's island, this place is closed off from the present, lying in another space and time as the embodiment of a Christian and aesthetic ideal. This quality can perhaps be seen more clearly in the context of geographer David Harvey's call in *Spaces of Hope* for a 'dialectical utopianism'.[85] He argues for a utopianism that is informed by the combination of transformative vision and pragmatic action. Here, then, Berkeley's project, while predating Harvey's term, can be read as an eighteenth-century instance of it.

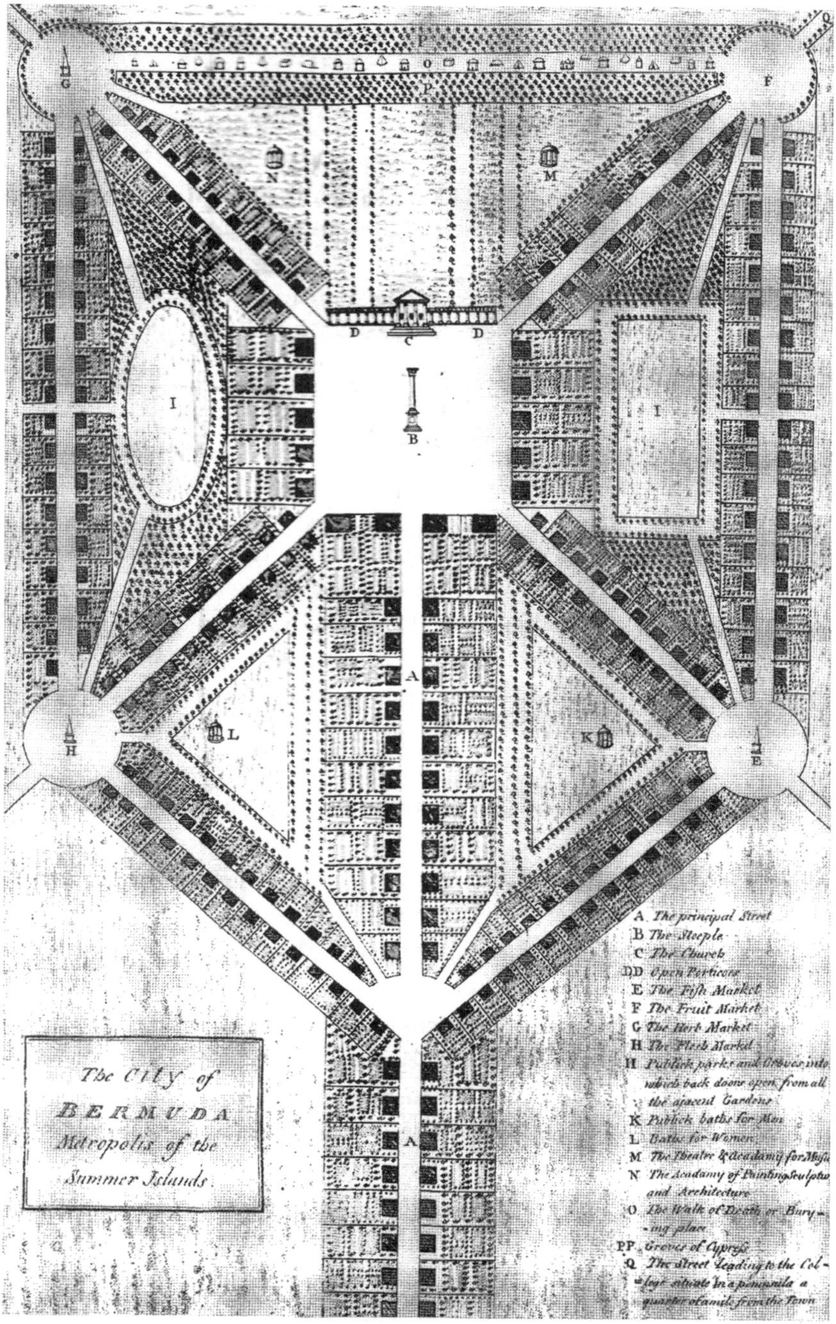

Figure 7: Plan for 'The City of Bermuda Metropolis of the Summer Islands'

Regardless of the outcome, opinions have differed, and will differ, about the Bermuda project. According to A.A. Luce, 'Berkeley's Bermuda Project is a topic of perennial interest'.[86] He tells of a letter written in 1851 by Revd W.C. Dowding to Primate Lord John Beresford, asking him to be patron of a scheme for 'the revival of Berkeley's College in Bermuda'.[87] This is a curious request, but nonetheless shows something of the interest Berkeley's project still generated over a century after it was first proposed. Moreover, John Mitchel (1815–75) in his *Jail Journal,* one of Irish nationalism's most famous works, mentions Berkeley's Bermuda plan. Mitchel had been deported from Ireland and spent time in Bermuda before he was sent to the penal colony of Van Diemen's Land (Tasmania). To be sure, to some the Bermuda project was a piece of quixotic folly. Hone and Rossi, concluding that Berkeley never founded his Platonic republic, called it an 'escapade'.[88] Others have viewed it as a scheme sound in principle but thwarted by a lack of funding and a decline in initial support.

Perhaps the true analysis lies in the *via media.* Bermuda could not have become 'the Athens of the West' because distance was a major problem. Bermuda is almost 600 miles from the nearest point on the mainland. If Berkeley's geographical information was incorrect, then he may not have realised the distances involved. A contemporary review of a book on Bermuda in Jean Le Clerc's *Bibliothèque choisie* places the islands of Bermuda about 'soixante lieues de terre'.[89] If Berkeley had access to this information, he might have come to think of Bermuda as not much further from America than the roughly sixty miles from Dublin to Holyhead in Wales. He could have seen his college as a Trinity College in the west, near, but not too near, the constraints of the mainland. Berkeley's plan for his Platonic republic eventually faded. His *Proposal* emerged out of discontent with the Old World as he looked hopefully to the New World, as he expressed poetically in 'On America'. As the Manuels observe, 'utopia is a hybrid plant, born of the crossing of a paradisiacal, otherworldly belief of Judeo-Christian religion with the Hellenic myth of an ideal city on earth'.[90] Berkeley's *Proposal* and his plan for the City of Bermuda represent such a hybrid plant, with its utopian seminary set in an ideal city. His city plan is the most Irish facet of his utopianism. If he saw himself and friends such as Thomas Prior, Samuel Madden and John Percival as leaders of a nation about to be reconstructed, then the city plan could be construed as a vicarious attempt at nation planning, set in the located elsewhere of Bermuda, and predicated on his personal vision. This utopian energy becomes analogous to a displaced rebellion, with an ideal city unrealised in

Bermuda but potentially realisable in a future Irish Utopia. Overall, Berkeley's utopianism is more complex than at first appears. In *The Querist* (1735), he is clearly exploring the idea of what might constitute a Utopia, even if he is not writing one. And so Berkeley's mis-mapping of Utopia in Bermuda comes to rest in the practical philanthropy of *The Querist*; his utopianism finds a home in the endless set of possibilities for the transformation of everyday eighteenth-century life.

The Pacific Utopia in the writings of Theobald Wolfe Tone

Tone is the intellectual ancestor of the whole modern movement of Irish Nationalism.
Patrick Pearse, *The Sovereign People*[91]

Utopian works rarely adopt a one-dimensional format, but are almost always multifaceted. Over sixty years after Berkeley first presented his *Proposal* and his plan for the City of Bermuda, another Irishman, Theobald Wolfe Tone (1763–98), subsequent founder of Irish republican nationalism, wrote his *Sandwich Islands Memorandum* (1790). Writing in *Archaeologies of the Future*, Fredric Jameson says 'utopia has always been a political issue, an unusual destiny for a literary form: yet just as the literary value of the form is subject to permanent doubt, so also its political status is structurally ambiguous'.[92] In disparate ways both Berkeley and Wolfe Tone could be said to have combined both the utopian and the political. Berkeley's discontent with the status quo in Europe formed the basis for the utopian kernel of his thoughts in his *Proposal* and in his plan for the City of Bermuda.

By way of contrast, Wolfe Tone's memorandum presents an interesting interconnection between republican and colonial utopianism in the late eighteenth century. For the late eighteenth-century imagination, Utopia represented the imaginative journeying into the unknown; sailing to the New World became a dominant motif. Thomas More's *Utopia* was the first Utopia to present the issue of colonies, and it does so, as Lyman Tower Sargent identifies, 'in a way that demonstrates that colonies are intended to support the home country, not primarily to fill the needs of the colonists'.[93] As in *Utopia*, where More links Raphael Hythloday's account of his visit to the island of Utopia with the real-life voyages of Amerigo Vespucci (1451–1512), a rich spectrum of projections appeared in print often based in part on the actual accounts of returning travellers, an example of which is James Burgh's

reformist Utopia, *An Account of the Cessares*, which appeared in 1764. It criticised contemporary English society by presenting the advantages and virtues
of a mythical South American republic. As Carla H. Hay argues, 'the Cessares
government epitomized the commonwealthman's ideal of a limited constitutional monarchy purged of corruption and faction'.[94] Moreover, Thomas
Spence's *Crusonia* (1782), Carl Wadstrom's *Sierra Leone* (1787), Wolfe Tone's
Sandwich Islands Memorandum (1790), Thomas Northmore's *Makar* (1795)
and Robert Southey's *Caermadoc* (1799) were all Utopias located in faraway
Africa, the Caribbean, South America and the Pacific.

In 1788 Tone, while studying law at the Middle Temple in London,
turned his hand to writing to earn some money. The Enlightenment and the
emerging concept of the global had generated major interest in faraway places
and people. Over the summer of 1788, Tone, his brother William and his
friend Benjamin Phipps read about the recent voyages of discovery. Within
the compass of such works were Narborough's *Account of Several Late Voyages
and Discoveries to … the South Seas* (1694), Ulloa's *Voyage to South America*
(translated from the Spanish, 1758), Woodes Roger's *A Cruising Voyage Around
the World First to the South Sea* (1712), George Anson's *Voyage Round the
World* (1748) and William Dampier's *A New Voyage Around the World* (1697)
(also beloved of Swift), the most recent edition of which was published in
1785, being the version Tone used along with the most recent editions of
James Cook's voyages published in the 1770s. During that summer Tone
wrote his first memorandum in collaboration with his brother William, an
officer in the East India Company artillery. It proposed the establishment of a
British military colony on the recently discovered Sandwich Islands as a base
from which to counteract the growing Spanish power and influence in the
Pacific. From an economic perspective he proffered that the landscape would
be suitable as a British site for growing sugar cane, cotton and indigo. In his
two volume *Life*,[95] Tone tells how he hand-delivered his work to 10 Downing
Street on 10 August 1788, to be given to Prime Minister William Pitt. He
later referred to it as 'my first essay in what I may call politics'.[96] Ten days later,
having received no acknowledgment, Tone wrote a letter to Pitt mentioning
his memorandum; that letter likewise went unacknowledged.

Despite the absence of a response from Pitt, Tone maintained an ongoing
interest in his plan. In 1790 he reformulated it with the assistance of Thomas
Russell (who was to become the future co-founder of the United Irishmen)
and the American republican veteran Thomas Digges. The revised plan was
written against the background of the Nootka Sound incident of 1790, when

Britain was in dispute with Spain over trading rights on the north-west coast of Canada. As Tone puts it, 'during the course of this summer, there were strong appearances of a rupture between England and Spain, relative to Nootka Sound … we enlarged and corrected my original plan'.[97] It was addressed to the Duke of Richmond and later to the foreign secretary, William Grenville, and it expanded upon the original plan by promoting a republican war of liberation in Spanish America. The idea for a war of liberation came from Thomas Digges. The revised memorandum – in a move reminiscent of James Burgh's mythical South American Republic – proposed creating a free republic in South America. It would have, as Tone wrote, 'her liberty guaranteed by England and North America, and a fair and equitable treaty of commerce between the three nations, which would, in effect, though not in form exclude the rest of the world'.[98] In essence, if established the military colony would provide a base from where England could move into South America and liberate the Spanish colonies there. Tone mentioned that through a series of contacts with an eminent American person, he was certain that North America would be willing to assist England in freeing the Spanish colonies. He asserted that America would not be induced to assist England in an open expedition against Spain, but would work with England in assisting the Mexicans and others in their wish for liberty and independence. Following on from this, the revamped memorandum included references to freedom and recommendations on republican forms of government and the benefits to England of creating a free republic in South America, while also noting the important strategic benefit to England of a successful military colony in the Sandwich Islands, which could always be used to political advantage. Moreover, he noted that the islands possessed many natural advantages, many harbours and a well-stocked landscape. Indeed, with these great advantages Tone argued that whether viewed in a commercial or a political light, the settlement could be more successful than any other colony hitherto attempted. In the first few lines of his memorandum, Tone quoted from Cook's writing: 'the Sandwich Isles, from their situation and productions, bid fairer for becoming an object of consequence in the system of European navigation, than any other discovery in the South Sea'.[99] Tone's plan is best understood in the context of many other projects for British colonial expansion in the years following Cook's voyages to the Pacific. As Nigel Leask points out, 'in 1783 James Matra had proposed a distinctly dystopian convict settlement in New South Wales as a means of clearing out England's overcrowded prison hulks after American independence had closed down England's previous penal dumping ground'.[100] Four years later Matra's plan was accepted by Pitt, and the first fleet set sail with convicts on board, arriving on 26 January 1788 at Port Jackson, or, as it would later be called, Sydney Harbour. This meant, inevitably, that events in Nootka Sound focused on the desirability of a strategic base in the Pacific, and Botany Bay was on the wrong side of the ocean. Among the thicket of ideas and plans for British colonial expansion, Tone believed that a plan such as his had not been tried since the days of ancient Rome. In a word, wrote Tone,

> The idea is to construct a settlement on somewhat of feudal principles, to reward military attendance and exertion by donative lands, to train the rising generation to arms and danger, to create a small but impenetrable nation of soldiers, where every man should have a property, and arms and spirit to defend it, to temper the ferocity of the natives by the arts of European culture, and to call forth from the tomb, where for a century it has slept, the invincible daring of the old bucaniers [*sic*], uncontaminated by their disgraceful debaucheries in peace, and their still more infamous barbarities in war.[101]

Tone proposed that 500 men under the age of thirty should be selected from different marching regiments, although he believed that ten times that number would voluntarily sign up to the plan. However, he argued that those chosen for the nascent mission should have a wide knowledge of the trades most needed in an infant colony. Moreover, he suggested that

> the officer commanding the expedition, should labour most strenuously to gain the friendship of the natives, and, in process of time, should try the experiment of training a few battalions, like our Seapoys in India; that, at the end of seven years, the soldiers should be allowed their discharge, with the option to return to England or stay in the Country.[102]

The Sandwich Islands were not empty but were in fact inhabited, and an expansionist settler Utopia such as Tone's undoubtedly prefigured a dystopia for the indigenous inhabitants. Up until the late twentieth century, utopian literature was almost in its entirety written by the colonisers or their supporters. More's Utopians did not think the inhabitants of the area to be important, and this thinking is frequently reiterated in utopian literature located in colonies. While Tone's *Sandwich Islands Memorandum* is an example of this kind of thinking, he is pragmatic in calling for the officer commanding the expedition to gain the friendship of the 'natives'. Tone's plan for the military colony was partially based on a classical republican model. It sits easily with the martial virtues exemplified by the expansionist 'republic of increase' extolled by James Harrington, Henry Neville and other 'commonwealth-men'. The choice of the Sandwich Islands – renowned for its fierce 'natives', who had murdered Cook in 1779 – may have been motivated by more than its strategic position to the American continent. According to Leask, 'It also underlines Tone's conscious rejection of the sensuous and epicurean paradise of Tahiti, celebrated by Diderot in his *Supplement to Bougainville's Voyage*.'[103] Tone explained that his plan was inspired by the military colonies of ancient Rome, but it is also suggestive of the philosophy of the Irish Volunteer movement, which had widespread Protestant support and had provided the genesis for Henry Grattan's successful bid to gain legislative independence for the Irish parliament in 1782. Set in this context, it is not difficult to view Tone's memorandum as a model for the secret society of United Irishmen founded by himself and Russell a year after they had reworked the *Sandwich Islands Memorandum*. The vision Tone cherished for the United Irishmen was that they would 'subvert the tyranny of our execrable government; to break the connection with England, the never-failing source of our political evils; and to assert the independence of my country'.[104] Meanwhile, in their revolutionary manifesto Tone and Russell urged 'our countrymen in general to follow our example, and form similar societies ... for the promotion of constitutional knowledge, the abolition of bigotry in religion and politics, and the equal distribution of the rights of man through all sects and denominations of Irishmen'.[105]

The early modern Utopia imagined new social formations emerging from the contact, real or imagined, between the Old World and the New World. Berkeley's utopian projection predicated on the island of Bermuda envisioned the creation of an 'Athens of the West'. During the later stages of the eighteenth century, the discovery of the Sandwich Islands 'opened' – as Wolfe Tone expounded in his pre-revolutionary *Sandwich Islands Memorandum* – 'an extensive prospect of public benefit'.[106] Utopianism is multifaceted. The utopian element in Berkeley's thinking in his Bermuda project was ultimately reconfigured in his practical philanthropy at home. Moreover, Wolfe Tone's memorandum represented a way station in the trajectory of the emergence of his radicalism.

CHAPTER 5

'To the Limits of the Lunar World':
Extraterrestrial Voyages and Utopia

What about my writing a 'City of the Moon?' Would it not be excellent to
describe the cyclopic mores of our time in vivid colours, but in doing so – to
be on the safe side – to leave this Earth and go to the Moon?

Johannes Kepler[1]

To behold an island in the air, inhabited by men, who are able (as it should
seem) to raise or sink, or put it into a progressive motion as they pleased.

Jonathan Swift[2]

S o far I have identified a utopian propensity in eighteenth-century Irish
culture. The more realistic utopian projections of Berkeley and of the
founders and supporters of the early Dublin philosophical societies and
the Dublin Society coexisted within a milieu where literary works of utopian
satire also emerged as an integral fictive facet of eighteenth-century Irish utopianism. While Berkeley and the Dublin Society worked towards a utopianism
of improvement, the satirical extraterrestrial and lunar narratives by writers
such as Jonathan Swift, Murtagh McDermot, Margaret King Moore (Lady
Mount Cashell), Francis Gentleman and others provided a more imaginative
register from which to criticise and challenge contemporary society.[3]

In *The Power of Satire*, Robert Elliott argues that '*Satire* is notoriously a
slippery term, designating, as it does, a form of art and a spirit, a purpose
and a tone'.[4] His use of the term, he argues, 'depends upon context and
qualifying terms to convey the relevant sense of *satire* intended at any given
time'.[5] In developing the link between Utopia and satire, Sargent refers to the
function of some Utopias 'to hold the present up to ridicule and, in doing

so, many utopias use a typical tool of satire, exaggeration'.[6] He has particularly defined utopian satire as presenting 'a non-existent society described in considerable detail and normally located in time and space that the author intended a contemporaneous reader to view as a criticism of that contemporary society'.[7] Northrop Frye speaks of a utopian satire as 'one in which social rituals are seen from the outside, not to make them more consistent but simply to demonstrate their inconsistency, their hypocrisy, or their unreality. Satire of this kind holds up a mirror to society which distorts it, but distorts it consistently.'[8]

The intertextual hybridity of Utopia and satire provides the framework for eighteenth-century Irish-authored extraterrestrial voyages. Both Gentleman and Swift wrote satires, and it is useful to note how they defined this mode within the context of their eighteenth-century world. In 1772 Gentleman, writing (under the pseudonym of Sir Nicholas Nipclose, Baronet) in *The Theatres: a poetical dissection*, says, 'If Satire is a useful species of writing, it can only deserve that title by being keen.'[9] Swift, in the preface to his *A Full and True Account of the Battel Fought Last Friday Between the Antient and Modern Books in St. James's Library* (1697), says, 'Satire is a sort of glass, wherein beholders do generally discover everybody's face but their own, which is the chief reason for that kind of reception it meets in the world, and that so very few are offended with it.'[10] The author of a pamphlet entitled *The Antisatyrist: a dialogue. To which is prefixed, a short dissertation on panegyric, and satyr* (1750) argues that, 'as for Satyr, it is a sort of Wormwood, infused, sometimes in ordinary Ale, and sometimes in choice White-wine: but, at the best, it is a disagreeable Medicine, fit for none, but squeamish, disordered Stomachs'.[11] Gentleman and Swift evoke a satiric mode that is both keen and benign in their individual critiques of contemporary society. Taken in Robert Elliott's sense 'in context', such satire comes to merge with the utopian. Utopia is, as Nicole Pohl writes, 'inseparable from the imaginary voyage'.[12]

Early colonies in space

While voyages within the earth and beyond to the limits of the lunar world occasion expressions of utopian desire, lunar voyages, popular since Lucian and Plutarch's *The Face of the Moon*, further challenged the boundaries of the cosmos; they were not located in another place on earth but offered new sites for utopian alternatives. The new discoveries in science combined with the format of a journey to another world facilitated critical commentary on the known world, and provided a large but 'safe medium to criticise contemporary society'.[13] It is not surprising that this distinctive body of literature on cosmic voyages is satirical. While cosmic voyages are both 'imaginary' and 'extraordinary', they contain an essential difference, as Majorie Hope Nicolson puts it, 'since they lead not to the outposts of civilisation upon our maps, but away from this earth to some other world, usually in the heavens',[14] thereby stretching the scale of human imagination and possibility. To better understand their provenance, it is helpful to link cosmic voyages of the eighteenth-century literary tradition to earlier texts. Utopias and cosmic voyages share a long connection. For 2,000 years, the moon has been peopled and explored through humanity's imagination. Lunar travel had long been an earthly dream. For centuries, philosophers, scientists, satirists and dreamers considered the possibilities and merits of undertaking trips to the moon. Peter Leighton's *Moon Travellers* (1960) was subtitled *A dream that is becoming a reality*. As Leighton observes, 'the world, educated by now as to the prowess of Russian and American scientists and technicians, is ready to accept as only a question of time that men will be following the monkeys, dogs and rabbits into space and that their first destination will be the Moon'.[15] Leighton cites Professor Chlebzevitch of the Soviet Union, who commented that 'at the turn of this century journeys to and from the Moon will become a routine business, the Moon will be just the seventh continent of our world and men will be mainly concerned with exploiting its mineral wealth'.[16] While the first prediction has long since been realised, the second remains elusive, and journeys to the moon have yet to become a 'routine business'. Yet Leighton, in foregrounding these points, is following in the trajectory from which a particular utopian tendency emerges, the point at which the imaginary journey may become real. From 1600 literary Utopias based on extraterrestrial worlds became increasingly prominent. This, as Frank and Fritzie Manuel have observed, occurred 'when moon travel dependent upon breaking through the gravitational pull and attaining a state of weightlessness for most of the journey became a theoretical scientific possibility'.[17] Indeed, the possibility of life on the moon was considered by Johannes Kepler in *Somnium*, published posthumously in 1634. Kepler created a voyage to the moon as a mixture of fantasy and realism. With Kepler, we are not in Utopia or Arcadia but on the telescopic moon itself. Our guide is a scientist. In this way Kepler's *Somnium* differs greatly from other cosmic voyages. As Nicolson notes:

Nonscientific writers spent their originality chiefly upon inventing ingenious means for getting to the Moon and on descriptions of the voyage. Their moon-worlds often prove conventional Utopias or mere convenient vehicles for satire on political and social customs in this world. Kepler, on the other hand, bent his efforts to describing the moon-world as Plutarch had presupposed it, as the telescope had shown it.[18]

The influence of *Somnium* continued into the nineteenth century. There are reminiscences of its moonscape in Jules Verne's *From the Earth to the Moon* (1865) and in H.G. Wells' *The First Men in the Moon* (1900). Kepler succeeded in transforming the ancient Lucianic literary tradition into the modern scientific moon voyage. *Somnium* was therefore familiar to all subsequent writers of cosmic voyages during the seventeenth, eighteenth and nineteenth centuries. Moon travel was adaptable; it could combine science, fantasy and even theology, as the creation and manner of life of extraterrestrial beings allowed scope for utopian invention. As Brian Aldiss argues:

> Kepler established no utopias there. But utopias were still being built. A confusion of wonderful voyages with utopias is of long standing; once a writer has got his travellers to his obscure region on Earth, or to another world, or to the future, he must find something for them to do, and on the whole writers divide fairly sharply between those who have their protagonists lecture and listen to lectures and those who have them menaced by or menacing local equivalents of flora, fauna, and Homo Sapiens.[19]

Such utopian invention permeated the contour maps of the literary-voyage landscapes created by John Wilkins, Francis Godwin and lesser-known Irish writers such as Murtagh McDermot (*fl.* 1720s), Francis Gentleman (1728–84) and Margaret King Moore (*c.* 1771–1835). The utopian visions created by these eighteenth-century Irish authors share the common factor of a journey to another world. Ultimately, they are discovery narratives, evoking the alternative space of the distant sphere. To be sure, in certain details both McDermot's and Gentleman's narratives share a connection with, among others, Wilkins and Godwin. Bishop Wilkins in *A Discourse Concerning a New World and Another Planet* (1640) describes a chariot; Gentleman's narrator Sir Humphrey Lunatic in his *Trip to the Moon* (1764) also speaks of a triumphal chariot or chair. Humphrey Lunatic meets with Wilkins while he is in the lunar world. Godwin's character Domingo Gonsales in his *The Man in the Moone* (1638) comes to connect in Nicolson's analysis with Swift's *Gulliver's Travels* (1726). As she puts it, speaking of Gonsales on the moon,

> As he remained among them, however, Domingo discovered, as do all travellers to Utopia, degrees and differences among lunarians as among men in this world. Many passages here anticipate *Gulliver's Travels*. Domingo, the mortal, found himself classed among the least of the lunarians as Gulliver found himself among the Yahoos, since one's social status in Godwin's moon-world depended in part upon his height and stature, in part upon his ability to bear the varied kinds of light Domingo found in the moon.[20]

Godwin's Gonsales starts his journey to the moon from 'the island of Tenerife one of the Canaries, which is famous through the world, for a hill upon the same called El Pico, that is to be discerned and kenned upon the sea no less that ten leagues off'.[21] Ninety years later, McDermot, while climbing the same hill, is enveloped by a whirlwind and transported to the moon.

Space, dystopia and 'A Voyage to Laputa'

Jonathan Swift in a letter to Charles Ford dated 14 August 1725 says: 'I have finished my Travells [*sic*], and I am now transcribing them; they are admirable Things, and will wonderfully mend the World.'[22] The *Travells* were published by Benjamin Motte on 28 October 1726 as *Travels into Several Remote Nations of the World*. 'A Letter from Capt. Gulliver to his Cousin Sympson' first appeared in the 1735 edition and is dated 2 April 1727. The name Sympson may allude to William Sympson, the pseudonymous author of *A Voyage to the East Indies* (1715). The letter opens:

> I hope you will be ready to own publicly, whenever you shall be called to it, that by your great and frequent Urgency you prevailed on me to publish a very loose and uncorrect Account of my Travels; with Direction to hire some young Gentlemen of either University to put them in Order, and correct the Style, as my Cousin Dampier did by my Advice, in his Book called, 'A Voyage Round the World'.[23]

Unlike Lemuel Gulliver, the putative cousin William Dampier was a character in real life. Born near Yeovil in Somerset in 1651, Dampier was a privateer, one of those brave but none-too-scrupulous adventurers who equipped themselves with ships and set off to make as much money as they could. He charted large sections of the Australian coast, and amassed a large botanical collection. Dampier noted all the weather patterns he saw and the ocean currents he experienced. He died in 1715, but as late as 1922 the science journal *Nature* described his charts of the Pacific Ocean as 'containing as much information about the winds in the Pacific as any of the modern works on the same subject'.[24] Undoubtedly, Dampier caught the attention of Swift as he did later of Wolfe Tone. William Le Fanu records that Swift owned a copy of the third edition of William Dampier's *A New Voyage Round the World* (1698).[25]

If Dampier's work influenced Swift in his writing of *Gulliver's Travels*, it is also possible that Swift was influenced by Robert Boyle (1627–91). Swift could well have owed the idea for *Gulliver's Travels* to Boyle's *Occasional Reflections on Several Subjects, Whereto is Premis'd a Discourse About Such Kind of Thoughts* published in London in 1665. Boyle therein says that he had

> thoughts of making a short romantic story, where the scene should be laid in some island, of the southern ocean, govern'd by such rational Laws and Customs as those of *Utopia*, or the *New Atlantis*; and in this Country he would introduce an observing Native, that upon his return home from his Travels made in *Europe* should give an account of our countries and manners under feign'd names, and frequently intimate in his relations (or in his answers to questions that should be made him) the reasons of his wondering to find our customs so extravagant and differing from those of his country. For, more I imagine, that by such a way of proposing many of our practices, we should ourselves be brought unawares to condemn, or perhaps laugh at them; and would at least cease to wonder to find other Nations think them as extravagant as we think the manners of the *Dutch* and *Spaniards* as they are represented in our travellers books.[26]

It is noteworthy that Boyle makes reference to More and Bacon, two utopian writers whose work influenced Swift in writing *Gulliver's Travels*. Gulliver refers to Utopia directly in the letter to his Cousin Sympson:

> If the Censure of the *Yahoos* could any Way affect me, I should have

great Reason to complain that some of them are so bold as to think my Book of Travels a meer Fiction out of mine own Brain, and have gone so far as to drop Hints, that the *Houyhnhnms* and *Yahoos* have no more Existence than the Inhabitants of Utopia.[27]

And in Bacon's *New Atlantis* Swift found his analogue for Gulliver's 'Voyage to Laputa'. Bacon had followed the course of More's *Utopia*, but differently, as A.L. Morton argues:

Bacon, unlike More, was not concerned with social justice. He, too, was a Humanist, but by the beginning of the seventeenth century Humanism had run cold: hence, the difference between *Utopia* and *New Atlantis* is not so much a difference of content as a difference of purpose, a shift of interest and a lowering of temperature.[28]

A 'Voyage to Laputa' is uniquely Swift's own extraterrestrial journey. As Nicolson argues, at one level

Swift's island of Laputa is a flying chariot, harking back to the devices of Godwin and Cyrano, to Lana's Canoe and Gusmão's Passarola. From another angle, the 'Voyage to Laputa' is a voyage to the moon, a conspicuous departure from other adventures of Gulliver, all of which take place in the terrestrial world.[29]

As the 'Voyage to Laputa' begins, there is nothing to suggest that this journey is to become a conspicuous departure from the other adventures of Gulliver. At first it follows the style of the others. Gulliver sets out on 5 August 1706, there is a storm at sea, and the ship is overtaken by pirates. Gulliver is set adrift on a solitary journey:

as to myself, it was determined that I should be set adrift, in a small Canoe, with Paddles and a Sail, and four Days' Provisions, which last the Japanese Captain was so kind to double out of his own Stores, and would permit no Man to search me. I got down into the Canoe, while the Dutchman, standing upon the Deck, loaded me with all the Curses and injurious Terms his Language could afford.[30]

Gulliver had taken his geographical location about an hour before the pirates boarded the *Hope-Well*, and found he was in 'the Latitude of 46N and of Longitude 183'.[31] These coordinates would place Gulliver in the North Pacific, south of the Aleutian Islands. After drifting among islands, on the fifth day he settled on an island, on a perfectly clear day, and the sun became obscured by the sudden appearance of an inhabited extraterrestrial world:

> A vast Opaque Body between me and the Sun, moving forwards towards the Island: It seemed to be about two Miles high, and hid the Sun six or seven Minutes, but I did not observe the Air to be much colder, or the Sky more darkened, than if I had stood under the shade of a Mountain. As it approached nearer over the Place where I was, it appeared to be a firm Substance, the Bottom flat, smooth, and shining very bright from the Reflection of the Sea below. I stood upon a Height about two Hundred Yards from the Shore, and saw this vast Body descending almost to a Parallel with me, at less than an *English* Mile distance. I took out my Pocket-Perspective, and could plainly discover Numbers of People moving up and down the Sides of it, which appeared to be Sloping, but what those People were doing, I was not able to distinguish.[32]

Following the example set by his predecessors, Gulliver took out his 'pocket-perspective' gradually; the 'Flying Island' came closer, so he could observe what people were doing: 'the Reader can hardly conceive my Astonishment, to behold an Island in the Air, inhabited by Men, who were able (as it should seem) to raise, or sink, or put it into a Progressive Motion, as they pleased'.[33] Gulliver's actual journey above the terrestrial world begins as he is drawn up to the 'Flying Island':

> they made signs for me to come down from the Rock, and go towards the Shore, which I accordingly did; and the flying island being raised to a convenient Height, the Verge directly over me, a Chain was let down from the lowest Gallery, with a Seat fastened to the Bottom, to which I fixed myself, and was drawn up by Pullies.[34]

Laputa hovers over the larger island of Balnibarbi, over which the king of Laputa also presides. On alighting, Gulliver is surrounded by a crowd of people whose 'outward Garments were adorned with the Figures of Suns, Moons, and Stars, interwoven with those of Fiddles, Flutes, Harps, Trumpets,

Guitars, Harpsicords, and many more Instruments of Music, unknown to us in *Europe*.[35] When brought for an audience with the king, Gulliver notes: 'Before the Throne, was a large Table filled with Globes and Spheres, and Mathematical Instruments of all kinds.'[36] The Laputans have what Gulliver calls contempt for practical geometry, which they considered to be servile and vulgar, and he remarks that

> they are very bad Reasoners, and vehemently given to Opposition, unless when they happen to be of the right Opinion, which is seldom their case. Imagination, Fancy, and Invention, they are wholly strangers to, nor have any Words in their Language by which those Ideas can be expressed; the whole compass of their Thoughts and Mind being shut up within the two forementioned [*sic*] Sciences.[37]

The key sciences were mathematics and music, but the Laputans also possessed a strong disposition towards news and politics, as they were 'perpetually inquiring into Public Affairs, giving their Judgements in matters of State; and passionately disputing every inch of a Party Opinion'.[38] They lived under 'continual Disquietudes',

> never enjoying a Minute's Peace of Mind; and their Disturbances proceed from Causes which very little affect the rest of Mortals. Their Apprehensions arise from several Changes they dread in the Celestial Bodies. For Instance; that the Earth by the continual approaches of the Sun towards it, must in course of Time be absorbed or swallowed up. That the Face of the Sun will by Degrees be encrusted with its own Effluvia, and give no more Light to the World. That the Earth very narrowly escaped a brush from the Tail of the last Comet, which would have infallibly reduced it to Ashes.[39]

The Laputans are so perpetually alarmed 'with the Apprehensions of these and the like impending Dangers, that they can neither sleep quietly in their Beds, nor have any relish for the common Pleasures or Amusements of Life'.[40] Visitors to Laputa notice that the inhabitants have their heads inclined either to the right or to the left, with one eye turned inwards and the other constantly looking up towards the zenith. As they are constantly absorbed in intense speculations, they require a physical stimulus to speak or pay attention to the discourse of others. This has given rise to the custom whereby the rich employ certain servants, called '*Flappers*', or '*Climenoles*', who carry bladders filled with small stones or dry peas. With these they gently strike the mouth of the speaker and the right ear of his intended listener. They also apply flaps to their masters' eyes to prevent them from walking into obstacles or bumping into other people.

In the centre of the island there is a chasm about fifty yards in diameter, from whence astronomers descend into a large dome, which is known as the Astronomer's Cave, or Flandona Gagnole (a near anagram of London, England), situated at a depth of some one hundred yards beneath the upper surface of the Adamant: 'The place is stored with great variety of Sextants, Quadrants, Telescopes, Astrolabs, and other Astronomical Instruments.'[41] Swift, however, was less concerned with the external features of his flying island than with the principles by which it flew. This in part was contingent upon one 'mineral', adamant. In the Astronomer's Cave, Gulliver views a loadstone of prodigious size and resembling a weaver's shuttle: 'this Magnet is sustained by a very strong Axle of Adamant passing through its middle upon which it plays, and is poised so exactly that the weakest Hand can turn it'.[42] By means of this loadstone the island can rise and fall, and move from one place to another. By these motions the island is conveyed to different parts of the monarch's dominions, and presides over the terrestrial world of Balnibarbi and its metropolis, the city of Lagado. The astronomers spend the greater part of their lives observing the celestial bodies, which they do with the assistance of telescopes the strength of which far exceeds those available in the terrestrial world. This advantage has allowed them to make discoveries much further away than astronomers in Europe.

It is through the creation of the flying island of Laputa that Swift examines the contemporaneous relationship between Ireland and England. The Laputans rule over the distressed inhabitants of Balnibarbi, who are constantly on the cusp of rebellion. The Laputans are often tempted to lower their island over the Balnibarbians, destroying them forever:

> If any Town should engage in Rebellion or Mutiny, fall into violent Factions, or refuse to pay the usual Tribute, the King hath two Methods of reducing them to Obedience. The first and the mildest Course is by keeping the Island hovering over such a Town, and the Lands about it, whereby he can deprive them of the Benefit of the Sun and the Rain, and consequently afflict the Inhabitants with Death and Diseases. And if the Crime deserve it, they are at the same time pelted from

above with great Stones, against which they have no Defence but by creeping into Cellars or Caves, while the Roofs of their Houses are beaten to pieces. But if they still continue obstinate, or offer to raise Insurrections, he proceeds to the last Remedy, by letting the Island drop directly upon their Heads, which makes a universal Destruction both of Houses and Men. However, this is an Extremity to which the Prince is seldom driven, neither indeed is he willing to put it in Execution, nor dare his Ministers advise him to an Action, which as it would render them odious to the People, so it would be a great Damage to their own Estates, which lie all below, for the Island is the King's Demesne.[43]

The kings have always been reluctant to allow the island drop directly upon the inhabitants of Balnibarbi because, as Declan Kiberd argues, 'this may signal a reluctance to imperil the English monarchy and constitution by an outright military repression of the other kingdom'.[44] The rebellion sparked in the second city of Lindalino (a play on Dublin), where citizens use magnetic towers to foil the path of the flying island, can be construed as a version of the Wood's halfpence affair: 'this Incident broke entirely the King's Measures and (to dwell no longer on other Circumstances) he was forced to give the Town their own Conditions'.[45] Swift's involvement in the defeat of Wood's halfpence coincided with his work on *Gulliver's Travels*. It arises in allegorical form in five paragraphs that describe the rebellion of Lindalino against Laputa.[46] After seeing all the curiosities of the island of Laputa, Gulliver is happy to leave, and so travels to Balnibarbi and the Metropolis of Lagado. In Lagado he finds 'the people in the streets walked fast, looked wild, their eyes fixed, and were generally in Rags'.[47] Of the countryside, he says, 'I never knew a Soil so unhappily cultivated, Houses so ill contrived and so ruinous, or a People whose Countenances and Habit expressed so much Misery and Want.'[48] In conversation Gulliver learns that about forty years earlier certain persons had gone up to Laputa and after five months came back with 'a very little smattering in Mathematics, but full of Volatile Spirits acquired in that Airy Region'.[49] These people had 'procured a Royal Patent for erecting an Academy of PROJECTORS in Lagado'. In this academy the professors discuss new rules relating to agriculture, building, new instruments and tools for all trades and manufactures, where

one Man shall do the Work of ten; a Palace may be built in a week, of Materials so durable as to last for ever without repairing. All the fruits of the Earth shall come to Maturity at whatever Season we think fit to choose, and increase an Hundred Fold more than they do at present, with innumerable other happy proposals.[50]

Gulliver visits the Academy of Projectors at Lagado, a research institute staffed by 'projectors' working on schemes for the material benefit of the country, including a scheme for extracting 'Sunbeams out of Cucumbers'[51] and an astronomer had undertaken 'to place a Sun Dial upon the great Weathercock on the Townhouse, by adjusting the annual and diurnal Motions of the Earth and Sun, so as to answer and coincide with all accidental Turnings by the Wind'.[52] An architect had uncovered a new method for building houses by beginning at the roof and working downwards to the foundation. Another project comprised a scheme for abolishing all words, which was seen as a great advantage in terms of health and brevity:

> For, it is plain, that every Word we speak is in some Degree a Diminution of our Lungs by Corrosion, and consequently contributes to the short-ening of our Lives. An Expedient was therefore offered, that since Words are only Names for *Things*, it would be more convenient for all Men to carry about them, such *Things* as were necessary.[53]

The projectors are involved in schemes for improvement that are not, it appears, based on real needs. As Thomas Duddy puts it, 'it is a world in which there is learning without understanding, knowledge without wisdom, rationality without reasonableness, and enquiry without responsibility'.[54] They believe themselves to have worthy, or 'improving', ends. Ultimately, they fail to provide realistic and practical solutions to real problems. Their schemes appear absurdly impractical, or, as Duddy puts it, 'they demonstrate the ignorant utopianism of the academicians, especially their contempt for natural processes and the laws of nature'.[55] Swift's satirising of all the curiosities of the Academy of Lagado may be seen within the broad context of his long-held aversion to 'New Science'.

The Academy at Lagado thus connects with or is influenced by Bacon's *New Atlantis* (1662), and also with the early Dublin societies before the RDS. Bacon is the link connecting More with Swift. As Bacon wrote, 'our method is continually to dwell among things soberly ... to establish forever a true and legitimate union between the experimental and rational faculty'.[56] Swift in *Gulliver's Travels* unifies this experimental and rational faculty. The information Bacon gives us about the political and economic organisation of Bensalem shows that *New Atlantis* belongs to the history of science as much as to the history of Utopia. Bacon's profile of the members of the House of Solomon resembles Swift's Academy of Projectors, dedicated as they are to 'enlarging of the bounds of human empire, to the effecting of all things possible'.[57] The House of Solomon's scientific research has led to the development of submarines and flying machines. Streams, cataracts and windmills are used to provide energy. Caves deep beneath the buildings are used for the production and preservation of metal, while high towers have been built for astronomical and meteorological observations and experiments. 'Perspective' houses are devoted to experiments in optical science and to the production of telescopes, microscopes and other optical devices. Acoustic experiments are carried out in the 'Sound' houses, which also manufacture musical instruments, such as the violin-piano, and devices to reproduce natural sounds. The people of Bensalem can, for example, acquire knowledge of any language within a matter of months. In Bensalem there is 'also a mathematical-house, where are represented all instruments, as well of geometry as astronomy, exquisitely made'.[58] Similarly, in Laputa's Astronomer's Cave 'the place is stored with great variety of Sextants, Quadrants, Telescopes, Astrolabs, and other Astronomical devices'.[59] As Boyle had referred to Bacon and More, the influence of Bacon and More also permeates 'A Voyage to Laputa'. Having left Balnibarbi, Gulliver journeys to Glubbdubdrib, the 'Island of *Sorcerers* or *Magicians*', where he can choose anyone from among all the dead from the beginning of the world to the present time and command them to answer any questions he should wish to ask them, only on condition that his questions be confined to the times in which they lived. Swift places Thomas More as the only modern among the group, which includes Alexander the Great, Hannibal, Caesar and Brutus. In a long conversation, Brutus tells Gulliver 'that his ancestors *Junius, Socrates, Epamimondas, Cato the Younger, Sir Thomas More* and himself, were perpetually together: a *Sextumvirate* to which all the Ages of the World cannot add a Seventh'.[60]

Almost a century and a half after *Gulliver's Travels* was published, Richard Whately (1787–1863), archbishop of Dublin from 1831 to 1863, in his 'Lost Leaf of Gulliver's Travels' alludes to a newly discovered manuscript of *Gulliver's Travels* containing a passage that had not previously been published, and which appears to have been lost. Gulliver makes a return visit to the Academy of Projectors. He meets with many of the projectors he had formerly seen. As before, they are engaged in multifarious schemes. He found 'the one who was engaged in petrifying the hoofs of a living horse, the one who was extracting sunbeams from cucumbers, the agriculturist who was employing swine as plough-men, and the breeder of naked sheep, all very much as I had left them'.[61] The professor who previously had devised a machine for composing books was now intent on a scheme he considered to be of far greater importance, 'the constructing of a machine for performing the most abstruse calculations as accurately as the most expert arithmetician'.[62]

Gulliver engages with many projectors working on medical projects, including one 'who was contriving a composition which would have the effect of rendering the human body insensible to pain, so that a man might undergo the amputation of a limb or any other such operation, without feeling the slightest uneasiness'.[63] However, he hears of a scheme that he views as still more beneficial to mankind, if it could succeed.[64] A projector proposed to

> stop the ravages of one of the most dreadful kinds of pestilence that ever afflicted the human race, a painful, loathsome, and most dangerous disease, spreading by infection from one to another, raging like a fierce conflagration, and threatening to depopulate whole regions. His plan was to infect his patients, while yet sound in health, with a kind of venom obtained from the body of a cow.[65]

This would produce, the projector believes, a very slight and mild form of disease but which could have the effect of strengthening the constitution against the most dangerous diseases. Gulliver finds it a strange notion to counter a disease with a disease, but the projector appears to have no doubt as to its success. Gulliver also finds newly invented telescopes much greater in size than those he has seen previously, and he is assured that several new planets have been discovered, and a great number of small ones. The astronomer could 'distinguish any object on the moon as large as a good-sized gentleman's house'.[66]

Among the political projectors Gulliver found one who greatly interested him with his description of a scheme for the humane reformation of criminals. He proposed 'that any one convicted of an assault and robbery, should receive the sentence of a long term of imprisonment and hard labour, but should be well fed and lodged, should do only a moderate amount of work, and should be released long before the end of the term, and left at liberty, with money in his pocket'.[67] It was expected that this leniency would elicit gratitude from the prisoner and 'awaken all the good feelings which had been latent in his breast, and thus produce a reformed character'.[68] Gulliver asked the projector what had been the result of the experiment so far, and the projector admitted that, in most instances, 'the first use that the released criminal made of his liberty was to commit some fresh outrage'.[69] He hoped, however, 'that in time this humane and generous proceeding would bring criminals to a better mind'.[70]

Gulliver's journey to Laputa, and in particular his visit to the Academy of Lagado, may be predicated on Swift's long-held disavowal of the 'New Science'. Swift attacks such science in most of his work, as in *A Tale of a Tub* (1704), where he writes of the intention to erect a large academy where members 'are to be disposed into the several schools of this Academy, and there pursue those studies to which their genius most inclines them. The undertaker himself will publish his proposals with all convenient speed.'[71] He proposes among other things a school of swearing, a school of critics, a school of hobby horses and a school of spleen. In satirising the experimenters, Swift not only seems to satirise the 'new science' or 'bad science' but also its presentation in utopian terms. This parallels Salomon's House in *New Atlantis*, where objects of genuine amazement in Bensalem appear as objects of parody in Laputa.

Swift's satirising of the projectors and their impractical schemes for improvement clearly finds a real-life parallel in Irish life: namely, in the Dublin Philosophical Society founded in 1683, and in the Irish associational life in the four decades after the Glorious Revolution, where a small community of learned individuals devoted themselves to scientific and intellectual pursuits. As the founding of the Dublin Society in 1731 was subsequent to *Gulliver's Travels*, we do not know how Swift would have portrayed its work, but it seems that he is using the utopian realist ideal to satirise modern science. The utopian ideal of improvement and betterment is thus challenged in an explicit parody where 'bad science' is inert, the antithesis of progress, of improvement. It is the antithesis of the utopian ideal itself. However, Whately, in having Gulliver revisit the Academy of Projectors in his 'Lost Leaf', reclaims the utopian among those schemes, identifying those that are ultimately for the betterment of humanity, most notably in the areas of medical science and social justice.

Utopia is inseparable from imaginary journeys, and in his projection of an imaginary world, Swift provides an exposition and critical analysis of social facts. To assist the process of comparison, Utopias provide us with a guide who, as Peter Ruppert observes, 'explains the marvellous transformation in utopia to a startled visitor who represents the author's society'.[72] Here, then, is an exercise in estrangement. Moving from the known world, the reader is presented with the alternative world of the text while remaining tangentially and critically connected to the known world.

As a utopian satire, *Gulliver's Travels* defamiliarises and thereby illuminates existing societal standards, values and norms. For Suvin, the critical impact of the literary Utopia lies in the capacity to distance from, or make strange, existing social relations and point towards better ones. The estrangement effect defamiliarises extant values and practices. Swift produces an estrangement effect in *Gulliver's Travels*, as it 'both defamiliarises a familiar world and seeks to acquaint the reader with a strange, uncanny, and fantastical world'.[73] Cognitive estrangement thus defines what is potentially the most pertinent effect of the utopian fiction discussed in this chapter. In *Swiftiana*, Charles Henry Wilson, writing in 1804, captured the cognitive estrangement invoked by Swift in Gulliver's voyages to Lilliput and Brobdingnag in a way that is also relevant to Laputa:

> For the whole of the two voyages to Lilliput and Brobdingnag arises one general remark, which, however obvious, has been overlooked by those who consider them as little more that the sport of a wanton imagination. When *human actions* are ascribed to *pigmies* and *giants*, there are few that do not excite either contempt, disgust, or horror; to ascribe them therefore to such beings was, perhaps, the most probable method of engaging the mind to examine them with attention, and judge of them with impartiality, by suspending the fascination of habit, and exhibiting familiar objects in a new light. The use of the fable then is not less apparent, than important and extensive, and that this use was intended by the author, can be doubted only by those who are disposed to affirm, that order and regularity are the effects of chance.[74]

In Laputa, Swift is 'exhibiting familiar objects in a new light': the flying island representative of England, and Balnibarbi as Ireland. Swift's Laputa is a negative Utopia. It is for Gulliver a dystopian space, a space he is happy to leave. As he puts it, 'having seen all the Curiosities of the Island, I was very desirous to leave it, being heartily weary of those people'.[75] The inhabitants are a 'people under continual Disquietudes, never enjoying a Minute's Peace of Mind'.[76] They are so perpetually alarmed that 'they can neither sleep quietly in their Beds, nor have any relish for the common Pleasures or Amusements of Life'.[77] Swift and many other 'improvers' of eighteenth-century Ireland envisaged a complete transformation of the Irish landscape and infrastructure. Yet none of their projects had been brought to perfection. Swift and his contemporaries observed a polity on the brink of collapse. Ironically, their assertions of the country's extreme poverty and the parlous state of its institutions were only outnumbered by the ingenious and hare-brained schemes they proposed for its transformation from a foundering state into a wonderland affording unlimited gratification of political and economic desire. Swift's flying island presages the need for the renovation of Ireland, through the 'making new' of a dystopian space. He challenges 'improvers' and projectors to take their heads out of the clouds. As Swift wrote, 'these voyages were intended as a moral political romance; to correct vice, by shewing its deformity, in opposition to the beauty of virtue; and to amend false systems of philosophy, by pointing out the errors and applying salutary means to avoid them'.[78] Thus, Swift's flying island, fundamentally satirical, provided an estranged space to comment on contemporary society, providing a series of cautions and warnings about modern times, and through its estrangement effect offered the possibility of the renovation of Ireland.

A Trip to the Moon by Mr. Murtagh McDermot: containing some observation and reflections, made by him during his stay in that planet, upon the manners of the inhabitants (1728)

Gulliver's Travels inspired many imitations; as Sargent phrases it, '*Gulliver's Travels* gave rise to an entire subgenre of literature, loosely known as Gulliveriana, in which a traveller visits one or more countries inhabited by speaking animals or odd humans'.[79] Welcher and Bush have noted that 'of the more than sixty such responses published in the eighteenth century, about eighteen are direct imitations of *Gulliver*, attempting to reproduce something of its style, intent, and design. Four of the imitations have settings in outer space'.[80] Two of these Irish-authored works are by Murtagh McDermot (1728) and Francis Gentleman (1764, 1765). Their design and their references to Swift place their work among Gulliveriana, but their moon settings distinguish them from all other Gulliveriana. McDermot's *Trip to the Moon*, appearing within two years of *Gulliver's Travels*, was the first Gulliverian imitation of the eighteenth century. It is Irish in terms of its origin, its narrator and its terrestrial setting in that McDermot tells us that he set sail from Dublin and returned to it at the end of his voyage. The work was published as *A Trip to the Moon by Mr. Murtagh McDermot: containing some observations and reflections, made by him during his stay in that planet, upon the manners of the inhabitants.*[81] No records have turned up of an actual author of that name at the time. The name, while not unrealistic, is particularly apt: the surname is correct for someone associated with northern Irish counties, and McDermot in his narration tells us he is from the north of Ireland. The name Murtagh appears in a Gulliverian pamphlet, *The Asiniad: a second satire upon a certain wooden-man revived by the pseudonymous Martin Gulliver* (1730). Murtagh is the servant of Ventoso and, in this short mock-heroic satirical poem,

> Murtagh! A dull Dog, empty-pated,
> Murtagh! successless and ill-fated.

He had made an audacious expedition to the moon. His name, meaning 'windy', could derive from McDermot's having been transported to the moon by a whirlwind. Part of the subtitle of *The Asiniad*, 'a second satire upon a certain wooden-man revived' (referring to a carved wooden statue on Essex Street in Dublin, then the publishing district), may connect with a 1721 pamphlet written 'By Dr. Sw-ft', *The Blunderful Blunder of Blunders*, which dwells at some length on 'the Wooden Man in Essex Street'. These possible links may be intentional and may be clues to the authorship of all three works – or they may not. Nonetheless, the author of the Martin Gulliver pamphlet must have had a knowledge of McDermot's *Trip to the Moon*. If Martin Gulliver sought, therefore, to cultivate an interest in McDermot's *Trip to the Moon*, it is altogether hard to demonstrate if it had any impact among the reading public.

Whoever Murtagh McDermot was, he had his *Gulliver* well in hand as he wrote *A Trip to the Moon*. The dedication of the work is 'to the Worthy, Daring, Adventurous, Thrice-renown'd, and Victorious Captain Lemuel Gulliver',[82] and it embraces Swiftian humour in its location, being 'a Dedication in the Rear', as McDermot puts it:

> Shall a Poet find a Patron, and not a Lunatick? Let it not be said, *Gulliver's* alive, or the *Laputans* had e're now crush'd us, by coming down to mourn him; yet his Lustre dazzles; he cannot be conceal'd: His Fame rings loudly in the Moon: *To Clods of Earth I tell it.*[83]

Like Gulliver, McDermot is drawn to a fantastical place by a natural phenomenon, a whirlwind. He learns the local language. The lunar language, which is unpronounceable and indecipherable, resembles Houyhnhnm speech. He is an acute observer and recorder. He has the same blend of curiosity, conceit and naivety as Gulliver. McDermot is both traveller and narrator of his story. His moon voyage took place in June 1718. He first identifies his family, education and occupation as background to his narrative. He decides to turn sailor, embarking in Dublin on the *Runner* under Captain James Anderson, who, with his crew, sets sail for the Canaries. On arriving at Tenerife, he writes:

> On the 12th of August following, we arriv'd at *Tenerife*, being driven thither by stress of Weather, for our Design was to land at *Palma*, to take in sugar; we got in *Santa Cruz* Bay, which is to the North East of the Island, and rode in 17 Fathom of Water. The Storm continued for some Days after we had providentially cast Anchor; during which Time, my Curiosity and Rashness prompted me to ascend the *Peak*.[84]

The following morning, McDermot begins his ascent of the mountain peak, and from there a whirlwind arises and transports him to the moon. He records:

> After I had been rais'd from the Mountain, I was carried at such a rate for a while, that I almost lost my Breath; but the Force of the Whirlwind gradually abating, my Passage became more easy, till I came to a Place of Resting. This was a Space between the Vortices of the *Earth* and *Moon*, where the Attraction of neither prevail'd, but the contrary Motions of their Effluvia destroy'd one another.[85]

Almost certain that he would die during the course of his journey, McDermot nevertheless reaches the moon and is rescued from his distress by the Lunarians:

> I was quickly remov'd into the Sphere of the *Moon's* Attraction, more than I intended; for two thirds of my Body being attracted by the *Moon*, the rest soon follow'd, so that I was carried with incredible swift-ness, which still increase'd my fall towards that Planet. It was my good Fortune to fall into a Fish-pond, which our sharp-sighted Philosophers mistake for a Part of the Sea, and call it *Sinus Rorum*; but I hope they will not be so bold as to deny what I say, since they all confess that they never were there.[86]

Drawn from the fishpond by the king's fishermen, he is brought before the king. His guide Tckbrff advises him that the king 'was an absolute Monarch, was an ambitious Tyrant, he was one that never troubled himself about the Good of his People; but if ever their Interest interfer'd with his even unlawful Diversions, it was entirely neglected; he was a great Lover of Pleasure, and of every thing that was new, which he was pleas'd to call polite Learning, (tho' he was often fond of, and encourag'd the greatest Absurdities)'.[87] McDermot speaks freely with the king, and gives him an account of the traditions of his terrestrial society, explaining to him as well as he could 'the Difference between *Whig* and *Tory*, *Protestant* and *Papist*, and told him with what Zeal every Man maintain'd that Opinion which he embraced thro' Ignorance, Prejudice, or Interest, with daring to examine his Principles by an infallible Rule, lest he should see any Reason for renouncing that Error he was so fond of'.[88] McDermot, a sharp observer of the lunar inhabitants, notes that the

> Generality of them were kind and affectionate to each other, which produced in them an Openness of living, whereby they held all Things in common. When they went abroad, they left their Homes open, and knew not what a Lock was. It was usual with them to assist each other in their private Concerns, without the Expectation of any Reward, other than the little kindness, if required.[89]

Here, McDermot's account, despite his earlier information that the king was a tyrant, evokes a utopian commonwealth. The inhabitants are kind and affectionate to one another, and all things are held in common. On finding such a society, McDermot believed that he was 'settled for life'.[90] Tellingly, while McDermot lauds lunar society, Tckbrff believes that McDermot's homeland was a better place, and that only honest men lived in Ireland. He wants to be among them, believing that 'the King and the People are so blended, that it is impossible for the one to subsist without the other'.[91] McDermot's response is that his people are the most refractory and rebellious in the entire solar system. McDermot, while writing a Gulliverian imitation, thus diverges sharply from Swift on the possibility of a utopian society. Swift, in 'A Discourse Concerning the Mechanical Operation of the Spirit', lists 'Utopian *Commonwealths*' with such fanciful objects of human longing as the philosopher's stone, the elixir of life, and the squaring of the circle as products of mankind's 'fanatic enthusiasm'.[92] McDermot, however, locates a utopian commonwealth on the moon, and in an echo of Plato also manages to find the philosopher's stone in a subterranean cavern with philosophers and poets working at anvils and

spinning sonnets, odes and epigrams. However, McDermot's utopian commonwealth is contradictory, for after all the lunar king is a despot and a
tyrant willing to enslave his people. Read in this manner, McDermot's work
can be more readily apprehended. His utopian projection as an imaginary
voyage allegorises the potential conflicts and rebelliousness of his homeland.
The tyrannical facets of lunar society can, dystopically, emblematise his own
society, while those clearly utopian elements of lunar society represent what
his terrestrial world might emulate. The Lunars were, he discovers, followers
of the Pythagorean doctrine:

> Whatever they practis'd, they confidently affirmed that they had his
> express Command for, or else they made him to mean Things as they
> serv'd their Interests by giving his Thoughts a new Turn, and by making
> their Comments upon his Writings as authentick as what they were
> design'd to explain.[93]

McDermot's most original idea in *A Trip to the Moon* incorporates
Pythagoreanism. One sees the suitability of this doctrine as a moon religion,
with its theory of transmigration, its interest in astronomy and music of the
spheres, and its general eighteenth-century reputation as an enthusiastic sect.
In his preface, McDermot alludes to transmigration to add verisimilitude to
his own account of his transportation to the moon. He speaks of those who
deny that transmigration of souls from one body to another is possible. He
posits that it is possible, as Pythagoras argues, for souls to pass from one body
to another, and so asks if it is probable that transmigration of an inhabitant
from one planet to another may not also occur. He brings the most convinc-
ing argument for it: as he puts it, 'I went, I saw, I return'd.'[94] He learns on
the moon that Pythagoras had been there and had transformed himself into,
among other things, a bailiff, a hangman, an emperor and a lawyer. He finally
sets himself up as a philosopher and calls himself Pythagoras. The Lunars
embrace all the Pythagorean principles: transmigration, asceticism, geometry,
objects in temples, and, ultimately, worship of Pythagoras rather than the gods.
McDermot then juxtaposes them with features of Catholic teaching, such as
the doctrine of purgatory, fasting and abstinence, and reliquaries. He expands
on this difference between the Lunar philosophers and their earthly fellows:

> I will not take upon me to say that all the Philosophers which we had
> upon Earth were first in the *Moon*, tho' I have been often tempted

to believe it, from the Conformity of the Opinion of several earthly Philosophers to those religious Sects in the *Moon*; for I observ'd that there were *Platonicks* and *Cynicks* there: The former affected magical Transports, and pretended that they kept a Courier constantly to bring them Intelligence from Heaven.[95]

McDermot knew the traditions of contemporary science. He uses terms such as 'effluvia' (studied by Boyle) and 'Vortices' (used in Cartesian cosmogony and Isaac Newton's gravitational theory). He refers to comets, moon maps, Hume's ideas on causality, and Descartes' psychology. In using these terms McDermot highlights experimental science, and his utopian commonwealth on the moon is the imaginative landscape in which science and society can cohere. Such experimental science, including the use of gunpowder, was to be the basis for McDermot's mode of transport in returning to earth. Whereas Gulliver was desirous to leave both Laputa and Balnibarbi as quickly as possible, McDermot contemplates living semi-permanently on the moon, and spends two years there: 'Hitherto I had liv'd as happily as I could expect at such a Distance from mine own Country; and now I began to think seriously of settling in the *Moon* for the Remainder of my Life.'[96] Nonetheless, he constructs a device made from a network of wooden tubs and a long trail of gunpowder, and does return to earth. This apparatus 'has sometimes been described as the first description of rocketry as a means of inter-planetary travel'.[97] His mode of propulsion, a whirlwind combined with gunpowder, come from Lucian (*c.* 120–*c.* 200) and from Savinien Cyrano de Bergerac's *Histoire comique des états et empires de la lune* (1656). He recounts his preparations for the journey:

> I design to place myself in the Middle of ten wooden Vessels, placed one within another, with the Outermost strongly hooped with iron, to prevent its breaking. This I will place over 7000 Barrels of Powder, which I know will raise me to the Top of the *Atmosphere*. I should here observe, that there were several Mountains out of which they dug Gun-Powder, which was made fit for use, as Salt is on the Earth, by exposing it to the intense Heat of the Sun in some Parts that are very near the Equator. The Mountains were called *Pfefwhthbz*, or the *Devil's Warts*. But before I blow myself up, I'll provide myself with a large pair of wings, which I will fasten to my arms in my Resting-Place; by the Help of which I will fly down to the Earth.[98]

McDermot's fictive construction of a network of wooden tubs and a long trail of gunpowder could indeed be the first description of rocketry as a means of interplanetary travel.

In Guinea after retuning to the earth, he finds a ship captained by 'a very civil Gentleman, one Mr. *Jacob Broome*', and joins his crew and sets sail for England.[99] On board, McDermot gives an account of his voyage to the moon, and finds that the captain exempts him from the work of a common sailor and makes him his companion so he could converse with him about his extraordinary travels. Arriving in London on 12 September 1720, Broome gave McDermot money to cover his onward journey to Dublin on the condition that he would publish his adventures. After arriving in Dublin on 27 September, McDermot learns that his friends had since travelled to the north of Ireland. As he puts it, 'Thither I follow'd them, being sufficiently tir'd with Rambling; and there I resolved to spend the Remainder of my Days in Quiet.'[100]

When McDermot published his *Trip to the Moon*, he wanted it, as Swift did with *Gulliver's Travels*, to have some verisimilitude. He viewed his journey as venturing forth on behalf of his countrymen to gather information on their behalf, or, as he observes,

> I went, I saw, I return'd; I ventur'd my Life many Times for the Information of my *Countrymen*, who, I hope, will shortly by their own Ingenuity, confirm what I have said. There is one Objection against this Piece, which I think ought to be remov'd. It may be said, that the Author never has been in the *Moon*, since he relates very little, but what is observable among us, for he talks of *Plays*, *Coffee-Houses*, *Balls*, *Ladies*, *Tea*, *Intriguing*, *Pythagoreans*, and other Things, which may be easily apply'd to our selves, and are in use among us. To this I answer, First, That to condemn a Man without Sufficient evidence, is contrary to our *Irish* statutes, neither can such Evidence be bad, till some Body arrives from the *Moon*, who I am sure will bear Witness to all I have set down.[101]

McDermot adds a codicil to his work: in an advertisement in which he draws on a story he had read in *Dickson's Newsletter*, he notes, 'Reading, June 5th, 1727. Yesterday a *Whirlwind* took up into the Air, near 100 Yards from the Ground, four Hay-Cocks in a Field near this Town, each weighing 200 Pound, and carried them to another Place half a Mile off.'[102] McDermot's championing of this story clearly aims to add to the plausibility of his own utopian projection. If a whirlwind could cause four cocks of hay to be transported beyond half a mile, is it not possible that a whirlwind, albeit a larger one, could transport a man, such as himself, from the top of a mountain to the moon? McDermot remains conscious that 'some may imagine my being in the MOON to be only a mere Dream; but why one should not be as likely as the other, I shall leave it to the Judgment of the Reader after he has read the Foregoing TRIP'.[103] Ultimately, he realises that readers may think his story fantastical and that such an event could not have occurred or was merely a dream or fanciful tale. A *Trip to the Moon* is a *jeu d'esprit* laden with references to contemporaneous technical and scientific advances. In the imaginary geography of the moon, McDermot finds a liminal landscape in which to discourse on science, learning, politics, religion, customs and manners. It is fundamentally a work of utopian satire, a homage to Lemuel Gulliver and the Laputans, and it remains a work of proto-science fiction, combining scientific knowledge and the world of the imagination in an eighteenth-century Irish context. The enigmatic McDermot, therefore, combines satire and science in a utopian projection that locates a utopian commonwealth on the moon. He creates a topos wherein his image of the utopian journey functions as an estranged pre-vision of what Ireland could become.

Francis Gentleman, *A Trip to the Moon. Containing an account of the island of Noibla* (1764, 1765)

Francis Gentleman, playwright and essayist, was born on 23 October 1728 in York Street, Dublin, the son of a British army captain. The details of his early life and ancestry are obscure, but it is known that he was educated at the grammar school in Digges Street, Dublin from the ages of ten to fifteen. In 1749 he was cast by Thomas Sheridan (1719–88), manager of Dublin's Smock Alley Theatre, as Aboan in Thomas Sourtherne's (1660–1746) *Oroonoko*, and afterwards in minor supporting roles. He then unexpectedly inherited £800 from an uncle in the East Indies, which was, according to its beneficiary, reduced by three quarters by his lawyers. This event was to establish a pattern of thwarted expectations, financial insecurity and debt that would continue for the rest of his life.

After this loss he left for London and embarked upon his career as a man of letters. In 1751 Gentleman published his adaptation of Ben Jonson's *Sejanus*, the first of many revisions of Jonson, Shakespeare and others in line with the tastes of eighteenth-century audiences. Around this time he also wrote a tragedy, *Osman*, which was produced in Bath in 1754. He produced a considerable body of literary and theatrical criticism, and he developed a peripatetic career as a supporting actor, moving between London, Scotland, the north of England and, finally, Dublin over the next three decades. Gentleman's most significant work, however, was on criticism, *The Dramatic Censor*, published in two volumes in 1770. Addressing the increasingly literate theatre-going public of the late eighteenth century, these volumes were a theatre-goer's guide. The key figure for Gentleman was the actor David Garrick (1716–79), with whom he had been associated since 1751 and whose self-identification with Shakespeare he enthusiastically endorsed. Gentleman was fulsome in his praise of the actor, and *The Dramatic Censor* is of special interest for its accounts of Garrick's major Shakespearian roles, including Macbeth, Romeo and Richard III.

In his two-volume work *A Trip to the Moon* (1764, 1765), Gentleman uses the pseudonym Sir Humphrey Lunatic. As Welcher and Bush have noted, the first printing of a play by Gentleman, *The Modish Wife: a comedy* (1775), carries an introductory essay entitled 'A Summary View of the English, Scots, & Irish Stages' which is mainly an autobiographical sketch. The author says that some little while after his play was first produced in Chester in 1761, he went and settled for four years in

> an agreeable and reasonable markettown, about twenty miles from *York*, called *Malton* … During my residence here, I wrote a thing in two volumes called a *Trip to the Moon* which had uncommon praise in that part of the world, and was not severely treated by those critical dictators, the Monthly Reviewers, yet the success of that publication was no way considerable.[104]

This is Gentleman's sole reference that we know of so far to his claim of *A Trip to the Moon* being his own work. While he draws on literary antecedents such as Savinien Cyrano de Bergerac (1619–55), he remakes the motif of the moon voyage as a vehicle for his critical and visionary ideas. His experiences with lawyers and patrons, his work on fables, his composition of an opera, and his many years as an actor all contribute to this work. Gentleman's narrator Sir Humphrey Lunatic alludes to Bergerac and notes:

> I form'd great expectations from a piece which once fell into my hands, called Bergerac's *Voyage to the Moon*; the title indeed gave me particular

pleasure as I hope to find somewhat very extraordinary in the contents; yet was I vastly deceived for tho' there are strong marks of Genius in that production, upon the whole I could discover nothing very interesting; however the thought of a journey to the Lunar World struck very deep, and all calculations, all my wishes, were ever after assiduously employed on the effecting such a jaunt.[105]

Here, then, Gentleman draws a direct thread of connection to an earlier lunar narrative. He has Humphrey Lunatic read Bergerac's work, and it sets the tone for his own journey to the lunar world, *A Trip to the Moon. Containing an account of the island of Noibla. Its inhabitants, religious and political customs, &c. By Sir Humphrey Lunatic, Bart.* Noibla is an evident reversal of Albion, and *A Trip to the Moon* opens with a glossary of forty-three words and phrases from the Noiblan language. Gentleman, as a dramatist, introduces his glossary as he would the dramatis personae. The Noiblan language reveals its English origins through a series of anagrams: Noibla/Albion, Nodnol, the capital city of Noibla is an anagram of London, and Notlam, the island's Spring of Purification, is named after Malton near York, where Gentleman lived for a time. After introducing the glossary, Sir Humphrey, in the style of Lemuel Gulliver, gives an account of himself and his family. It contains an account of his ancestors from the time of the first baronet of his family:

> Though the following piece is not of a biographical nature, the Author thinks it necessary to give some short account of himself and his family, that thereby forming a kind of acquaintance with his readers, they may pursue their journey together through the Lunar World with more cordiality and pleasure.[106]

He then describes the Lunatics as a 'considerable family, ever since England was England', and describes how

> to make a complete detail of genealogical particulars, would be a work of insufferable prolixity and ostentation; wherefore the Author will only revert to his Great Grandfather, the first Baronet of *his* part of the family; and proceed from him in a direct line, without regard to several other distinguished collateral branches.[107]

Humphrey Lunatic's biography of his ancestor Sir Whimsical Lunatic and his father, also Sir Humphrey, reveals that they had always questioned public affairs. Sir Whimsical is remembered as one who might have been eminently advanced in the state,

> but, like a true LUNATIC, being fond of opposition, and disdaining to run with the stream long, he began to find fault with the conduct of Public Affairs; openly declaring that the plan of PLATO'S REPUBLIC, with some Alterations and Amendment of his own, would be the only sure Foundation for our National Happiness.[108]

And so Sir Whimsical provides a link to classical Greece and to the earliest work we now call a Utopia, and thus evinces his own desire for a much better society in his own time. The senior Sir Humphrey is remembered as one who had been involved in politics for thirty-five years, and as part of a strong opposition had been the main cause of removing a dozen ministers of state, 'most of whom he thought honest till in office'.[109] However, the present Sir Humphrey has decided to find a different means of immortalising his name and embalming it for posterity. He has studied the whole planetary system, and he hopes that his trip to the moon will show 'that he deserves as exalted a place in the Rolls of Fame, as any LUNATIC that ever made a figure in life'.[110] Humphrey Lunatic's journey to the lunar world occurred during a period of sleep:

> Slumber instantly fell up on me, and from thence I dropp'd into a profound sleep. How long this soft Semblance of Death remained upon me I cannot say; but imagine Reader, if thou cans't, my surprise, and let me add some terror also, when upon waking, I found myself seated in a kind of Triumphal Car, surrounded by a great number of human figures, not one of which I had the least idea of yet all showing many marks of respect, and murmuring out an extraordinary kind of joy.[111]

His journey to the lunar world differs from McDermot's. McDermot is transported by a whirlwind from the top of a mountain in Tenerife to the moon. Lunatic tells us that at the end of May, while taking a nightly walk of contemplation, he climbed a hill whose top was shaded by trees. There was a great silence, broken only by the lulling notes of a nightingale. He came upon a vale beside a stream 'skirted by a venerable Grove, whose branches, as SHAKESPEAR has it, were silvered by the MOONSHINE'S watry [*sic*] beams; that Planet having then filled its Orb with most unusual Lustre, wrapped up in pleasing Melancholy, Slumber insensibly fell upon me, and from thence I dropp'd into a profound Sleep'.[112]

Lunatic's journey to the lunar world is therefore only realised in the dream-world of deep sleep. Drawn from the place where he had slept, he was taken 'to the limits of the lunar world'.[113] His destination is the island of Noibla, 'the most favoured spot of all this Lunar World'.[114] His host and guide on the journey to Noibla informs him that his being chosen for the trip was 'an operation not a little facilitated by some sympathetic pamphlets thou hadst in thy pockets'.[115] They included 'three of WHITEFIELD'S SERMONS, half a dozen North-Britons, and as many schemes for paying off the National Debt by Jacob Henriques'.[116] Thus, Humphrey Lunatic's transportation to the lunar world was far from arbitrary, for he was selected on the basis of the political and social beliefs he held in the terrestrial world. George Whitefield (1714–70), the evangelist, produced some 18,000 sermons during the course of his lifetime. From the time of his ordination in 1736 he delivered many sermons throughout England, Scotland and Ireland. It is therefore possible that Gentleman heard such sermons and subsequently incorporated the reference to Whitefield into *A Trip to the Moon*. During his sojourn on the island of Noibla, Humphrey Lunatic is introduced, as in the typical utopian tour, to many aspects of society, such as the Noiblan laws, the manner of elections, food, and the management and education of youth. Sir Humphrey thus concludes: 'it is a country much to be admired, and a people in many points highly deserving imitation'.[117] For example, when he first arrived in the city and was brought to the Notlam, or Spring of Purification, he drank from the holy spring and was sprinkled with water while a maiden uttered the words 'may content ever dwell here, and social happiness be the reigning Principle'.[118] This rite of purification was effected to instil both wisdom and virtue, but it clearly registers a utopian element since through undergoing such a purification process the individual would become wiser and more virtuous as the society as a whole would, as the Noiblan maiden states, be a place where social happiness would be a reigning principle, a holy commonwealth. The works of religion, however, are not sold there, for they do not have currency. Thus, the coin they have is 'but social intercourse and mutual regard'.[119] Humphrey Lunatic had wanted to make a payment in coin after the rite-of-purification ceremony, but his Noiblan guide admonishes him, and says that among them there is no envy or discord, saying also that 'after that could'st thou imagine any Regard would be paid to such Dross as Gold? Did we want to introduce

Flames among our Fields, Dearth among our Cattle, Dissentions among our Families, Bloodshed into our Cities, Diseases into our Bodies.'[120]

The guide took some pieces of gold from Lunatic's purse and held them in each hand before addressing the multitude in a clear utopian mode:

> Behold, my Friends and Brothers of the Island of Noibla, the most favoured spot of all this LUNAR WORLD, behold, ye Sons of natural and untainted Liberty, the Fiend who, having got Footing on the Terrestrial Globe, rules every Government and every Individual, of all Sexes, Ages, and Degrees; for the Sake of Bits like these, dug, by half-fed Slaves, out of the Bowels of the Earth, to pamper Pride and Luxury; thousands and ten thousands march into the bloody Field of War, hung round with the most destructive Weapons of Cruelty, to mutilate and butcher their Fellow-Creatures; for these their Clergy pray; their Lawyers wrangle; their Physicians kill: For these Fathers and their Sons, Mothers and their Daughters, Brethren and Sisters, run into the most uncharitable Dissensions: Gilded with these, Vice claims Respect while thread bare Virtue stands shiv'ring and helpless at the unhospitable [*sic*] Doors of Luxury and Pride.[121]

Here, the Noiblan speaker views his own society in utopian terms that echo More's utopian narrative. This is the most favoured spot in all of the cosmos. The inhabitants are viewed as pure and untainted, and he compares life on Noibla to life on the terrestrial globe. Each is represented in dystopian terms as a place where avarice, luxury and vice reign. It has become corrupted by the evils wrought by money and gold. The speaker offers a critique of the social evils of luxury and pride that have infected the terrestrial land, and makes a call to reason: 'Oh Reason, where is thy Power? Mount, mount for Shame thy Throne, nor longer abdicate thy judgement-seat, lest usurping Passions create universal and incurable Confusion.'[122] If reason is to be the salvation of the dystopian terrestrial world, by contrast he continues to portray Noibla as Utopia. It is free of gold, of luxury and pride, which he views as fatal influences and a bane to social happiness. Tellingly, he notes:

> No Blood stains our Fields; no Fears shake our Peace; that Religion is Gratitude, no interest; that Inclination, moderated by Prudence, joins every Couple here; that Sons, when arrived in Discretion, enjoy equal advantages with their Fathers, whom therefore they never wish

to bury; that such Failings as we have amongst us cannot either be hid or rendered less shameful by such tinsel covering; that here no Tongue will move, no Virgin yield her Honour for mercenary Bribes![123]

Through a series of micro-narratives facilitated by his guide, Lunatic thus gives an outline of many aspects of Noiblan society. Among them is an account of the legal practices on Noibla. In the House of Justice, or Requecex, laws are enforced on all matters relating to the administration of the city of Nodnol. The island is divided into 100 districts, each under a city and each under the guidance of a magistrate called the Namredal, who sits each week to adjudicate on complaints. He refers for direction to laws drawn up in 'a plain concise style, without the intricacy and incumbrance multiplied, which serve only to explain away the sense and diminish the force of the original design'.[124] He has the power to summon a council of citizens to assist him. If the Namredal is displaced as incapable, he is deprived of his rights as a citizen and banished to the mountains of Neroma. Once a year all the Namredals of the island meet and consider the general state of the inhabitants; disputes are resolved and six citizens from each district enter into a minute inquiry of every Namredal's administration during the year. He is either given an honorary certificate or rendered incapable of that office ever after. The honour and respect of the citizens are the rewards for their labour. The office of the Namredals is the only office of pre-eminence, 'all other CITIZENS being upon an equal footing'.[125]

In the rearing of children the guide asserts that the method of treating children is very different from that of Lunatic's world: they are reared 'to become Sparks to animate Virtue, not Flames to destroy it'.[126] A few days after its birth, a child is taken from its mother and given to the care of some other woman,

who may, by corrective, constitutional qualifications, alter the child's natural defects; if he is born of a Mother cold and phlegmatic in her Disposition, he is put to one of a sanguine Habit; and thus the contrast is observed in other cases, so that a due Temperament is formed from the earliest.[127]

Young people are sent to the Snoissapans, or public schools, where professors are rewarded solely in exemptions from other offices and avocations, so that 'each person knows the Sphere he is to move in, and is solely answerable for his Conduct in it'.[128] The pupils are instructed in the principles of morality, the tenets of religion, social duties and the laws of the island. Each individual learns 'how to conduct himself in private and social, and, by the last, in a political Capacity; from this Method he becomes his own Divine, his own Lawyer, his own Magistrate'.[129] Because they do not trade with any other country, or among themselves, 'the Arts of Trade, and consequently Fraud, are unknown'.[130] What are called in the terrestrial world 'polite accomplishments'[131] are looked upon on Noibla as useless and 'pernicious superfluities, since they not only engross much time, but also afford great occasion to Vanity'.[132]

Sir Humphrey, then, develops another line of commentary by way of his accounts of earthly personages who have been taken up to Noibla. The transported person of Bishop John Wilkins plays a central part as host and guide to Humphrey Lunatic. His *A Discourse Concerning a New World and Another Planet: the first book, the discovery of a new world; or, a discourse tending to prove, that 'tis probable there may be another habitable world in the moone* had been published in 1638. Wilkins, a Namredal, greets our narrator as 'Brother of the nether Globe',[133] and recalls how he arrived on Noibla:

> Tho' to all Appearance I died, and was laid in Earth with the usual solemnity yet the strict, unwearied attention I had paid to the LUNAR WORLD, obtained me a Translation to this happy spot, where I have continued ever since in Ease and Respect, without a wish to gratify, a fear to perplex, or any visible decay.[134]

Other transported inhabitants of Noibla include Alexander the Great, Peter the Great of Muscovy, Cardinal Wolsey, Henry VIII, Queen Elizabeth, Oliver Cromwell, Caesar, Pompey and Cato. In a Dantesque gesture, these former inhabitants of earth are punished or rewarded according to their actions on earth. Henry VIII, for example, 'has brought with him hither all his Spirit of RELIGIOUS REFORMATION; it still remains so active and impetuous that he never lets our AVOZENS [priests] alone; who hear him indeed; but as often laugh at the vain Effects of Innovation, to the no small Mortification of his Pride'.[135] Cardinal Wolsey, 'that puffed-up mushroom of Fortune, in return of his most exorbitant insolence, is here reduced to the office of keeping the Ruvenal [the square]; that is, sweeping it every day and tolling the Elknitan ['Bell of Noon'] before the citizens dine'.[136] Queen Elizabeth is allowed precedence of all females in Nodnol and would have been chosen for the magistracy 'but for the Caprice of having sacrificed a Favourite to ill-grounded Resentment or Jealousy, and the Cruelty of having even agreed to the Execution of so amiable a Princess as her Sister of SCOTLAND'.[137]

Humphrey Lunatic also gives an account of what he calls 'several of the Literati transferred from Earth to the Moon'.[138] In the artistic and literary life of the island Homer presides over epic poetry in Nodnol, assisted by Virgil and Milton. Francis Bacon, John Locke and Isaac Newton are vested with the superintendence of all philosophical transactions. Tacitus and Clarendon preside over history. In drama, Shakespeare is dignified with the title of Delineator of Nature and is head of the theatre, or ESTRALAM, although his work is as critically examined and reviewed as one who had never written before. Joseph Addison was 'admitted as a good man than a great Poet, on account of his Integrity, his zeal for Morality and Religion while he was on Earth, has been naturalised a CITIZEN, and enjoys the post of Secretary to the NAMREDAL'.[139] Through Addison's intercession, Swift is appointed his assistant. Swift, however, does not enjoy any Noiblan privileges because it had been proved that

> he paid more Attention to Politics than Divinity; that Ambition not Piety was his ruling Principle; that he ever took more Delight to censure that commend; that he anatomised Characters with as little Remorse as Surgeons do Bodies; and that he was guilty of unheard of Cruelty in regard of Vanessa.[140]

Solely through Addison's interest and his avowal that Swift 'had done many extensive and well-appropriated Charities'[141] was Swift admitted. However, despite admission to Noibla, the dean's situation is indifferent,

> for his Pride ill brooks so subordinate a State, and his perverse Nature is mortified at the Tranquillity he sees around him; he never enjoys any Satisfaction, unless he meets some of his Countrymen wearing Badges of their Vice or Folly; and then, DIOGENES-like, he gratifies his malicious Temper with cynical Sneers and biting Sarcasms.[142]

Humphrey Lunatic further learns that Alexander Pope has been accepted on Noibla, while Ben Johnson had been excluded because of 'first, his abominable Principles bordering on theism; and next, his Ingratitude to SHAKESPEAR, either of which was sufficient to shut him out'.[143] Johnson has been banished to Erishnover (the Mountain of Blood), where 'he drags on a tedious and

despicable Existence'.[144] Pope, while well regarded by Homer, is seen as having
'a shameful Envy of his Contemporaries',[145] and wears a laurel wreath mingled
with sprigs of nightshade and is 'almost continually tormented with the jests
and Railery of COLLEY CIBBER, BEAU NASH, AND JOHN RICH, late
Manager of *Covent-Garden* THEATRE'.[146] Only lawyers and clergy above the
degree of curate are allowed on Noibla. While acknowledging that abuses can
occur within the press, the 'LIBERTY of the Press, however it may be abused
(and no human institution is perfect) ought to be most carefully preserved, as
an unreserved Monitor to KING, STATESMEN, AND PEOPLE'.[147]

A Trip to the Moon includes a moral, philosophical and ideological interrogation that is the nexus of this utopian satire. Gentleman describes a
non-existent society in great detail, thereby critiquing and criticising contemporary, namely English, society. Through the voice of his Noiblan guide,
the island of Noibla is presented as a place of invariable felicity, a Utopia. This
is counterpoised against the dystopian space of his own terrestrial world. The
narrative is then strengthened as those earth-bound characters are translated
to the island of Noibla to be challenged and reformed. This Utopia is both
open and dynamic, for the open-endedness is wrought from the narrator's
and citizens' questioning of the core of Utopia itself. Through the persona of
Wilkins the awareness of the limitations of Noibla is stressed:

> There is a general and amiable tranquillity here but then it is founded
> upon principles which entirely restrain progressive knowledge; all here
> think themselves sufficiently wise, sufficiently happy; they seek to know
> no more than they are already acquainted with, nor to possess any
> Thing better than what their Fathers have enjoyed: This will appear to
> you a mental lethargy, and undoubtedly it is such; but many advantages
> accrue from such mode of thinking.[148]

Humphrey Lunatic adds a commentary on his own thoughts:

> When alone a vast variety of ideas crowded upon each other in my
> imagination; First, my unaccountable conveyance to the LUNAR
> WORLD, surprising and inconceivable in its Nature; next that peculiar
> and kind reception I had met in it; the novelty of those ceremonies I
> had gone thro; the happy situation, the tranquil equality of the people
> I had, as it were, dropp'd among; with many other circumstances which
> do not now occur; moreover I felt some degree of uneasiness, that I

knew not how I was to return, nor when, nor if at all; but sleep, like a kind friend, came to my assistance, and, by its oblivious influence closing up the Eye of memory, relieved me from those Anxieties which my new and extraordinary situation had occasioned.[149]

And so Humphrey Lunatic confirms the utopian nature of the lunar society: the happy situation and equality of the people is a realisation of his ancestor Whimsical Lunatic's vision of such a society in the style of Plato's republic as the foundation of national happiness. In closing the first volume of his travels, he speaks of 'this extraordinary Progress': the 'kind Readers, after conversing and travelling so far together, I hope on friendly terms, you think it fit that for a while at least, we should part: if you are inclined to accompany me any farther in this extraordinary Progress, I shall attend your Call, and in the mean time I bid you heartily farewell'.[150]

The second volume of *A Trip to the Moon* was published a year after the first volume in 1765. Gentleman's use of the island of Noibla again provides a frame for his literary and political thoughts. Humphrey Lunatic, at the beginning of volume two of his *Trip to the Moon*, refers back to the reception given to his first volume:

> FELLOW-TRAVELLER, according to Promise I have again met you, in order to continue our *Tour*, and I doubt not but the same Degree of good Humour, the same Flow of Spirits, the same commendable Curiosity on your Side, and the same friendly Disposition to gratify it on mine, will render our farther Progress both pleasant and profit-able. Before we set off, however, let me express my Hope that you will not prove like a learned and ingenious *Critic* upon my *former* VOLUME, who declared a general Approbation of the Matter and Conduct, were it not that he deemed the Ascent of a Mortal to the Moon impracticable.[151]

Gentleman does not tell us who the critic of his former volume was, but that volume provides an ample frame for his thoughts, digressions, fragments and musings. He includes a sequence on the drama of Shakespeare that coheres with Gentleman's own biography, as he had adapted several of Shakespeare's plays. In an extended scene a drama takes place in the Noiblan language, with the audience entertained by Addison with a piece called *Temple of Virtue*, while Bolingbroke presented a dramatic revue called *The Europeans*. According to

Noiblan custom, all citizens are actors by turns, and every author introduces his own work. Addison introduces his work, and the narrator remarks on the difference between Addison's terrestrial persona and his changed persona on the island of Noibla, 'for he, who could never utter any Thing declamatory in the other World, having, by Custom, cast off that childish Diffidence, or perhaps irrational Pride, which closed his Lips there, is now become one of our most eloquent and most powerful Speakers'.[152] Gentleman's use of anagrams, foreign words, digressions and observations is indebted to the pattern of Gulliverian narratives. As I have noted, in his first volume Gentleman has Swift act as Addison's assistant. In the second volume he gives a satiric evaluation of *Gulliver's Travels*. He states, referring to Henry Fielding's (1707–54) *Shamela*, that

> We may say of her Life, as a learned Bishop did of JONATHAN'S Gulliver, that the Story was well enough, but must be a confounded Lye; and that the Book ought to be burnt by a Jury of Females, as Locke's *Essay on Human Understanding* was by the Convocation of Oxford, for tending to confuse and mislead with impossible principles.[153]

The extended dramatic performance thus draws Humphrey Lunatic's narrative to an end. The audience parts, and the dramatic performance and the volume ends:

> There remains no Room for the Criticisms that passed between QUEEN ELIZABETH, SHAKESPEAR, and Sir HUMPHREY upon the *Dramatic* Action of NOIBLA, which gave Occasion to many Strictures upon that of our World. – Much curious Matter also, of various Nature, is left untold, and many kingdoms of the Moon are yet unvisited.[154]

Both volumes of *A Trip to the Moon* are fundamentally satirical, providing a work that allows Gentleman to fashion a lunar Utopia in the tradition of Gulliveriana. Each of his techniques, degrees of intelligibility and ambiguity, anagrams and added letters is part of the Gulliverian mode. Gentleman portrays Swift in both volumes of *A Trip to the Moon*. It could be argued that his fictionalised Sir Humphrey – a naive narrator commenting on the world he visits – is primarily imitating Gulliver.

A Trip to the Moon is rooted in its time and place, and reproduces the stage scenery of a particular world. The island of Noibla acts as both a redemptive and retributive site. The roll call of the 'remarkable personages translated from Earth'[155] who are treated on Noibla according to their follies and foibles on earth ensures that Gentleman's mirror reflects an English society clearly through the prism of his own world view. Gentleman, in the distant space of Noibla, has created a hybrid work that draws on the combined traditions of medieval dream-vision formulas, early lunar voyages and undoubtedly the satire of Swift.

A History of the Customs, Manners, and Religion of the Moon. To which are annexed several specimens of lunar poetry; and the characters of the most distinguished personages (1782)[156]

The anonymous work entitled *A History of the Customs, Manners, and Religion of the Moon. To which are annexed several specimens of lunar poetry; and the characters of the most distinguished personages* (1782) also stands as a creative and critical utopian satire of its time. The author opens with an account of the character of Ilphinzingo and his imaginary voyage to the moon:

> The 390th Revolution of Saturn was accomplished, corresponding by the present calculation of time with the year 521 from the building of the Imperial City of Ahilkildyhou, when the great Ilphinzingo was born; this appears from the authentic monuments now preserved in the Archives of the Sacred Castle of Zablemunrow; the only remains now existing of that ancient and once deemed immortal City, formerly the Pride of the Monsemugian Empire and the Admiration of the World; it was situated on the most inaccessible part of that vast chain of mountains, by mortals called mountains of Moon, but by the immortal Genii Belgalzafin.[157]

Ilphinzingo is admired by mankind because he has discovered an easy and pleasant way of journeying through the wide expanse of the heavens: 'floating through the downy undulations of soft ether to Orbs before unknown to human eye; far beyond our Stars and planetary Worlds'.[158] In this voyage Ilphinzingo 'visited many worlds, and not only planted colonies in some, but even wrote accurate Accounts of his Travels and observations made in forty five thousand different Orbs of which many are now lost and others sadly mutilated'.[159] The author explains that 'the following genuine, authentic and interesting history of the Moon has, however, escaped the Wreck of Time'.[160] In this lunar voyage Ilphinzingo is transported to the moon on board a flying machine called the *Butterfly*:

> I embarked on board the Charming *Butterfly*, well man'd – equip'd and furnished with every thing necessary for a six Months Voyage: we extended our pinions from the lofty Top of Orlorn Pike with a favourable Gale, and soon got clear of the cloudy atmosphere which surrounds the Earth, and crossed the wide ethereal Ocean, and arrived in the confines of the Lunar World round which I resolved to make a circuit and discover the variegated face of that Planet.[161]

Having performed a circuit of the moon, he lands in Titty, one of the fortunate islands. He sees the lunar inhabitants in the roads and in the fields, singing, dancing and running to and fro. Their dress

> consisted of Feathers of a monstrous size, stuck very close on a Cap of conic form, which covered the Head – from thence downward to their knees, the fore Part of their Body like a bristled Porcupine, was embellished with Steel Spikes of about 18 inches in Length, equal to about eight of our Measure: Behind they trailed vestments of purple fringed with Gold; the rest of their Form was habited as usual, with this Difference, that the Dress was black, which I understood to be the orthodox colour of the Country.[162]

Beginning what emerges as a utopian report, Ilphinzingo finds the natives to be perfectly harmless. He makes his way to the city and is addressed by a magistrate, whose language he does not understand and who leads him into the presence of the king, who at that time was taking a ride round the palace on a wooden horse, supported on the shoulders of two great orang-utangs. During his stay on the moon he makes a visit to three temples. In the Temple of Oliboli he finds 'a Branch of Gold, in the center of which is a small chair ornamented with brilliant diamonds and covered with a canopy – here the High Priest took his seat'.[163] In the Temple of Althuhi he finds a 'superb monument of Lunar Grandeur erected on a rising ground in the center of the City; the Portal looks towards the rising Sun, the Façade is of burnished Gold supported by five hundred Columns of Emeralds; a thousand different Statues of Amethysts appear in the Niches'.[164] At the Temple of Quawquaw he finds a burial ground where malefactors were executed and interred. The space was surrounded by 'the melancholy Yew'.[165] The walls surrounding the entrance were decorated with human bones, 'nettles and the deadly night-shade hung a dreary gloom' and 'mangled limbs and gibbeted malefactors lined the porch'.[166]

Ilphinzingo then discovers the labyrinth of wisdom. Inside the labyrinth – in yet another link to the scientific and improving societies of the author's own world – he finds the most learned men of the kingdom 'in close dispute concerning the most important Truths: I accosted the Philosopher Tantahaw whom I found walking alone; his countenance was lively tho' by a continued thoughtful Habit it had lengthened into Solemnity; being Presupposed with his philosophic Mien'.[167] Together they discuss the arts and sciences, particularly astrology, astronomy, architecture, botany, building, biography, chemistry, embalming and equity, and much more. Ilphinzingo, surprised by the philosopher's universal knowledge, was told that the attainment of knowledge was by no means so difficult. Indeed, there were many academies and universities on the moon. As he puts it, there are

> North in the Moon, some hundred miles from the metropolis, Academies and Universities where all possible science is taught in a few months at a very cheap rate, but those schools are only frequented by the most necessitous persons, on account of the length of the journey – the inclemency of the climate and the savage manners and dialect of the Inhabitants; but above all what prevents persons of consequence from attending them – is a disorder universal in that country.[168]

Alternatively, the students who do not undertake the journey to the far-flung academies and universities can

> send a letter to the Chief Northern University enclosing ten small pieces of Gold, like two medals, with a man's head on one side and some National Hieroglyphics on the Reverse; in return for this he receives from the University a small writing on skin, with an Hieroglyphic Impression annexed to it, on a waxen Body: instantly the students become in possession of all the effectual ... beneficial and efficient branches of literature, and may practice as a Professor in any science.[169]

Thus, in the Labyrinth of Wisdom the most learned men of the lunar world gathered. Ilphinzingo's curiosity was roused when he saw a man strangely dressed 'carefully shrinking from our approach'[170] and trying to conceal himself among the crowds. Tantahaw, the philosopher, told him that he was one of the most celebrated wits of the age whose downfall had come about as a result of the potency of his satire directed against distinguished personages. He observes that the wit had 'turned the edge of his Satire against several first rate Personages, who thought their distinguished Situation would amply justify an Excess of Folly and Vice, and impose Silence on the Tongue and Pen of Man – his downfall was decreed'.[171] This most celebrated wit can only allude to Swift, here banished to the moon because of the keenness of his satire. Ironically, this figure's existence in the author's highly satirical work negates somewhat the purpose of his banishment, as his chosen medium of satire continues to exist. Tantahaw recounts that when 'Swift's' downfall was decreed, no man willingly came forth as his accuser. However, a woman who had grown enormously rich through a series of crimes and prostitution, and whose vices the wit was said to have satirised, accepted a bribe and levelled 'a scandalous charge'[172] against him. Tellingly, others who had felt the sharpness of Swift's satire joined in the cry for his punishment. The 'unbefriended Wit'[173] was then sentenced, as the author puts it, 'to wear that ridiculous Garb, which is a Fool's Dress, and to pass a Year in the Gallery of Fools; this being deemed the most severe Sentence which they could pass on a Man of Learning, Wit and Judgement'.[174]

Prior to the passing of his sentence, 'Swift' had applied for a licence for a play of his to be performed before the public; however, his request was refused and he wrote a lengthy letter in response. He asked to be allowed to enjoy the fruits of his labour, and felt that he should not be punished because a capricious individual had levelled charges against him. He requested that he be allowed to continue in the service of the public, and asserted that 'I never profited by flattering their Passions, or falling in with their Humours; as upon all Occasions I have exerted my little Powers, as indeed I thought it my Duty, in exposing Follies'.[175] 'Swift' argues that he never lost credit with the public because they knew he was motivated by principle, and that he never received any reward or protection from any other than his public.

The author, in describing his lunar society, finds – as in the previous discussed lunar texts – a safe medium from which to criticise contemporary Dublin life. The lengthy title of the work, I would argue, refers to Dublin itself, as its customs, manners, religion and characters of certain distinguished personages are reconfigured on the moon. The moon setting provides that safe distance from which to hold the present up to ridicule. In his introduction, the author, speaking of the Church, refers to 'the mitred Heads of that respectable Body being now so totally immersed in Politicks, and the promoting of their own private Interests, that they cannot even find *Time* for the Discharge of the Duties of their Function'.[176] This sets the tone for his assessment of clerical politics throughout the work. The first verse of a poem presented to Ilphinzingo on the moon, entitled 'The Decision', could be said to make a direct connection with an actual Dublin prelate, William Cradock (also Craddock) (*c*. 1708–93), who was appointed dean of St Patrick's Cathedral, Dublin after the death in 1775 of Dean Francis Corbet, whose incumbency had lasted for twenty-eight years, the longest in modern times. Cradock remained Dean until his death in 1793:

> To Zaman's bosom Crabbock sped
> By Fate untimely taken;
> To court the honours of the Dead
> A croud of High Priests came.[177]

The poem is based on those who present themselves for preferment to succeed Cradock as archbishop. Cradock's successor as dean of St Patrick's was English-born Robert Fowler, who served for a short period in 1793–94, and who developed a reputation as an absentee prelate. Although not directly referred to in the poem, it is probable that the author is referring to him and, indeed, his father, the archbishop of Dublin.

> Whilst round his Vulture Eyes he cast,
> To find if an Hibernian dare
> Look for Preferment and he there[178]
> And will 'hold' D – b – n in Commendum.[179]

The author of this work must have been familiar with the workings of St Patrick's Cathedral in the post-Swift period. Those years were of considerable importance in the narrative of the Church of Ireland. Politicians adopted policies, writes Kenneth Milne 'that vitally affected its life as the established church, and that these policies impacted with some force on the cathedral'.[180] St Patrick's was the only cathedral that had retained the right to elect its own deans. However, this was not without controversy. Swift's appointment in 1713 had been made by the Crown, but when he died in office, in 1745, the chapter, or general assembly, of the cathedral opted to elect a new dean, as it believed it was entitled to do under the rules governing the cathedral. The Crown thought otherwise, and (as was also the case some fifty years later when the aforementioned Dean William Cradock died) instituted legal proceedings against the chapter of St Patrick's and the archbishop of Dublin, who had already accepted the chapter's choice of Gabriel James Maturin for the position. Because Swift had been such a controversial, popular and outspoken dean during his tenure, it is possible that the Crown sought to control the choice of his successors as much as possible. Before the legal proceedings against Maturin's appointment took place, he died, and the chapter appointed Francis Corbet, who was in due course succeeded by William Cradock, who was also elected by the chapter. The Crown did not challenge the appointment of Cradock. However, a vigorous campaign was launched when the chapter chose Robert Fowler as successor to Cradock after the latter's death in 1793. The Crown instituted a case against the choice of Robert Fowler based on – it may be assumed – some shortcomings on his part. His father, the archbishop of Dublin, had been involved in some asset stripping of diocesan properties, and had, as Anthony Malcomson puts it, arranged the 'unprincipled' promotion of his only son Robert, a man of allegedly ill-repute.[181] Fowler's father had also appointed him precentor of St Patrick's, which was within his remit, and this paved the way for him to be elected dean by the chapter when the position became available. As it happened, Fowler was elected dean in October 1793. In December the Crown gave notice of a suit being initiated, and as a result Fowler resigned in April 1794. In the same month his father appointed him archdeacon of Dublin, and the chapter appointed James Verschoyle as dean, and continued over subsequent decades to resist challenges to its right to the election of deans. While the 'vulture eyes' referred to in the author's verse could refer to either Fowler senior or junior, the line 'look for Preferment and he there' could refer to the fact that Robert Fowler was in an advantageous position in St Patrick's to claim the deanery when it arose, and upon gaining the position of dean both he and his father as the archbishop could not fail to hold Dublin *in commendam*, an example of the interplay between churchmanship and politics in the latter half of the eighteenth century.

While the author of this utopian satire-in-miniature has Ilphinzingo embark on an imaginary voyage, a 'grand tour' of the heavens where the cultivated plains and rocky mountains 'exhibited a scene at once enchanting and novel',[182] the putative 'gallery of fools', 'the conventicle of fanatics', 'the porch of tatlers', 'the hall of justice', among others, represent facets of the characteristics of earthly inhabitants – their vices, foibles, inventiveness, satire and tranquillity. In this brief utopian projection, the journey to the lunar world allegorises contemporary life, as the author holds a mirror up to Dublin society. This mirror is solely directed towards the machinations around status, preferment and politics in the terrestrial Church. Thus, it is a composite Utopia, integrating an imaginary journey, a utopian satire and a cautionary tale for potential satirists, which has Ilphinzingo – to be on the safe side – leave this earth and go to the moon.

Lady Mount Cashell's lunar Utopia

Margaret King, later Countess of Mount Cashell, was born in Henrietta Street in Dublin. In her early years her parents Lord and Lady Kingsborough moved to their estate, Mitchelstown Castle in County Cork. In 1787 Mary Wollstonecraft accepted the position of governess to three of the five daughters of Lord and Lady Kingsborough on a salary of £40 per year. By all accounts, Wollstonecraft's stay was not a happy one as both herself and Lady Kingsborough disagreed on many matters. Her thoughts about the Kingsboroughs appeared in her first novel, *Original Stories from Real Life* (1788). She based the character Mary – the heroine, an unhappy girl of wealthy parents – on her young Irish pupil. Wollstonecraft had been dismissed from her position within a year, and moved to London to become a professional writer. Nonetheless, Wollstonecraft's influence on Margaret was to remain a feature of her life. In one of her letters Margaret writes:

> Almost the only person of superior merit with whom I have been intimate in my early days was an enthusiastic female who was my governess … for whom I felt an unbounded admiration because her mind appeared more noble and her understanding more cultivated than any others I had known.[183]

Selene – an unpublished, three-volume novel written in Italy in the early 1820s – bears the subtitle *Memoirs of Matthew Ivy, Quondam Esquire of Ivy Castle, Supposed to be Written by Himself, and Prepared for Publication by Basil Fitz Edward.* The preface is written by Fitz Edward, who tells how he met Matthew Ivy, the author of the first-person narrative that follows. Matthew's mother dies when he is still a child, and he is adopted by a rich uncle, Jonathan, who declares that the boy will be heir to Ivy Castle. Over the course of seven years Matthew is schooled at home by a private tutor, and indulged by his uncle, whose passions include the study of Arabic and the Irish language. When he goes to university, Matthew falls into bad company, and after his uncle's death fails in his attempt to pursue a political career. He marries a woman whom he discovers has been having an affair with his dearest friend, resulting in her pregnancy. The lovers elope, and Matthew decides to commit suicide rather than endure the public shame of a divorce. While searching for a pistol in his uncle's bureau, he discovers a narrative entitled 'A Voyage to the Moon' and a set of balloons, which he inflates before using them to set off on a journey that brings him to the moon. Upon the moon he is impressed by the volcanic lunar landscape, by the giant unicorns with grass-green eyes, eight legs and two tails of purple, green and gold. The Seleneans have yellow skin, are taller and thinner than humans, and have an extra organ in the middle of their foreheads; this functions as a kind of sixth sense, which allows them to see the meaning of words, and so to gain an understanding of the true nature of wisdom. Following on from this, they value benevolence above wealth, virtue over self-indulgence, justice over self-interest. Some characters wear green cloaks evocative of Ireland, while the better sort of Seleneans wear purple underclothes to distinguish themselves.

Similar to McDermot and Humphrey Lunatic, after a time Matthew wishes to return to earth, completes his homeward journey, and makes his way to England. There, he is unrecognised as the heir of Ivy Castle, and makes a living as a translator while searching for his two brothers, whom he has not seen since childhood. He meets a young woman named Eleanor and marries her, having found out that his first wife is dead. They adopt his first wife's son and settle in the country. An extract on the title page from Canto 34 of Ariosto's *Orlando Furioso*, which details the strange landscape first glimpsed by Orlando after his arrival on the moon, places *Selene* within the tradition of lunar narratives stretching back to classical times. *Selene* encompasses facets of More's *Utopia*, Swift's country of the Houyhnhnms and Voltaire's El Dorado. The Seleneans never engage in war, murder is unknown to them, and the hardest punishment given to those found guilty of wrongdoing is to deprive them of sunlight while sentencing them to hard labour on public projects for specific periods of time. Consequently, soldiers, barristers and attorneys are unheard of. Among Seleneans celibacy is popular, marriage at a young age is unheard of, and when it does take place at a later stage it is based on mutual respect and companionship. Seleneans only permit a handful of books, censors review everything that is written, and those texts regarded as unsuitable are destroyed at a public event known as the Feast of the Books once every three years. The Seleneans look after their health, and renounce alcohol and all excess. They have no system of currency and no taxation, and they repudiate all falsehood and injustice. Matthew discovers that at one time all Seleneans were equal but that an aristocratic race evolved, and their physical strength and intellectual prowess set them apart from all others. Every three years a chief is chosen from the elite, and all the noblemen over the age of twenty-five years and plebeians over the age of fifty can vote in the elections. If it is shown that the elected chief is unworthy of office, the appointment does not go ahead.

In the early 1790s many in the circle of Lady Mount Cashell professed a genteel classical republicanism or an enlightened patriotism that could exist alongside the hierarchies and structures of their own class. Claire Connolly has argued that *Selene* 'imagine[s] interplanetary travel as a way of highlighting injustices in Ireland'.[184] However, Anne Markey suggests that this argument is difficult to sustain, 'not least because the only two Irish characters to feature in the three volumes are a drunken priest and a proselytising, avaricious Catholic nurse'.[185] That said, Lady Mount Cashell's Irish background must have influenced her political views and her depiction of life on the moon. As Markey points out, 'the principle of toleration that underpins Selenean attitudes to religious practice and belief reflect her disapproval of the injustice enshrined in the Penal Laws, many of which were still in operation in Ireland at the time *Selene* was written'.[186] In addition to her critique of contemporary politics and social mores, Lady Mount Cashell casts a satirical eye on the English publishing industry in the late Romantic period. Matthew discovers that, whereas in Selenean practice only a few books of real merit are published each year, English booksellers print a vast number of inferior works. In London, after his return from the moon, he secures work from a bookseller doing translations of second-rate romances, and he comes across many works replete with vacuous sentiment and dull moral philosophy, and this prompts him to try a superior fiction, which he offers to his employer. When the bookseller Mr Adamson sees the one-volume manuscript, he suggests that it needs to be extended to at least three volumes to get a good price, but he agrees to read it. He likes it, but gets a successful novelist called Mr Amplify to amend some parts so that Matthew can see how to make the necessary improvements. One of these adjustments involves the expansion of a passage of some forty words into several paragraphs running to over 400 words, to which nothing of any substance has been added. In spite of Adamson's assurances that the book could be expanded into four volumes, Matthew puts it aside and commences work as a reviewer for a periodical of literary criticism. *Selene* draws attention to the power of the bookseller in determining literary taste and convention. Adamson's refusal to print a one-volume novel and his recruitment of Amplify to improve on Matthew's efforts may seem satirical, but according to Barbara M. Benedict, booksellers were the most influential people in English publishing during the Romantic period, often telling 'printers, and sometimes authors too, what to produce'.[187] *Selene*, as a work of utopian satire partly set on the moon, presents a critique of English politics and social mores while also conveying insights into the English publishing world in the final years of the 'long eighteenth century'.[188]

Combined, these lunar and extraterrestrial works of utopian satire represent a distinctive facet of eighteenth-century Irish utopianism. In each case the extraterrestrial voyage functions as a device for estranging readers from the familiar world, enabling usually satiric perspectives to be set up. Estrangement is a necessary component of these Utopias. It allows a critical distance through spatial separation, as the imagined 'good place' is set apart from the present. The lunar realms are guided by different values from the authors' own, and organised through diverse and different socio-political arrangements. The journey to, and topos of, the extraterrestrial world functions to hold contemporary society (or in the case of *A History of the Customs, Manners, and Religion of the Moon* specific aspects of it) up to ridicule and analysis. The author of *A History*, while presenting a cautionary tale on the perils facing the occupational satirist, also allegorises the conflicts of the society from which he emerged, reflected and refracted on the moon but rooted firmly in and around clerical politics in contemporary Dublin. Swift's 'Laputa' comments on society, and ultimately offers the possibility of the renovation, or the 'making new', of Ireland. The fantasy-adventure writer McDermot finds a utopian commonwealth on the moon, and provides a counter-space in which the experimental science of rocketry as a means of interplanetary travel and satire cohere in a work of proto-science fiction. Gentleman's moral, philosophical and ideological work is enveloped in the kernel of a utopian society. His ancestor Whimsical Lunatic's vision for a Plato's republic is recovered on Noibla and counterpoised with the dystopian space of the terrestrial world. Lady Mount Cashell's *Selene* takes the form of a travel account, combining elements of an adventure narrative set in a classical republican government with utopian satire while drawing attention to contemporary English literary production. The presiding spirit of Swift and the leitmotif of the extraterrestrial world as a space from which to criticise or comment on a parlous contemporary society is a unifying element in all of these works, whilst the authors independently grapple with the plausible alternatives to which a reconfigured terrestrial world might aspire.

CHAPTER 6

Dark Caverns:
Samuel Madden's Futurism

Leaving the beaten Tracts of writing with Malice or Flattery, the accounts of past Actions and Times, have dar'd to enter by the help of an infallible Guide, into the dark Caverns of Futurity, and discover the Secrets of Ages yet to come.

Samuel Madden, *Memoirs of the Twentieth Century*[1]

I could not with ease look back on the World, I resolved to look forward and consider what might happen, since I abhor'd to reflect on what had.

Samuel Madden, *Memoirs of the Twentieth Century*[2]

The variegated nature of Irish utopianism reveals a succession of Utopias to be found in fiction, verse, speeches, songs and manifestos. So far I have recognised a clear utopian propensity in Irish culture of the eighteenth century, one marked by twin discourses of improvement and satire. The utopian projections of George Berkeley together with the imperative to improve and the sense of advancing the public good of the founders of the Dublin Society combined disparate improving visions in the public sphere, while the extraterrestrial and lunar narratives of Jonathan Swift, Murtagh McDermot, Francis Gentleman and others presented utopian satire as a means of fictional discourse through which to allegorise and criticise contemporary society.

In this chapter I focus on one Irish-authored text. It stands as a high point in the literature of utopian satire predicated on an imagined future society conjoined with the inaugural time-travel Utopia – it is Samuel Madden's *Memoirs of the Twentieth Century*, published anonymously in 1733. For many years Louis Sébastien Mercier's *L'an deux mille quatre cent quarante* (*Memoirs of the Year Two Thousand Five Hundred*) (1771) was presumed to be the first literary Utopia set in the future. We now know that it was not the first, and was predated by Madden's *Memoirs* by thirty-eight years. Drawing on Sargent's specific definitions of the disparate textual forms of the generic literary Utopia – eutopia, dystopia, utopian satire, anti-Utopia and critical Utopia[3] – I define a 'future Utopia' as a non-existent society described in considerable detail and combining one or all of these elements: utopian satire, time travel and prophecy, and being located in a chronologically specified future that the author intended a reader to view as a comment on contemporaneous society. While all authors of Utopias locate the new society in a place different from their own, the significance of Madden, and so often celebrated of Mercier, was that their Utopias were located not in another place on earth, such as the Antipodes of the South Seas, a lost valley such as Shangri-La, one of the polar regions or, indeed, underground in a cavernous society – that is, in places not yet explored by Westerners. Instead, these new works of the eighteenth century shifted the location to the future. That said, it is not so much that they created a new category of a future Utopia but that they changed in a radical way the former provenance of Utopia from an honoured place to be found contemporaneously with the author's own time to another place in the future. This has deep implications, because it strongly supports the idea of historical development, even progress. And so the move is not to some parallel or lateral society but to a future society that grew from the contemporaneous author and reader's own present. This remains a significant change because it implies that humanity through its own efforts can get there.

So who was Samuel Madden, and what do we know about him? Samuel Molyneux Madden, Church of Ireland clergyman, writer and philanthropist, was born in Dublin in 1686. He was the second son of John Madden MD (d. 1703) of Manor Waterhouse, County Fermanagh – who was one of the original members of the Irish College of Physicians – and Mary Molyneux (d. 1695), a sister of William and Thomas Molyneux. Samuel Madden received his BA from Trinity College, Dublin in 1705 and his DD degree in 1723. In 1709 he married Jane Magill, and they had five daughters and five sons, and employed the progressive Church of Ireland clergyman and philosophical writer Philip Skelton (1707–87) as a curate and tutor to their children. After his father's death, Madden inherited the estate in Fermanagh. Upon ordination he became rector of the parish of Galloon (which included Newtownbutler, the nearest place to the family estate), to which was added (in 1727) the adjacent parish of Drumully, at that time in the gift of the Madden

Figure 8: Portrait of Samuel Madden by Robert Hunter. Trinity College, Dublin
Art Collections. Reproduced by kind permission of the Board of the University of
Dublin, Trinity College, Dublin

family. He had a notable involvement in the civic life of the area, was an active
author, and through the Dublin Society promoted his ideas on agricultural
improvement, architecture, philanthropy and education.

In 1732 Madden's *Proposal for the General Encouragement of Learning in
Dublin-College* was published. It was a seminal pamphlet in which he proposed
instituting a system of prizes for students in the quarterly examinations at
Trinity College. It was dedicated to Hugh Lord, archbishop of Armagh and
primate of all Ireland. In this *Proposal* Madden asks the named cleric for
his support, and notes that such approval would encourage other clergy and
gentry to support it. He lays down what he calls 'the naked skeleton of this
plain and easy scheme; which by God's Blessing may produce very happy

effects, if it be pursued with that honest zeal and warmth which may be hop'd for from many people of worth among us'.[4] It was to provide the basis of his soubriquet of 'Premium Madden'. Madden writes of 'some additional Motives and *Premiums* for Diligence, which might operate perpetually, and keep up a constant and almost a daily Emulation for Application and Study in their Pupils; we should soon find such an Improvement thereby among the whole of our People'.[5] And so Madden's words foreground the socially transformative logic of the utopian mode, for diligent and worthy students will ultimately bring benefits to the whole of society.

Madden's plan for the encouragement of learning was adopted by the university, and he contributed £600. With this resolve he also funded a series of annuities from 1740 for the Dublin Society. In 1745, with the help of his friend the eminent lexicographer Samuel Johnson (1709–84), he published a panegyric poem in memory of Hugh Boulter, the long-serving archbishop of Armagh and Whig privy councillor, and which was dedicated to Frederick, Prince of Wales. He also penned an anonymous panegyric to Lord Chesterfield, and prefixed a 200-line metrical epistle to the biography of Philip of Macedonia by Dublin-born classicist and historian Thomas Leland (1722–85), which was published in 1758.

In his *History of Irish Periodical Literature*, Richard Robert Madden recounts what he calls the earliest notice he had found of the illustrious benefactor Dr Samuel Madden in any Irish newspaper. He cites the *Dublin Evening Post* of 14 November 1732: 'Last Saturday, a number of gentlemen, educated in Dr. Sheridan's school, entertained him at the Eagle, on Cork Hill, where they entered into a resolution to support some reduced young gentlemen at the University, bred under him.'[6] Undoubtedly, this gathering would have been aware of Madden's recently published *Proposal for the General Encouragement of Learning in Dublin-College* and were willing to support it. In her correspondence, Mary Delany records a visit to the Madden estate in Fermanagh in August 1748, and of both Madden and his estate she notes:

> *He is a very remarkable man*, and to give you a just portrait of him would take up more time than is allowed me at present. The place is pretty; a very fine wood of all sort of forest trees, planted by Doctor Madden just by the house, surrounded by a fine river. He has been a great planter and benefactor to his country on many accounts and a great encourager of the premiums and charter-schools.[7]

Delany provides a clear link between both Madden's domiciliary milieu and other major aspects of his career, that of a benefactor and philanthropist.

Madden in the age of Walpole

In 1733, the year in which Madden's *Memoirs of the Twentieth Century* was published, the author was forty-seven years old. George II had been king since 1727, and Robert Walpole had been prime minister for over ten years and was to remain so until his forced resignation in February 1742. Walpole, born in August 1676, was the son of a Norfolk country gentleman, and was educated at Eton and King's College, Cambridge. He was politically ambitious: a Whig since his Cambridge days, he fought his first general election in 1701 without success. He was elected in 1701 for Castle Riding, where his father had been MP, and in 1702 was elected to a more important Norfolk borough, the port of King's Lynn, the seat he was to represent until he was created Earl of Orford in February 1742. By the time of the accession to the throne of George I in 1714, Walpole had a reputation as one of the leading Whig parliamentarians. His rise had been rapid, and he was, by the standards of the day, a good party man. Swift, a Tory, wrote of 'his bold, forward countenance, altogether a stranger to that infirmity which makes men bashful, joined to a readiness of speaking in public'.[8] A pamphlet of 1716 referred to Walpole's vivacity, fine parts, deep judgement and penetration, another to his wisdom and 'golden tongue'. A pamphleteer of 1711 called him 'pragmatical, noisy and impertinent'.[9]

To understand both Walpole and Britain in this first half of the eighteenth century, it is necessary to appreciate the seventeenth-century background. This was the period in which the subsequent generation of leading politicians was born and grew up. Of the leading Whigs, Stanhope was born in 1673, Townshend and Sunderland in 1674, Walpole in 1676, Argyll in 1678, Ilay in 1682, Pulteney in 1684 and Newcastle in 1693. Of the leading Tories, Strafford was born in 1672, Shippen in 1673, Bolingbroke in 1678 and Wyndham in 1687. These were years of great instability and conflict. The primary interconnected causes were religious, political and dynastic. The religious conflict was pivotal in the major events of the seventeenth century. The English Civil War can best be understood as a war of religion. James II (reigned 1685–88) was ousted in the so-called Glorious Revolution largely because of the fear that he would try to enforce his own Catholicism on his subjects. However, religion was not solely a matter for politicians. Those people who were in the wrong Church were deprived of a wide variety of what would today be considered rights but were then thought of as privileges, such as the right to vote or to be an MP, to hold political and government office, to establish schools or to go to university.

The anti-Catholic sentiment that accompanied the Popish Plot of 1678 and the violence that was directed against Dissenters (the burgeoning denominations of Protestants who were not members of the Church of England) testified to the force of religious passion in the politics of the period and the extent to which such fervour was by no means confined to those who had political power. The overthrow of James II had been prefigured in the Exclusion Crisis of 1679–81, when an attempt had been made to prevent him from succeeding his brother Charles II in favour of a Protestant heir, and again in the rebellion of Monmouth and Argyll in 1685. After James' overthrow there were two claimants to the throne. The supporters of James and his descendants, known as Jacobites, were especially strong among the Catholics in Ireland and the Catholics and Episcopalians in Scotland. The throne itself was held by Protestants: first James' daughter Mary and her husband William III of Orange, then, because they had no children, by Mary's sister Anne and, after her death without issue in 1714, by the Lutheran Electors of Hanover, whose claim descended from the German marriage of James I's daughter. Their claim was recognised by Parliament in the Act of Settlement of 1701, but, in dynastic terms, they were clearly further from the Stuart line than James II's son James, who claimed the throne from exile in France that year as 'James III' on the death of his father.

The political atmosphere of the period was one of hovering conflict and violence. Plots such as the Rye House Plot of 1683, a scheme to assassinate Charles II, were suppressed with violence. Judge Jeffrey tried and executed many of Monmouth's followers, only to end up dying in the Tower of London himself when the political climate changed. It was a time when an unsuccessful politician could expect parliamentary impeachment, exile, imprisonment and even execution. Such was the political world in which Walpole grew up, and, indeed, Walpole himself was imprisoned in the Tower by his Tory opponents in 1712. The longevity of Walpole's ministry, from 1721 to 1742, did not eliminate instability. The Jacobite rebellion of 1745 was ample evidence of the continued problem posed by dynastic conflict. It was only with the Battle of Culloden in 1746, when Bonnie Prince Charlie, leading the army of Scottish Highlanders on behalf of his father 'James III', was defeated by

George II's younger son, the Duke of Cumberland, that the Hanoverian dynasty was really safe. The nature of politics and government during the period of Walpole's twenty years as prime minister is a recurring theme of writers during this time. Nearly all of the major writers of the period (Swift, John Gay, Alexander Pope, Samuel Johnson and Henry Fielding) adopted an anti-government stance, which was reflected in their works.

In the summer of 1711, aiming to consolidate intellectual support among Tories, Henry Bolingbroke had founded the Brothers Club for men of learning, wit and breeding as a counterbalance to the Whig Kit-Cat Club. This aristocratic and intellectual circle included Swift, John Arbuthnot and Bolingbroke, and was soon joined by younger poets, such as Pope and Gay. The Scriblerus Club evolved out of the Brothers Club. For the next thirty years this group of wits and satirists were, as Isaac Kramnick puts it, 'committed to scourging the follies from mankind, directed their offensive against the corruptions of the new England'.[10] Walpole met only token opposition after he came to power in 1721. From 1727–30 the situation was transformed with the appearance of Bolingbroke's opposition newspaper *The Craftsman* on 5 December 1726, and so a sustained critique of Walpole's ministry began. Kramnick quotes a pamphleteer describing the mood as *The Craftsman* was inaugurated: 'all hands were employed and engines set to work, manuscripts were circulated, the press loaded, coffee house talkers, table wits, and bottle companions had their instructions given them'.[11]

These years also saw the publication of Swift's *Gulliver's Travels* and Pope's *Dunciad*, and the premiere of Gay's *The Beggar's Opera*, all of which were, at least in part, intent on maligning Walpole and his administration. Estimates of *The Craftsman*'s circulation vary, however; Johnson's estimate had it high: 'It was more read and attended to than any political paper ever published, on account of the assistance given to it by some of the most illustrious and important characters of the nation. It is said 10,000 of that paper have been sold in one day.'[12] That said, whatever its circulation, its impact was evident, as Laurence Hanson puts it: 'it raised the whole tone of political controversy in the press, for the criticisms which it made were both pungent and well informed'.[13] *The Craftsman* excelled in barbed wit and biting satire that focused the ire of its reading public on one individual as the object of all its vilification, Walpole. As J.H. Plumb writes on Walpole and *The Craftsman*, 'Walpole hated it, hated it furiously and bitterly.'[14] Samuel Madden also spoke about *The Craftsman*; however, unlike his fellow Irishman Swift, Madden was, or at least appeared to be, a dedicated supporter of Walpole. In a letter written to Walpole some time after 1727, Madden offered his services in a literary capacity, and admitted that *The Craftsman* had a 'greater Reputation for Wit, & Talents for dispute' and that it was 'a superior Master of the arts to catch the Crowd'.[15] Thus, Madden recognised the popular, literary and intellectual appeal that the newspaper had captured. Contrary to the spirit of Christian forbearance that a clergyman such as himself might be expected to practice, he made the following recommendation:

> Begin an attack against them in a method & manner entirely new & that there was no way so effectual to defeat them, as to turn their own Cannon against them & ridicule them; for besides that this is no reasoning age nor our People so fond of strong arguments as biting Jests, I was persuaded if once the laugh could be turn'd against them the mob would desert them & they must be undone.[16]

The exact date of this letter from Madden to Walpole is not known, but it is clear that Madden is against the opposition newspaper *The Craftsman* and is pro-government or appearing to be pro-government. Clearly, he is proposing an idea as to how it could be defeated and undone. He argues that should the techniques of *The Craftsman* be adopted and adapted by pro-government writers and used to turn their satire and ridicule back upon them, what he calls the 'mob' would decamp and cease to support those anti-government writers. Madden asserts that Walpole's opponents can be defeated, but, interestingly, does not expand upon how such a plan was to be produced and effectively executed. While Madden was not alone in expressing such sentiments, there is no evidence to suggest that he became one of Walpole's penmen.

A letter written by William Pulteney, Earl of Bath, in 1733 to Walpole expresses the view that critics of *The Craftsman* are 'the shameless crew, who write against their Country, as they would write against their God, for hire'.[17] He argues that 'the Ribaldry, which these Scriblers employ, hath been and will continue to be despised, not answered'.[18] He defends the writings of *The Craftsman*, saying that they endeavour to revive the 'Spirit' and to 'confirm and propagate the Doctrines of Liberty'.[19] During Walpole's administration, pamphlets were regularly issued by J. Roberts, the government printer, in which the position of his government was presented by writers such as Bishop Hoadly, Daniel Defoe, Lord Hervey and Horatio Walpole. Writing about *The Craftsman* to Thomas Sheridan in 1727, Swift says, 'It is certain that Walpole is peevish and disconnected, and stoops to the vilest offices of hireling

scoundrels to write Billingsgate of the lowest and most prostitute kind and
has none but beasts and blockheads for his penmen, whom he pays in ready
guineas very liberally.'[20] Swift's comments were accurate: a covert parliamentary investigation in 1742 into Walpole's conduct in office revealed the extent
of his purchase of penmen. The sum of £50,000 had been paid during the
years 1732–42 to authors and printers of newspapers, the most popular of
these being *The London Journal.*

Thus, Bolingbroke's *Craftsman* and many contemporary writers alluded to
Walpole in their works. Gay in *The Beggar's Opera* made an implied comparison between the criminal world and the world of politics. In Swift's *Gulliver's
Travels*, 'Flimnap, the Treasurer', thought to be an allusion to Walpole, does a
dance on a rope to entertain His Majesty and the court. Whoever jumps the
highest without falling succeeds in the office, and chief ministers themselves
are commanded to show their skill to convince the emperor that they have
not lost their faculty: 'Flimnap, the Treasurer, is allowed to cut a Caper on the
strait Rope, at least an Inch higher that any other Lord in the whole Empire.'[21]
The exercise in rope dancing is a felicitous metaphor for the contortions contemporary politicians went through to obtain and retain power. The theatre
became increasingly politicised from 1728 following the first performance of
The Beggar's Opera. Writing in the first volume of his *Dramatic Censor*, Francis
Gentleman records an anecdote about Sir Robert Walpole, against whom Gay
chiefly brandished his pen. The characters Peachum and Lockit engage in a
satire about their accounts:

> When you censure the age,
> Be cautious and sage,
> Lest the courtiers offended should be:
> If you mention vice or bribe,
> 'Tis so pat to all the tribe,
> That each cries that was levell'd at me.[22]

Walpole was seated in the stage box, and Gentleman records his supposed
response:

> In respect of this song, which showed an agreeable and politic presence
> of mind; being in the stage-box, at the first presentation of the opera, a
> most universal encore attended Lockit's song, and all eyes at the same
> time were fixed on Sir Robert, who, noting the matter, joined heartily

in the plaudit, and encored it a second time with his single voice; which not only blunted the poetical shaft, but gained a general huzza from the audience.[23]

On that occasion, and from this account, it would appear that Walpole's response defused the potency of the allusions to him evident in *The Beggar's Opera*. However, allusions to him occur and recur throughout the period. Criticism was voiced through literary works, and Walpole as a character was an obsession with writers more or less loosely associated with the opposition. Some years later, in the early 1730s, Lord Hervey, a supporter of Walpole, recalled in a letter to Henry Fox dated 25 January 1733 a visit to the theatre in Goodman's Fields to see James Ralph's adaptation of a Restoration play, *The Fall of the Earl of Essex*. When the actor who played the leading role delivered his lines, 'Abhor all Courts if thou art brave or wise,/ For then thou never shalt be sure to rise,/ Think not by doing well a Fame to get,/ But be a Villian & thou shalt be great',[24] Hervey records that 'Her Grace of Marlborough cry'd charming; & clapt her Hands so loud that we heard her cross the theatre into the King's Box'.[25] This story shows how sensitive and attuned audiences were to political allusions in literary works. As a supporter of the opposition, the duchess had seized the opportunity to show her contempt for Walpole. Although he is not mentioned by name in the passage, audiences would have had very little difficulty in reading an allusion to Walpole in the final line. The word 'Courts' in the first line evoked not only the entourage of kings and queens but aimed at a whole coterie of Whig supporters who maintained Walpole in power. In the final line the use of the adjective 'great' would have been enough to bring up the image of Walpole as a corrupt politician. The opposition writers often ironically referred to Walpole as 'the Great Man', so that the term 'great' came to have very negative overtones. In referring to this clear undercurrent of political allusion present in numerous eighteenth-century literary works, Bertrand Goldgar uses the term 'argot', in which certain words developed layer upon layer of political meaning and connotation to the point where the mention of words such as 'screen' or 'brass' conjured up the image of Walpole as a corrupt politician.[26] What was happening politically during the twenty years of Walpole's ministry clearly influenced the literary works of the period.

Unlike his fellow Irishmen Swift and Berkeley (Berkeley believed that Walpole, in refusing to pay a £20,000 grant, was chiefly responsible for defeating his Bermuda project), Madden was and remained a supporter of Walpole.

As I have noted in his letter to Walpole, Madden had determined that an aggressive campaign against *The Craftsman* would be effective, and in the same letter he also commented on the difficulty for anyone confronting government propagandists: 'you know well Sr. how vain it is to reason with anyone, who will never be convinc'd or silenc'd, but will still have the last word.'[27] In their striving to criticise Walpole, Madden here seems to suggest that such dogged opposition will be difficult for pro-government writers to match without an aggressive campaign on their part. Did Madden receive a response from Walpole? Did Walpole take any note of what Madden had said? Was such a situation likely, or would Walpole have kept an impersonal distance between himself and correspondents such as a Church of Ireland clergyman with a novice literary career? We do not know if Madden tried to keep his association with Walpole a secret. Some supporters had done this, motivated by a wish to avoid any backlash in their surroundings should their political persuasions become widely known. However, the letter does show Madden's own point of view, and could explain some of the questions surrounding his subsequent suppression of his anonymously published *Memoirs*. That said, the bifurcated nature of Madden's career at that time seems stark. He was a Church of Ireland clergyman running his family estate. He was aware of the early Dublin societies, and was developing his plan for the encouragement of learning in Trinity College. In 1731 his brother, Revd John Madden (vicar of St Ann's and later dean of Kilmore), and his uncle, Thomas Molyneux, were among the founding members of the Dublin Society. Madden was to become its first patron. Madden's milieu for his literary efforts is clearly set within the flux of the eighteenth-century political life going on about him. However, the contrast between his utopianism as manifest in his practical support and patronage of the Dublin society and as expressed in his *Memoirs* reveals a character whose utopianism is far more complex and disparate than at first appears.

Memoirs: pre-vision and futures of the past

It was against the background of this political and literary milieu that Madden published his *Memoirs* in March 1733, and the book caused enough of a stir that it was suppressed by him shortly after its publication. There is, as John Nichols puts it, 'something mysterious in this history of this work, which was written by Dr. Samuel Madden, the patriot of Ireland; who projected a scheme, in 1731, for promoting learning in the College at Dublin by Premiums'.[28] According to Nichols,

> a thousand copies were printed, with such very great dispatch, that three printers were employed on it (Bowyer, Woodfall, and Roberts); and the names of an uncommon number of reputable booksellers appeared in the title-page. In less than a fortnight, however, 890 of these copies were delivered to Dr. Madden, and probably destroyed. The current report is that the edition was suppressed on the day of publication. And that it is now exceedingly scarce, is certain. Mr. Tutet who has a copy of it, never heard but of one other ...[29]

Madden had already dedicated his play *Themistocles* to the Prince of Wales, and may have acted as chaplain to him. They had certainly carried on a correspondence. Frederick, Prince of Wales, served as the tenth chancellor of Trinity College, Dublin from 1728 to the year of his death in 1751. In 1733 he was not yet officially part of the opposition to his father George II's government. Madden is explicit in viewing this dedication as a public espousal of his regard for the Prince of Wales. As he puts it, 'possibly I had been less liable to Censure, if I could have contented my self with paying You in private the secret Homage of my Heart, without giving any publick Testimony of that infinite Regard which I pretend to bear you'.[30] Madden speaks of his 'uncontested Virtues so universally acknowledged by all'.[31] He expresses his 'sincerity of heart',[32] which should remain 'unsuspected of the little Arts of fawning sycophants'.[33] While distancing himself from fawning sycophants, Madden clearly admires the Prince of Wales, but he also expresses admiration for the king and queen. He writes that he sees the prince 'as the Heir apparent of the best Man and Woman, the best King and Queen, that ever adorn'd a family, or blest a Nation'.[34] Madden's dedication is dated 25 January 1731, two years before *Memoirs* was published. He is clearly dedicating this in anticipation of Frederick becoming king (this was not to happen). Alternatively, it could have been written by Madden to accompany any subsequent work of his, not necessarily *Memoirs*. He views the Prince of Wales as an 'amiable character',[35] and he speaks of the Britain that would emerge under his reign in utopian terms, as King Frederick would 'make us the happiest of Nations, and the best of Subjects under a race of Princes, against whom the little Clamours and Arts of Faction at Home, will be as impotent and contemptible, as the inveterate Malice of Rome, and the Enemies of our Peace Abroad'.[36] However, Madden's view of Britain as a Utopia under the new king is contrasted with the image of those who he views as threatening the 'happiest of nations',[37] namely factions at home, the Church of Rome and any other enemies of Britain's peace abroad – essentially, any enemies of his Utopia.

Madden's fulsome praise for the Prince of Wales may have been heightened to garner some perceived advantage for himself and his plans for practical improvements during the Walpole years. The printing of a thousand copies seems to contradict Madden's claim that only fifty copies would be published. In the first preface to *Memoirs* he explains that only fifty copies were to be published, or, as his narrator puts it,

> For my part, I have acted with the utmost Caution in suppressing or publishing any Particulars, and as it is to be fear'd if after all my Care this Book should grow too common and be in everyone's Hand, it may be applied to ill purposes, by letting the meanest of the People see, *uti digerit omnia Calchas*, I have given order to print but fifty Copies, which I compute will answer the number of Persons in Great Britain, who are Wise and Honest enough to be trusted with such a Jewel.[38]

It is clear, however, that Madden viewed the work as directed towards a private readership or, at any rate, a select readership. None of this is to deny, though, that the printers printed as many as a thousand copies, but it may offer a reason as to why Madden sought to suppress them – not solely because of content but also because of quantity.

The sacred text of the *Comte de Gabalis*, Cervantes' *Don Quixote* and the writings of Jean-Louis Guez de Balzac are among the coterie of literati Madden alludes to in his first preface to *Memoirs*.[39] The narrator – interestingly, not specifically identified as Madden – is, we are told, descended 'in a direct line by the Mother's side, from a Son of that famous Count *Gabalis*, in the seventeenth century, whose History is in every one's Hands'.[40] He questions whether Balzac 'ever toil'd more than I have done to give full Satisfaction in this Introductory Discourse, to the profound Readers and Judges of these Times, who have the Glory and Advantage of being Witnesses to the birth of this admirable Production'.[41] The narrator clearly establishes his literary credentials, and wants his 'admirable production' to find a worthy readership, conscious of the 'treasure'[42] they are being offered. After alluding to those literary titans, he begins an account of his own august origins:

I was born also under the most fortunate of all Planets, and to make my Nativity still more Happy, in one of the *Ember*-Weeks, and with a Cawl, or certain Membrane about my Head; both which as the learned Jesuit *Thyraeus*, (an Order I particularly Reverence) observes, in his Tract *de apparitione Spirituum*, are Circumstances, that render such Children more likely than others, to gain the Acquaintance and Familiarity of the *Genii* design'd for their Conduct.[43]

The narrator here expresses his admiration for the Jesuits, specifically the German Jesuit theologian and preacher Hermann Thyräus. While this is inconsistent with the representation of the Jesuits in much of *Memoirs*, for the narrator it is central to establishing the uniqueness of his origins. Such origins are a prelude to his having been chosen for a visitation from the genii or celestial beings. He recounts the 'more material particulars'[44] of his history: he 'came into the World Heir to a good Family and Fortune, as well as a deal of Pride and Ambition, to distinguish my self from the common Herd of Mankind'.[45] He had spent considerable time travelling around the world so that he could observe something more 'than my Country-Seat and Neighbours in Summer, and London in the Winter'.[46] And so he travelled for three years and became 'as perfectly improv'd as any fine Gentleman of my Time'.[47] He believes that he became a 'sage politician and patriot'.[48] At this point he observes:

I bought a Seat in Parliament at a fair Purchase, for a good deal of Beef and Ale for the Mob, and a round Sum of Money to the worthy Electors, and determin'd to grow great by Voting according to my Conscience, and as the best Arguments should be offer'd me in Favour of those two dangerous Monosyllables, *Yea* and *No*.[49]

He chose his patrons wisely and received many fair promises, not only from his patron but from his patron's patron's patron, who was, we are told, a very great man indeed. He was 'trusted with several Secrets before they were in Print, and assur'd of succeeding to many tolerable places, before they were vacant; and was so much considered, that I never asked for anything'.[50] After some time our narrator realises that his patrons are offering him little more than empty promises, and he makes a decision to break with his patron and 'all my dear friends the courtiers', and

> set up once more for a good Conscience, on the other side. But, alas! I
> soon found this was the worst tim'd step I could have taken, for it both
> ruin'd my Character with the World, and my Tradesmen lost me my
> Election the next Parliament; and in a Word, left me to brood over my
> own Resentments, Disappointments and Despair.[51]

Thus, having made an unwise political move and under altered circumstances, he takes leave of the city and returns to his debt-ridden estate in the country. His life becomes a melancholy and embittered one. He 'began to hope for a thousand scenes of confusion and destruction to my Country and the Royal Family, and to see their Labours to make us happy, luckily overturn'd by some fortunate Calamities, which might destroy their interest with the people'.[52] For several years he gave himself up to reading, despising what he saw as the narrow paths taken by common scholars, and so, by contrast, he

> Studied all hidden Sciences, from magick to the *Jewish Cabala* and
> the Philosopher's Stone, and particularly turn'd my self to Astrology
> with vast Application, in hopes to find some propitious influence from
> the Heavens, to favour these reasonable expectations, since I saw with
> sorrow there was little to be hop'd for from the Earth.[53]

The impetus for *Memoirs* began with the arrival in the narrator's room of a celestial being on 20 January 1728. As he described it, he was lying in his bed

> When I was surprised to see my door which was fast lock'd, and my
> curtains which were close drawn, opening suddenly of themselves and
> a great light filling my chamber, in the midst of which I saw a beautiful
> appearance of something like what we usually imagine Angels to be.[54]

The Angel told him that 'he was my good Genius, and was come to show me nobler Prospects, that should be deriv'd to me and my family, as well as my Country, from the present Royal Line and their Posterity, than those I was drawing from my mistaken Principles in Political Astrology'.[55] The genius seems to be suggesting that the narrator is erring in his reading of political astrology, because greater knowledge and enlightenment of what the future holds both for the narrator's family and his country's politics will be forthcoming from him. He promised to keep up constant communication and correspondence with the narrator, and to give him 'at once some little intelligence of the great events that would happen under their glorious Government, not only to my country, but even my own house and descendants'.[56] Here, the enigmatic visitor sets out to provide information to the narrator not only on the future of his own country but also on the future of his family. To this end he presents him with several large volumes of letters which, he asserted, would be written by, or to, his great-great-great-great-great-grandson, who would be chief (prime) minister at the end of the twentieth century under George VI, a time that would also mark the last days of the world.

As soon as his visitor had left, the narrator began to read over the volumes of letters, and decided to publish a select portion of them. He decided not to make any alterations other than translating them into the English of what he calls these 'illiterate times'.[57] And so the narrator anticipates that radical changes in the language could be expected over the course of the next two centuries. In great detail he presents his reasons for deciding to publish the letters. First, he decides that having been 'enlightened, and having such wonderful discoveries revealed and instructed' to him,[58] he should give the public some foretaste of the fate of mankind in the ages to come. Second, by making the letters public and by showing the glory accruing to certain future ministers, he may lessen the reputations of those who presently have positions of power. As he argues,

> I saw it in vain to attempt their Ruin by downright Railing, throwing Dirt at random, and calling them at all Adventures Rogues and Knaves in Print; for they have so deluded the People, by the cursed success of their Administration, that they will not listen any longer to general Declamations, to witty insinuations or the boldest satyrs, without some few real facts to vouch them and prove they are well grounded.[59]

He believes that in showing the world that in time to come there will be far greater ministers than exist at present, namely in the form of his descendant, then they may pay a little more respect to himself, the ancestor of the future prime minister, who, as he puts it, '(out of that modesty so natural to all great Spirits) I shall not mention here'.[60] Therefore, the narrator, through the revelation of these letters, is showing the current government how badly it has handled the ancestor of the great man who will rule England at the end of the world.

Third, he recounts that the sages and politicians of the present could be kept from destroying the peace if they could be drawn to focus on the secrets of times to come. He believes that it is insufficient for the elevated elites of his time to know all that may be known, but they should aim at being masters of all that is not yet known. He recalls that whenever Augustus or one of the 'antients'[61] had a dream of the public and relating to the Commonwealth, it would be published either 'by the voice of the common Crier'[62] or written up for others to view it. And so he believes it would be criminal to withhold from publishing, as he wants to preserve

> Our country from all the confusion and madness, which the rest of the world will be involv'd in; and continue us in that happy situation, and that spirit of improving our Laws, Arts and Manufactures which I have shewn we shall enjoy in the following centuries, when the other kingdoms of the Earth are to labour, as it were, in actual convulsions, and be jumbled together, like the mountains and plains of Jamaica in the dreadful earthquake of 1692.[63]

He takes great care to ensure that his text, when published, should not be tampered with. To this end he says he has made an exact inventory of the number of syllables, words and sentences it contains in order to prevent imitation or bowdlerisation. He argues that while this may appear somewhat arrogant and conceited, the Turks had done as much for the sacred Alcoran and the Jews for their Talmud, because mistaking a letter could alter the world.

In what he calls a 'Coup d'Eclat', or a grand gesture, the narrator chooses to make three prefaces to this work, with the second and third in the middle and end of the volume. In the second preface, which begins on page 215, the narrator interrupts his readers in studying what he calls 'these admirable letters, and the amazing scenes of Futurity discover'd in them'[64] to answer his critics who accuse him of mere invention, and who suggest there could not be such beings as angels or genii assigned to mankind. The narrator, in a lengthy commentary, rejects such allegations, and draws on his knowledge of different religions and their fundamental beliefs in the existence of angels. He argues that 'it has been common opinion of all Nations, of all Religions, of all Ages, that every Man had a good Angel attending him'.[65] He argues that all the Pharisees in the ancient Jewish Church maintained the existence of angels, but many of them believed that every man had two assigned to him, one good, to protect him, and the other bad, to record his faults and ultimately to be his accuser. He refers to ancient authors to back up his thesis, including

Homer and Hesiod, and mentions that Seneca's hundred and tenth epistle to Lucilius maintained that every man had his genius and every woman her Juno attending on her. He notes that ancient writers who had such genii and who conversed with them included Hermes, Socrates, Aristotle and Cicero. These men, according to the narrator, were allowed to have their genii, 'who either appeared to them, or only assisted and watched over them privately'.[66] He mentions Bartholomaeus de Sybilla, and states:

> a good Angel is assigned to every one of us, from the moment we peep into the World; because, as he wisely and judiciously observes, the minute we are in danger of sinning, the care of the good Angel is necessary to defend us from the assaults of Satan; and that till we are born, we are sufficiently watched over by our mother's good Angel.[67]

He mentions that the Church of Rome had ventured to assign men in high and public stations not only an angel but an archangel. A man of consequence may sometimes be allowed thirty or more angels. He asks the reader why he would have said he received the work from his good genius when it would have been much more to his advantage to attribute all of these things to 'the force of my own learning and wisdom, and a happy foresight into future events'.[68] His descendants would come to know that he was 'the original inventor and author of this new and unexampled way of *writing the History of future times*, than that I was the bare transcriber, or translator of this prodigious work'.[69] He asserts it would have taken an enormous fund of imagination to have composed all that is to be contained in six volumes, and it shows that he could only have received such prodigious knowledge from the hand of a superior being. He argues that it is not unusual to have the death of particular persons foretold, 'as well as the place of their departure and burial, by the means of those surprising apparitions, called Dead Men's Candles; which are as frequently seen walking their rounds in that Country, as our watchmen are with their lanthorns every night in London'.[70]

The second objection is on the pretext that he has some skill in the worst sort of magic, or in the black arts. These critics suggest that through these means the narrator attained his amazing knowledge of futurity. He answers his critics with the riposte that if they really believed that he was a practitioner of the black arts, they would desist from making such claims for fear that he should use his powers against them. Another objection relates to insinuations that he had borrowed all the vast scenes of future events as depicted from his understanding thoroughly the celestial alphabet, which many of the greatest rabbis suggest is written by the 'divine Finger of the Creator of the Stars, plac'd in the Heavens in Hebrew Characters, and which contain all the various accidents which shall ever happen below'.[71] He provides an assurance that he will conceal nothing from the reader, and mentions his learned friend, a Mr Vincent Wing, an ingenious writer of almanacks who prefixes all his almanacks with these words: 'The Heaven's a Book, the Stars are Letters fair; God is the Writer, Men the Readers are.'[72]

The third preface of *Memoirs* is written by way of a postscript to the critics. It is an answer to the critics who make charges that the subsequent letters presage events which cannot possibly happen, and because of their improbability are consequently not true. He again asserts that they are 'not forgeries and impostures, but real facts'[73] that will be made public by an honest publisher. By way of example he asks readers to engage in some retrospection by looking back in history and contemplating how improbable it would have seemed to the original builders of the city of Rome if they had been foretold of how vast and powerful that city was to become through the ages. This includes what he calls 'the overturning of all others by that embryo state, the majesty of the pagan religion there, the birth and rise of the Christian, the breaking of the Roman Empire into several little scraps and pieces which are now miscall'd Kingdoms; the spreading conquests of the Pope and his Monks'.[74] He even asks who could have foreseen that Britain within a short space of time would have grown under what he calls 'the care of a few good Princes',[75] before noting that further progress for the country is to be foretold in his work. And as to trade and riches, he wonders how anyone could have foreseen how

> the new world prov'd the great nursery and prop of the old, which was so long a weak and sickly infant, hardly thought worth the rearing or owning, tho' it is now grown one great source, of the strength, wealth and prosperity of those kingdoms, who almost grudg'd its support.[76]

He appeals to time, which he calls 'the great parent of truth, for the verification of all I publish, and to posterity for that honour and deference, which I already behold them paying, to my faithful labours'.[77] And so he believes that with the passage of time his narrative's veracity will be confirmed.

Letters from the future

The letters Madden's narrator received on that winter's evening in January 1728 are those written to N----m, the narrator's great-great-great-great-great-grandson – who at the end of the twentieth century is both lord high treasurer and prime minister – together with N----m's answers. The letters *N* and *m* are the first and last letters of 'Madden' reversed. The correspondence to N----m are all addressed to the lord high treasurer, and his correspondents are all connected with places:

Stanhope: Constantinople
Hertford: Rome
Clare: Moscow
Herbert: Paris
N----m: Chelsea, London.

The correspondents write on various dates in 1997, 1998 and 1999. From the vantage point of the future they adroitly comment on conditions in Paris, Rome, Constantinople and Moscow. Stanhope, writing from Constantinople on 3 November 1997, gives a very detailed account of trade between England and the east. In a clearly utopian mode, Stanhope is lauding the success of his trade mission to the east. He has been engaged in talks with people, and assures his prime minister that these diplomatic manoeuvres will result in greater glory for Britain. He says that in a short time they will mutually sign an agreement whereby British products will not have any duties placed on them; as he puts it, 'our cloath and manufactures shall hereafter have no unreasonable Duties impos'd on them, as those of other Nations have'.[78] Stanhope humbly suggests that such successful trade negotiations on behalf of the English are not entirely his own doing but are also owing to the wisdom of His Majesty George VI, 'the strength, loyalty and wealth of his subjects, the terror which his fleet spreads over the ocean and the care and policy of his Ministers, and above all your Lordship, who now so happily preside over them'.[79]

Tellingly, Stanhope's trade negotiations with the Grand Visier of Turkey are backed by the military force of his king and his prime minister. Stanhope's wish is simply for his country to be powerful in trade and status throughout the world. As an envoy his focus is clearly on bettering the success of his country abroad. His greatest hope is that 'our native Country shall hereby be highly advantag'd'.[80] Stanhope portrays England as a potential Utopia that will become a better place as trade and military success advance. George VI has through his military stratagems forced his enemies to concede defeats: he has 'humbled France so far, as to oblige her to give up all her ports in the Channel, even Dunkirk and Calais itself into our hands, and taught all the powers in Europe the respect and almost dependence they owe us'.[81] Stanhope suggests that the prime minister's cares will now be based on keeping the general peace with the ultimate aim of promoting trade and profit. He then gives an account of Turkey from 1949 to the present time. The memoirs of his two predecessors in the post had fallen into his hands, and this, coupled with his own experience, had given him great knowledge. He offers an account of religion, namely the overshadowing of the 'Mahometan Religion'[82] by Christian missionaries and Jesuits. As he puts it:

> It is incredible, my Lord, what an harvest Christian Missionaries and Jesuits have reap'd thereby among this people. For being disguis'd as Physicians, Mathematicians, Astrologers, as Janizaries and Spahies, as well as under the appearance of all kinds of the best sort of trades, (and some of them even by the Pope's connivance circumcised and acting the part of Turkish Priests) they got so thoroughly both into the knowledge and confidence of all kinds and ranks of people here, and especially the better sort, that under pretence of proposing their own doubts, they soon overturn'd the established Religion, in the Minds of all persons eminent for their posts or learning.[83]

And so Stanhope lights on the dominant motif of *Memoirs*: religion. Madden's fear or distrust of the Society of Jesuits seems to mirror contemporary prejudices rather than anticipating any actual changes in society. In the future milieu of the late twentieth century, Madden has Stanhope accentuate the not uncommon eighteenth-century fear of the power and growth of the Jesuits. However, his letter is wrapped in the lexicon of expansionism; the growth of Britain's trade through a combination of diplomacy and war is presented as positive. Ultimately his aim is to see a stronger country: Britain as a Utopian country under the magisterial rule of George VI and his ministers. Britain as Utopia is part of Stanhope's capacity for utopian anticipation, and his visions of a *better* society are articulated through his letters proposing a Utopia reconfigured no place else but in Britain. The acceptable political expansionism of Britain is paralleled by the religious expansionism of the Jesuits that so concerns the narrator.

Stanhope juxtaposes the growth of the Jesuits with the decline in Muslims practising their own faith, which is portrayed in dystopian terms. Stanhope recounts how in the villages the Turks could be seen drinking all day and carousing in defiance of their Alcoran [Koran]. He adds that some had been heard to 'speak contemptuously of the stupid Prophet, who thought, (they said) by the blind Hopes of an imaginary Paradise above, to deprive them of the only Heaven Men could enjoy below, a cheerful bottle, and an open-hearted friend'.[84] In a curious way, the Muslims, in abandoning the hope of an imaginary paradise, are presented as having entered a dystopian space where collective hopes are distilled into 'the cheerful bottle', thereby foregoing and thwarting long-held hopes of an imaginary paradise above. As caveats and cautionary soundings about the Jesuits permeate Stanhope's letters, the Muslim Turks are presented as having been led into a darker world by the Jesuits in abandoning their faith. This abandonment is represented in dystopian terms: the hopes they held of an imaginary paradise become denuded of value, hopes formerly held dear recede. He argues that 'Mahometism' is now just like a pagan religion, and that this state of affairs has been brought about 'chiefly by the means and management of the Roman See, though she has almost renounced the Faith herself, yet out of political views labours to encrease [*sic*] her converts here'.[85] Thus, Stanhope links both religion and politics: the Church of Rome, portrayed as lacking in faith herself, seeks in political terms to increase her numbers in eastern Europe.

Stanhope gives an account of the state of the Turkish army and soldiery, its trade and revenue, and its laws and customs as they have been since 1949. They had suffered defeats in battles with the Germans and the Poles, and likewise had been vanquished by both the Muscovites and the Persians. This was brought about by 'decay'd valour and discipline'[86] among the Turks that saw them lose all their conquests in Persia and their territories round the Black Sea, together with the greater part of Transylvania, Moldavia and Wallachia. Their naval power had been significantly depleted after a defeat by the British, and they lost both Crete and Cyprus to the Pope and the Venetians. Their trade was also in a poor way due to the weakness of their vessels and what he calls 'the natural indisposition of the Turks to long voyages'.[87] He juxtaposes life in Turkey in the decline of its years with life in Britain. He suggests that every Briton must have honest joy when he sees himself

> Secur'd by laws of his own making, in his liberty, life and property, above the reach of the highest power and the strongest Arm; and in Peace

and Security under his own Vine and Fig-tree, enjoys from the best of
Constitutions, and (the usual and natural consequences thereof, the best
Princes, all the Blessing men can ask for as Freemen and Christians.[88]

Here, Stanhope views himself as a favoured Briton. Throughout his dispatches
from foreign lands to N----m, his utopian vision leads him to laud his country
and its espousal of the values of liberty, peace and security.

N----m responded to Stanhope in a letter sent from Chelsea, London,
dated 19 December 1997. Although Stanhope has spent twenty-five years
in Turkey, N----m compliments him on not having forgotten his native
country: 'you have not forgotten England so much, by your long residence
at Constantinople'.[89] In this letter N----m confirms that he will have a telescope sent to Stanhope, and gives an account of its extraordinary power to
allow the viewer to see 'real cities in the Moon, that seem nearly to resemble
our own, and what is still more, even mountains and seas in Venus and the
other planets'.[90] N----m also seeks to reacquaint Stanhope with the improvements made in science and the arts in England during his long absence. His
commentary on the scientific advances afforded by telescopes is allied with
his long discussion on England's great achievements in the arts and sciences.
N----m informs Stanhope about the premium models at Oxford, and about
the improvements that 'have been made here in the polite Arts; and also,
how far our Trade, and both the Laws and Manufactures of our Country, are
advance'd and regulated within these twenty-five Years, since you left us'.[91]

He recounts how a premium scheme had been established to fund those
who create the best picture, houses and statues each year. The king subscribes
£1,500 a year, and 'he has but one vote in determining who best deserves the
Premiums; and that parties and factions may be excluded'.[92] Accordingly, he
says that Great Britain has become the seat of the fine arts, and has drawn
many masters of the arts to it, confident of generous rewards for their labours
and merit. He states that 'we have better new Pictures and Statues in Great
Britain, than in all Europe besides; and perhaps Italy herself, will not, in a
little Time, be able to excel the Palaces we have built here, since this Scheme
has taken Place'.[93]

N----m confirms that the Royal College of St George at Oxford, founded
in the eighteenth century, had been vastly improved and a great square had
been built by His Majesty, which he named 'the College of the learned
World'.[94] There are apartments for fellows and lodgings for four new salaried
professors. One of these professors is employed in teaching agriculture and

gardening, 'and has (near the College) twenty Acres of Ground, which he employs in small Parcels, under the Plow and Spade, in different Methods and Experiments, in those two useful Arts'.[95] Another professor has been appointed the weather professor, and is obliged to keep exact diaries and indexes of all wind and weather patterns. He must note 'the Changes of the Air and Weather, with Deductions and Conjectures as to all Dearths of great Crops, healthy Seasons, and epidemical Distempers, and the Causes and Remedies of Famines and popular Sicknesses. He is to enter his Observations in regular Calendars.'[96] There are two professors of trades and mechanical arts. They divide all the trades between them, such as dyeing, weaving, tanning, carpentry, masonry, painting, brewing, baking, spinning, printing, glassmaking and such like. They are obliged to investigate all possible or probable methods of improvement in these trades. Each year they give their observations or inventions to the Board of Trade, which, after examining them, may allow the apprentices to publish them 'for the common Good'.[97] This forms a clear connection with the actual concerns of Madden's life. N----m, in speaking about premiums, improving projects and experimental gardens reflects Madden's own commitment to improvement. His fictive concerns cohere succinctly with Madden's philosophy expressed in his 1732 *Proposal* and also in his *Letter to the Dublin Society* in 1739.

Writing from Rome on 7 November 1997 Hertford recounts that he is well settled in the city in 'a most handsome and convenient house'.[98] He has had an audience with the Pope and is impressed with his visit, and says:

> The Pope, to say truth, how heartily soever he wishes our destruction, as the great bulwark of the Protestant cause and interest; yet is so sensible of his Majesty's wisdom and power, and the vast ascendant his fleets and arms have procur'd him, over all the affairs in Europe; that he shows the greatest readiness to comply with all our demands, and puts the best mien on it he can.[99]

More deliberately, the Pope in Rome is portrayed as both a religious and a political figure aware of the military strength of Britain, and who complied with all Britain's demands as relayed to him through Hertford. The Pope, we are told, has restored all privileges to Britain in the area of the Adriatic Sea. And so in 1997 we learn that the Pope employs what is called the Holy Office of the Inquisition, which, according to Hertford, is a mere engine of state to uncover heresy among any enemies of the 'Roman See'. Hertford confirms that a bull is to be published wherein the Pope has agreed to all the conditions it contains.

At a more covert level, Hertford's mission is to gather any intelligence relating to what he calls 'this overgrown State'.[100] It is Hertford's remit to gather intelligence on behalf of the prime minister and his government, as they are feeling the threat of the growth of this 'new Empire of the Vatican'.[101] He suggests that the new empire of the Vatican has 'risen of late to so prodigious a height, that it seems not only to rival, but out-grow the most extended limits of old Rome'.[102] He then relates as much information as possible about what he calls this 'Spiritual Monarchy'.[103] He relates how throughout the nineteenth century the Church in Rome had expanded and strengthened, and that the policy of this see had been for many ages to employ her 'ecclesiastics to preach up to the people in all parts of the Earth, the vast superiority of the spiritual office of priesthood'.[104] It is the Jesuits who become the focus of Hertford's displeasure and grievance. He argues that the Jesuits 'took care to build the prodigious superstructure of wealth, territories and power'.[105] He believes that the Pope and the order of Jesuits are but one and the same. They have amassed great treasure and power: 'the Pope and this Order (for they are but one and the same Body and Interest) have from their Provinces in Africk, their territories or empire rather of Paraguay in America, and their revenues from China, a fund so prodigious, that it exceeds all belief'.[106] The Vatican has amassed great wealth and power, but the Jesuits also have political power. Speaking of the courts of Europe, he says that there

> is hardly a great person in them, who has not a Jesuit for his confessor, nay his director. How few of its crown'd Heads are there, whose Prime Minister is not either a Cardinal Jesuit, or so absolutely under the influence of the Pope's Nuncio, that they may be said to be entirely govern'd and directed by them.[107]

Hertford then turns to the Protestant cause and the damage caused to it by the Jesuits, who have been 'able to divide and distract the Protestant Powers, to corrupt and pervert some of them, perfidiously'.[108] In education the Jesuits reign supreme: 'besides their being the general bankers and traders of the world, they have unjustly, and by the vilest means engrossed all the schools and colleges of Europe, and the sole Education of the youth there'.[109] They have control over the minds of princes and those in authority, but even preserve their empire with 'the lower ranks and degrees of men; to the poorest tradesmen, the common soldiers, and the very porters and rabble of the streets, who are all oblig'd to confession at least once a month or to be excommunicated and outlaw'd'.[110] The Jesuits are also the sole licensors of books, by which means nothing appears in public 'but what is season'd to their palate, and dressed up by their spiritual cooks so skilfully, as to please their Society'.[111] He refers to Pasquin, who had said that His Holiness had made his good brethren the Jesuits 'sole spectacle-makers to the world; by which means they were impower'd to make all things in print, appear dark or clear, fair or foul, great or little, as they pleased to represent them to the eyes of others'.[112] He computes that there are 170,000 known Jesuits in Europe alone, in a hierarchy where each member once a week gives an account of his conduct and observations to his rector, and he to the college, each college to the provincial, and each provincial to the nuncio, and each nuncio to the Pope, who is always general of the order. According to his intelligence gathering, there are 1,300 stationed in Britain in different places, some of them as tradesmen, *valets de chambre*, clerks, preachers and schoolmasters. He encloses a list of the names and last known places of residence of seventy-five of what he calls 'these traytors [*sic*]'.[113]

At the close of his lengthy dispatch Hertford combines anti-Catholicism with anti-Jacobitism. The Jesuits and the Holy See are seen as a threat and kept in check by the potential power of His Majesty George VI:

> it is most sure his Britannick Majesty is consider'd here, as the greatest obstacle to all these schemes of the Papal ambition; and how far the daily Terror of our Fleet on this coast, and his Majesty's Arms, Conduct, and personal Bravery, (hereditary to his house) may intimidate and cool the ardour of his hopes, is not easily to be imagin'd.[114]

However, Jacobitism is portrayed as a lost cause with but few adherents. Hertford describes a meeting with

> an old Gentleman who is actually the lineal Descendant of one of our ancient Kings, who abdicated his Throne thro' a violent Aversion to the Northern Heresy, and his Zeal to this See ... He is certainly Great Great Grandson, to the Person who is once or twice mention'd in the Histories of the glorious Reigns of George II. and Frederick I. under the Name of the Pretender.[115]

He is considered 'a piece of Antiquity'.[116] The Vatican allows him '2000 l. a Year, and a beneficial Place, of first Valet de Chambre to his Holiness'.[117] He is near eighty and is 'very constant at his Breviary'.[118] The whole description of this octogenarian is suggestive of a lost cause. He is attended only by 'a few Highland Gentlemen' and 'converses with none but a Rabble of Scotch and English Jesuits, and now and then an Italian Painter or Fiddler'.[119] Neither he nor his father ever took the title of king, nor does he have an heir, for his five children – all in occupations relating to the Catholic faith – are illegitimate. His links with Britain are completely severed to the point where he does not speak English. Hertford had met him at the opera, and they conversed in Italian.

In a lengthy letter Hertford again wrote from Rome, dated 7 January 1998 and to be delivered by 'a very worthy English Gentleman, Mr. Lumley',[120] he gives an account of an auction of holy relics that is to take place at the church of St Peter 'on Monday April 25th, 1998, from Nine in the Morning till eight at Night, and to continue till all be sold'.[121] This amazing event of 'selling publickly those venerable Remains, which the Bigotry and Zeal of their Ancestors had so long held sacred, is entirely occasion'd by the Avarice and Prodigality of the Cardinal's Nephew'.[122] Tellingly, the auction is being presented as an opportunity to disperse holy and precious items throughout all Christian nations in order to increase devotion and piety to them. The description of the relics is both painstaking and exceedingly satiric, a veritable tour de force in the use of detail, where Hertford presents a five-page inventory that shows a wide, if biased, knowledge of Catholic dogma. Some of the items he mentions are 'the Table on which Christ eat [*sic*] the last Supper, a little decayed … The Towel with which he wip'd his Disciples Feet, very rotten … Part of the Money paid Judas',[123] 'the holy Linnen-Cloath upon which St. John Baptist was beheaded, wants new Hemming and Darning … the brains of St. Peter, from Geneva'[124] and 'the Water-Pots of the Marriage at Cana in Galilee'.[125]

Writing from Moscow on 29 November 1997 the correspondent Clare writes on matters of politics. It appears that Britain had used her naval power to defeat the Russians in the Baltic, and Clare suggests that the Russians want to develop an accord with them to assist in matters of commerce. Clare notes that he will lose no opportunity in developing cordial relations with them, and comments that the people are vastly improved in every way, having made 'great advances in all polite Arts, as well as the learned Sciences'.[126] He notes that 'a Caravan for China went off yesterday, with near twenty British Merchants in their Company, all provided with sufficient Pass-ports, and allowed the same

Privileges with the Czar's Subjects'.[127] Clare advises that Russia would make a dangerous enemy but would prove a useful friend. He suggests that all efforts should be made to cultivate the czar's friendship, and asserts that he will do everything in Moscow to achieve that aim. In a lengthy digression Clare mentions Laplanders employed in Moscow to create fine gardens. They had the art of making sunshine and could create gardens of choice fruit, flowers and exotic plants. Clare suggests that such Laplanders employed in Britain could enhance life greatly. Gardens could be created under their direction with all the fruits, trees and flowers of France and Spain or even the East and West Indies. He asks 'how many Cures might our George the Sixth make, by settling a few acres by the year on our hospitals for the sick'.[128] Clare sees the Laplanders in utopian terms, believing Britain would be a much better place with their presence, as he notes 'but by the help of their improvements in our fields and gardens, we shall get, as it were, new Heavens, and a new Earth, as St. Peter speaks'.[129]

In a letter dated 8 March 1997 Clare, again writing from Moscow, refers to the prime minister's request that he give details on the Jesuits in Moscow. Clare speaks of 'the prodigious growth of that Society in Muscovy'. 'They have applied themselves to the study and practice of Physick with great success, and have had success in the Czar's Court and throughout his empire.'[130]

On 16 December 1997 Herbert writes from Paris on what he calls 'this unhappy kingdom'.[131] He finds that works at Calais have much improved the port, and at Dunkirk British ships could come and go without any hazard. He finds all the British garrisons in perfect good health and order, being 'well fed, cloath'd, and paid, and made a fine Appearance; especially when compar'd with those of the French in the towns I past thro', which were as naked and lean as Beggars'.[132] France has been ravaged by both famine and plague, has had an unsuccessful war with Germany and her naval affairs ruined by Britain, and is on the decline. 'King Lewis the twentieth' 'does not seem sufficiently resolute, or able, to mend the ill posture of his Affairs'.[133] He has 'grown a little crazy' and 'leaves his Affairs to his Ministers'.[134] The poor people 'pay taxes for all that they eat or drink or wear, to an excessive degree, even to their salt and bread'.[135] Meanwhile, 'the Luxury of the Nobility and Gentry is increas'd beyond all Bounds'.[136]

N----m, writing from London on 5 April 1998, responds to Clare's letters from Moscow of 29 November, 17 January and 8 March 1997 (in line with the Julian calendar then still in use, these years commence on 25 March). N----m responds to Clare's comments on the caravan that had left for China, and notes that previously any Chinese who had been brought to England had 'taught our people here to be as good potters, and to make as fine vessels as any in China'.[137] N----m asks that some Chinese be hired at any expense and 'sent to us by the return of the first caravan. Our chief want is painters and bakers, tho' the truth is, we are already such masters in this art'.[138] Despite his request that Chinese be hired for their skills in painting, baking and pottery, N----m concludes that England presently exports vast quantities of its superior-quality manufactured goods to China, and as for English pottery it is, he argues, 'better painted'.[139] N----m informs Clare that His Majesty wishes to maintain cordial relations with the Czar, and to have a resident, if not an ambassador, perpetually with him to, as he puts it, 'preserve a constant mutual intercourse of good offices between the two Crowns, and favour our traders thither all we can'.[140] N----m informs Clare that he is unlikely to be recalled from Moscow for these reasons, and says of him: 'I believe'd indeed by your long continuance in that Court as an Ambassador, you were almost chang'd into a perfect Russian.'[141]

Although N----m argues that Clare's comments on the Laplanders are most likely invented, and says that His Majesty, having read his letter, 'is of opinion, you have either a mind to laugh at us, or to make us laugh at you and your sun-shine'.[142] Nevertheless, N----m does ask Clare to inform him should he 'have heard or seen anything more, of the handy-work of these Sun-drummers'.[143] N----m returns to the theme of the Jesuits and to Clare's account of their growth in Moscow. He notes that many of the plans of the Jesuits had been adapted by His Majesty and his royal ancestors, and put into execution in England 'to the infinite service of the British Churches'.[144] N----m does not elaborate on what aspects of the Jesuits' plans had been so subsumed by the British Churches. However, he does return to one of the main themes of his letters: that of premiums. He implies that premiums are one of the ideas of the Jesuits that had been absorbed and adapted. The connection between the Jesuits and premiums was first made by Madden in his 1732 *Proposal*. Writing on the benefits of establishing premiums as incentives for the most diligent of students, Madden refers to the success of the Jesuits in this area in their schools: 'Whoever doubts of this may easily be convinc'd by the Conduct of the Jesuits, in most of their Schools all over Europe, and by the Effects of both Balzac and the French Academies annual Premiums in France.'[145] Here, then, Madden's practical *Proposal* of 1732 converges with the fictive imaginative landscape of his *Memoirs* of 1733. It highlights his spirit of improvement as both practically applied and imaginatively rendered.

N----m, in his letter, refers to Frederick III, who at the beginning of the last century had 'established premiums in our principal colleges, for those who gave their best proof of their scholarship'.[146] N----m argues that the Jesuits had only 'imitated the zeal, of one of our best Princes in the same century'.[147] His concern remains that 'the Russian Church must in a very little time, become a province of the Roman See, and embrace all her errors, superstitions, and idolatry, as the essential truths of Christianity'.[148]

The themes of religion, trade, politics and military engagement occur and recur throughout the letters. However, writing on 16 April 1998, from Constantinople, Stanhope confines himself to accounts of his meeting with the grand seignior and their discussions on scientific and astronomical matters. Stanhope has learnt to speak Turkish and this facilitates his conversations. The grand seignior had an interest in globes, watches and the like, and so Stanhope says that he had delivered to him from London 'Globes, Maps, Clocks of all kinds, and Watches; Dogs, Guns, Barges, Coaches, and, in a word, whatever I found him most desirous of'.[149] Stanhope and the grand seignior spent many hours conversing on the moon and the stars. The grand seignior wondered if there could be living creatures and, above all, men on the moon. Stanhope responded that he had 'great and weighty reasons to be persuaded of it'.[150] Together they spent hours looking through the telescope, which Stanhope claimed

> Could not only discern Hills and Rivers, but even objects like Towns and Forests in the Moon; and that, if the Inhabitants there were as large as some great Astronomers conceived them to be, I doubted not in time, our Glasses might be so far improved, as to see even Men and their actions there.[151]

And so Stanhope is aware of what his telescope may discern, but he is also aware of the fact that 'glasses' will be improved in the future and that much more of the world of the moon will be revealed. They pored over a vast map of the moon, which Stanhope had brought from London, with 'all the Seas, Rivers, Mountains, Hills, Valleys, Forests, and the supposed Towns that are so accurately laid down in it by the Selenographers'.[152] Before they parted, the grand seignior had decided to endow and have built an astronomical college to be staffed by the best professors in Europe. Stanhope requested of the prime minister that he should give orders that some excellent astronomers may be prevailed upon to set out with the next fleet for Turkey. They ponder on the wonderful discoveries that will be made: 'what discoveries shall we not make in the Heavens of new Stars arising, old ones decaying, unobserv'd Comets, with new Suns and Planets in their several systems, arranging in the thousands and ten thousands of the yet undiscover'd hosts of Heaven'.[153] When Stanhope writes his next letter from Constantinople, on 1 May 1998, the astronomical college has been established with great zeal and expedition. The grand seignior, though not very fond of travelling upon the earth,

> frequently makes the great tour of the Heavens, and visits all the con-
> stellations in their turns; and begins to be confident, that in another
> age, we shall not only be able to see the inhabitants of the Moon, which
> would be useless, without any other benefit, but to invent engines to
> carry us thither.[154]

In the closing years of the twentieth century, he alludes to another age, a future age, when inhabitants of the moon will not only be visible but 'engines' will be invented to transport people to it.

In an excursion with the grand seignior to his new house of pleasure, built with immense expense near Chalcedon, Stanhope recounts how in this 'earthly paradise'[155] the gardens are among the finest built in the European manner, and he describes the temples, vistas, porticoes, walks, flower beds and foun-tains that are all surrounded 'with so perpetual a serenity of the heavens, and fertility of the earth, that it looks like the Paradise, which God planted for the Lord of the world to dwell in'.[156] However, this letter contains a prophecy that the ten lost tribes of Israel are to be rediscovered in the twentieth century. A Rabbi Solomon from Tunis visits Stanhope and tells him that the ten tribes have been discovered in the centre of Africa. He says that they 'have a vast Empire there, and are very powerful, having near 50 millions of souls under their Kings'.[157] The Messiah is among them and has an army of 500,000 men; they are in motion to cross the deserts of Borno and Guoga, and, passing the Nile, to seize Egypt, 'and then the land of Canaan their Inheritance, and build up the fallen glories of mount Sion and Jerusalem'.[158] The rabbi had letters from the synagogue of Tunis that directed all faithful Jews to be on their guard 'for the Kingdom was about to be restor'd to Israel'.[159] As one of the few attempts at actual prophecy in *Memoirs*, it is the one that has proved true.

Accounts of events in France are provided by Herbert in a letter sent from Paris, dated 16 December 1997, in which he reports that he has just returned from a journey visiting the seaports and garrisons in France, all of which are in perfectly good order. The port of Calais is much improved, and he observes 'in the lowest neap tides at Dunkirk, our ships of war of forty guns can go out and come in without any hazard; the benefit of which I need not mention'.[160] He finds both men and officers of all the British garrisons to be in perfect good health and order, being 'well fed, cloath'd, and paid'.[161] By contrast the French troops he saw in the towns he passed through were hungry and unkempt. He argues that when troops are so ill paid and fed they will 'neither have heart and spirit in time of action'.[162] Herbert says that both France and Spain have for a long time been noteworthy for the mismanagement of their troops, and 'have paid dearly for their neglect, by so many terrible losses as they have met with for these last fifty years'.[163] France has been much on the decline due to the ravages of both famine and the plague and its unsuccessful wars with Germany. Further, it has been weakened by Britain ruining its naval affairs and impeding its trade. He notes that 'Lewis the nineteenth' and the present king, 'Lewis the twentieth', have had quarrels with the Holy See. The French king, during the reign of Henry VIII in England, had renounced the Pope's authority. In order to placate Rome, France had given up strong frontier towns in Dauphiné, which, as Herbert observes, 'the Pope keeps as Keys to enter the Gates of France from Italy, now that most of Savoy is his own'.[164] Relations with Spain are not good as there had been wars between the crowns, and Spain as victor has forced France to accept some 'very inglorious conditions'.[165] The French are no longer the fear of Europe that they formerly were, and Herbert concludes that 'the Pope is now the entire object of the fears of Europe, instead of the conquering French'.[166] According to Herbert, the truth is 'this Nation does not seem form'd for Empire, and tho' they've often made mighty efforts, and great conquests, they never preserve them'.[167]

The present 'King Lewis the twentieth' is portrayed as not sufficiently resolute; indeed, his clergy and people seem more desirous to support the Pope than to strengthen the hands of their king. It seems they are fearful that the king would exact revenge 'for their joining with Rome against him, if he should once recover his former power'.[168] The king, while not yet fifty years of age, has grown a little crazy, and leaves matters of state to his ministers. They are only 'mercenary rapacious Ministers'[169] who had pillaged the kingdom. The king is surrounded by sycophants and flatterers 'that are ever buzzing about the ears of great Princes, knowing it is impossible otherwise to support themselves'.[170] Herbert portrays France as 'this unhappy Kingdom':[171] the poor people groan under so many burdens, and they 'pay taxes for all that they eat or drink or wear, to an excessive degree, even to their salt and bread'.[172]

Meanwhile, the luxury of the nobility and gentry is increased beyond all bounds 'as if they were not only insensible of, but even rejoiced in the publick calamities of their fellow-subjects'.[173] Ultimately, Herbert sees France as having fallen now 'from the object of our Fears, to that of our pity'.[174]

Herbert, writing from Paris on 8 February 1997, gives an account of everyday life in France. He notes that public granaries in all the major villages are filled with plentiful crops, so that they have nearly two years' provisions to supply them should any shortage of food occur. On a political level efforts have been taken to prevent what Herbert calls 'the continual Fraud in the managing of the Finances'.[175] He speaks of 'the vile arts these Financiers, and Bankers of the Treasures of the State, made use of to enrich themselves'.[176] To prevent further such dishonesty, an edict had been passed and seven commissioners are to examine 'with the strictest care and fidelity, all publick accounts of the Nation'.[177] Such information is to be published annually and to be viewed by the public, noting any errors found in them whether by fraud or mistake. Any such lapses are to be repaid by the offender. Herbert notes that, as a result, 'it is hard to be believed with what honest severity, regularity, integrity, and economy, the Publick Finances here have been managed of late'.[178]

Writing from London on 24 February 1997 N----m responds to Herbert's correspondence from Paris of 16 December and 8 February. He notes that the king has read the letters and is happy with the account of the works carried out in the harbours of both Dunkirk and Calais. N----m further notes that the king is anxious that a planned audience between Herbert and the French king goes well, as he hopes that closer ties between France and Britain may benefit by, as he puts it, 'humbling the exorbitant power of the empire of the Vatican'.[179] N----m returns to the favoured theme of his letters: improvement. He speaks of the development of the state-run Royal Fishery and the Plantation Companies. The Royal Fishery, which operates out of sixteen ports, is obliged to employ at least 200,000 workers as coopers, shipwrights, smiths, sawyers, sailors, fishers and sailmakers; others are to be employed making nets, baskets, ropes and dressing, and spinning hemp and flax. At least 1,600 lame and 1,000 blind people are to be employed in rope and net-making. It is financed by shareholders. All 'common beggars and vagabonds, and all foundlings, when eight years old shall belong to the company, and be seiz'd by them, and kept in their work-houses for seven years, allowing them cloaths and diet, without wages'.[180] Without the taxes that the Dutch pay, the plan for the Royal Fishery is that it would train all these people for employment, and in selling to foreign markets would enable Britain 'to undersell all our rivals in this trade',[181] and 'to breed up every year several thousand seamen, and employ numbers of our useless poor, and import immense sums of treasure to our happy island'.[182]

Utopian in its tendencies to define how individuals working for the company have to live, the Plantation Company for the new colonies in the West Indies has three million acres, and the plan is that they are 'to be laid out and applotted equally to all planters who shall settle there, and build new towns'.[183] They also have large premiums for 'such limited quantities of iron, pitch, tar, hemp, flax, silk, indigo, wine or oil'.[184] These items will be imported from Britain, and the plan is that in a few years they will 'make us utterly independent of our neighbours in the North for all naval stores, which us'd to drain such immense sums from us'.[185] N----m notes that these two companies can only strengthen the wealth of the country. They will 'not only enrich us vastly beyond any of our neighbours but they also vastly increase our naval strength, employ our starving poor, and will so far enlarge and extend our colonies on the Continent'.[186] N----m argues that new bishoprics founded by His Majesty's ancestors, as well as those of Carolina, Barbados and Boston, should contribute to the reformation of manners and principles in the colonies 'and to keeping them firm in their allegiance to the crown'.[187] He notes that two colleges erected in the colonies by 'George the third' had gone a great way in civilising and improving the inhabitants. He reflects on 'the happy condition of our own country, and what it owes to that glorious Line of Hanover'.[188]

Madden stated in his lengthy title to *Memoirs* that six volumes would be published, only one of which ever appeared. However, questions remain as to why he had a substantial number of his newly printed book destroyed. It has been a matter of some speculation. It might have been suppressed by him in deference to Walpole, or it might have been suppressed by Walpole himself. I would argue that Madden's work is superior to most pro-government satires, and was neither suppressed by him in deference to Walpole nor suppressed by Walpole. It seems most likely to have been suppressed as a result of Madden's cloak of anonymity having been cast aside and his authorship revealed. As a clergyman he could have viewed partisan party writing as inconsistent with his vocation, and wished to remain anonymous. This is substantiated by reference to the first letter Madden wrote to Walpole and which seems to reveal his wish for general anonymity in party-political matters. Madden suggested the setting up of a newspaper 'as a vehicle for his [Walpole's] papers'.[189] He mentioned 'many of your & our Countries friends might hereafter come in to my assistance'.[190] He referred specifically to Dr Edward Younge, Sir William Yonge and George Lyttelton (who after entering Parliament in 1735 was to become a prominent member of the opposition and an opponent of Walpole, but who in the early 1730s wrote in favour of Walpole's government). However, Madden wished to remain anonymous, citing his personal belief that political writing was improper for a clergyman.

In the years following *Memoirs* Madden continued his correspondence with Walpole. Writers who sent their work to Walpole very often wrote of their willingness to alter the material to suit his taste. Writing from Ireland on 3 January 1740 Madden sent material 'to be publisht when & how you please, with whatever corrections those you entrust them with think best'.[191] He expands:

> I am sensible both my want of abillity [*sic*] & skill for such a Work & my distance from the scene of business, & being depriv'd of all proper instruction & information, must make them very defective; but if you think they are worth my own attendance or the care of others to alter or improve them, they & I are absolutely at your service, if such trivial things can be worth your service.[192]

Among the 'trivial things' is Madden's poem 'Bermuda'. He wrote to Walpole that he wanted to publish his poem as he 'is often mention'd in it with honour & that the War with Spain makes a number of Passages very seasonable for these times'.[193] This is a recurrent motif in the letters of pro-government writers: they are replete with references to works that either 'cannot appear at this time' or works that the author, as in Madden's case, considered 'seasonable'. I would argue that the combination of the loss of Madden's anonymity and his specific references to religion in *Memoirs* necessitated his suppression of it. Madden's major concern in *Memoirs* is the danger of a Catholic plot to take over and undermine Britain. Like Swift, he was opposed to Catholicism and to the new politics beginning to emerge. The combined threat from the 'overgrown state of the Vatican' and the 'prodigious growth of the Jesuits' form the central theme of the letters from the future. While such criticisms were not uncommon, Antonio Gavin's *A Master-key to Popery* was a bestseller of 1725. Madden, in locating *Memoirs* in the later half of the twentieth century – taking place far from the everyday world of eighteenth-century life – confirms in fact 'that all utopian fiction whirls contemporary actors through a costume dance no place else but here'.[194]

Thus, *Memoirs* speaks to the fears of its times. Yet in writing his history of future times, Madden, to use the words of Paul Alkon, 'created a viable form in the shape of a tale of the future that could work perfectly well as a framework for futuristic fiction in any of its modes'.[195] If Madden provided a framework for further future histories, he was also, according to Alkon, 'the first to write a narrative that purports to *be* a document from the future', and thus 'deserves recognition as the first to work with the rich idea of time-travel in the form of an artefact sent backwards from the future to be discovered in the present'.[196] Madden's work is also noteworthy, according to Alkon, because his was

> the first prose narrative to adopt the central technique of those modes of futuristic fiction formally distinct from previous traditions by virtue of inviting readers to imagine themselves looking backwards from a far future to their own present and immediate future, which are thus also to be regarded as the past.[197]

Memoirs is therefore seminal in being the first English-language work of prose fiction set in a chronologically specified future. The framework of Madden's narrative – documents transported backwards in time from the twentieth to the eighteenth century – differs from the idea of transporting a narrator forward to the future, a device used in Louis-Sébastien Mercier's 1771 *L'An 2440: un rêve s'il en fut jamais* (translated as *Memoirs of the Year Two Thousand Five Hundred*).[198] Madden had found a novel way of satirising and depicting contemporary life by describing it from a future vantage point. Speaking of *Memoirs*, Alkon writes: 'the first time-traveller in English literature is a guardian angel who returns with state documents from 1998 to the year 1728'.[199] The literary world of eighteenth-century Britain and Ireland was distinctive for its formal experimentation, especially in satirical works that parodied existing genres, and in the process sometimes created viable new forms. To be sure, Madden did create a viable new genre: the future history enveloped in utopian satire.

Memoirs represents a multidimensional perspective on Utopia: it deploys elements of satire, science fiction, myths of the earthly paradise, travel narrative and prophecy. As we have seen, *Memoirs* points to the gap between present and future, Britain and Europe, and prophecy and diatribe in an expanding world. By imagining another reality in a hypothetical future, Madden created a future history that enabled him to develop a satire on contemporary politics and religion. It is possible that Madden was not as vociferously pro-Walpole as his correspondence would indicate. Indeed, it is more likely that he was garnering favour on behalf of his improving projects that ultimately were the bedrock of his utopianism. He seems to have been – as evidenced by his dedication to Frederick, Prince of Wales – unimpressed by the current party system. This may be what *Memoirs* is all about: a satire on contemporary politics and religion but one which could be construed as conservative, or even Jacobite, as much as Whiggishly pro-Walpole. Swift, as an Anglo-Irish patriot, distrusted deluded single-mindedness (Jesuit and Presbyterian) at the expense of practical improvement. Madden may well be doing with time and futurism what Swift's *Gulliver's Travels* did with space and fantastical islands: satirising folly wherever it manifests itself. However, through the diverse voices of *Memoirs* Madden clearly maintained a thread of connection with his ideas for practical improvement, as revealed in his *Proposal* and in his *Letter to the Dublin Society*.

Madden's *Letter to the Dublin Society, on the Improving Their Fund; and the Manufactures, Tillage, &c. in Ireland* is clearly a practical and pragmatic presentation of his improving visions and can be linked to his *Memoirs*. N----m in *Memoirs* speaks in his letters of premiums, improvements in agriculture, trade, arts and sciences. In his *Letter*, Madden transposes such a vision to the geographical, political, cultural and economic milieu of his home country, while also foregrounding his social conscience. In the opening section entitled 'To the reader', he requests that his letter should be read 'with the same good will it was written with, and promote the honest Designs it proposes, for the service of our poor neglected People'.[200] In the substantive part of the letter Madden addresses the gentlemen of the Dublin Society, reassuring them that his plan and the measures he suggests to implement it would aid in making 'you one of the most useful Societies that ever was set up in Ireland'.[201] Madden suggests that all the learning in the world is mere foppery and folly 'where it does not contribute to the Good of Men; so it is as certain, that the highest and noblest labour of the Mind, is the contriving and providing for National Interests, and the real Service of one's native Country'.[202] Madden's utopian vision is aligned with his design for the betterment of his country. Here, then, Madden's utopian anticipation can be seen as his production of hopeful visions of a *better* society, one that is shaped through social practices. As he is dissatisfied with the way things are in contemporary Ireland, his narrative aims to offer a radical template for the better organising of the Dublin Society. Such a vision for an improved society is one that offers the possibility of a reconfigured Ireland. It should 'be capable of changing and absolutely mending the situation of Ireland, and placing its future prosperity and welfare, on the most immoveable foundations'.[203]

Central to Madden's mode of thinking is the concept of self-reliance. He believes that 'the remedies of all our evils, must begin from ourselves, rather than our neighbours, and chiefly from our own increase of industry'.[204] Madden paves the way for the positive creation of a better society based on self-reliance and practical application. Such practical application is predicated on the need for the Dublin Society to increase the number of its members and to increase the amount of financial resources available to it. He considers how this is to be done, what is to happen, when it is to be achieved, and what purpose funds are to serve when attained. Madden suggests ideas on improving Ireland's linen industry and ways to lessen the country's reliance on imports by developing industries for the manufacture of glass bottles, earthenware, iron tools, pots, knives, scythes, lace, paper, tapestry, sugar and salt. He believes that proper premiums, or encouragements, offered to interested parties (including skilled people from other countries who may be persuaded to come and settle in Ireland) would assist these developments. He proposes that a select number of acres in different soils and places near Dublin be developed as experimental farms for all aspects of husbandry. Such improvements could, in a number of years, contribute to what he calls 'the service of mankind'.[205] Madden's vision is summed up in his call to members of the Dublin Society 'to encourage our people to think for others as well as work for themselves'.[206] He is clear that his vision is inclusive and that it cannot be thwarted because 'it is neither Papist nor Protestant, Whig or Tory'.[207] This, then, is Madden's public-spirited plan for a better society. *Memoirs*, located in the future and predicated on satire and improvement, is the fictive precursor to his pragmatic and practical *Letter to the Dublin Society*; both provide important insights into the disparate journeying of Irish utopianism in the eighteenth century, and confirm that Madden belongs in the Tír na nÓg of both intellect and of imagination.[208]

CHAPTER 7

Conclusion: Some Vague Utopia

I know not what the younger dreams –
Some vague Utopia – and she seems,
When withered old and skeleton gaunt,
An image of such politics.

W.B. Yeats, 'In Memory of
Eva Gore-Booth and Con Markiewicz'[1]

Ralahine became as 'a city on a hill', and
attracted the attention of men of all classes.

E.T. Craig, *An Irish Commune*[2]

The world of utopianism in eighteenth-century Ireland created a body of textual works of utopian satire and whole categories of societies founded to promote an improving agenda or to provide charitable assistance. The *raison d'être* of those societies was to advance and pursue distinct purposes. They presented themselves as intellectual and improving societies, political societies, convivial, sociable and sporting societies, and regional societies. These categories are not and should not be thought of as fixed. The legacy of eighteenth-century Irish utopianism coalesced in subsequent nineteenth-century and twentieth-century utopian visions that may be collectively identified as offering a plurality of models, both in text and in social practice. Their structure is varied and moves from the utopian satire of Irish-born writers such as Edward Mangin (1772–1852) and John Banim (1798–1842) to the philosophical writings on radical and feminist utilitarianism of William Thompson (1775–1833) and Anna Doyle Wheeler (1785–1850), to lived utopian experiments in Ralahine, County Clare and others in west Cork, Dublin and Galway. Moreover, in keeping with this pattern, utopianism in the late nineteenth and early twentieth centuries took many forms. Horace Plunkett (1854–1932), George Russell (1867–1935), James Connolly (1868–1916) and others have demonstrated the extent to which the benefits of cooperation and politics were to become a central concern to the lives of ordinary people.

In the realm of utopian satire, Mangin's *Utopia Found: being an apology for Irish absentees addressed to a friend in Connaught. By an absentee residing in Bath* (1813) provides a nineteenth-century counterpoint to Richard Head's *Hic et Ubique: or, the humours of Dublin* (1663). While Head's émigrés view Dublin as Utopia and London as dystopia, Mangin, as an absentee landlord, represents London as Utopia. He resides in England, along with other absentees, because of the 'astonishing superiority of this Country over every other civilised nation upon the face of the earth'.[3] In drawing a comparison between England and Ireland he lauds the English climate and its political system, which he regards as 'the best that ever was devised by the wisdom of man for ensuring the happiness of his kind'.[4] The streets in London are perfectly clean and free from offensive smells. Moreover, in no part of the world are human life, health and property so secure as in that city. Mangin celebrates England's liberal hospitality to Irish wit, and wits, of the previous century:

> Ireland boasts (and boasts sufficiently) of Swift, and Steele, and Farquhar; of Goldsmith the Poet, and Barry the Tragedian, and Barry the Historical Painter: of Edmund Burke, and Richard Sheridan; of Grattan, and Curran, and Thomas Moore: but, mark the liberality of *this* country; England makes these very men (aliens as they are) the subject of *her* pride and exultation likewise, and on all occasions, kindly allows them to pass for her own.[5]

Here, then, Mangin's utopian projection represents, as did many of the eighteenth-century Irish Utopias, a commentary on colonisation and identity. His satire whereby the coloniser admits the most successful Irishmen into its ranks represents just one facet of nineteenth-century utopian satire indebted to works of earlier times.

By way of contrast, Mangin's near contemporary John Banim in *Revelations of the Dead Alive* (1824) has his narrator explain that he possesses the power of sleeping at will for long periods, and during these periods possesses the faculty of 'going out of himself', a form of self-activating clairvoyance. He 'lay down in a sequestered and silent arbour, with the rays of a spring sun dancing in through the trees, over and around me. I collected my mind as usual, and to the earth soon became dead.'[6] He had been enabled through consuming an unusual American plant to extend the periods of sleep to a length much beyond the usual. After a slumber of 198¼ days he is able to record and relate the events of the year 2023. For every day of his sleep he saw a year of time, so that when he came to life again he had observed what was, and what was to be, in the subsequent 198¼ years. The narrator recalls that for 'eight months altogether I lived in futurity'.[7] Banim's early biographer Patrick Joseph Murray notes that *Revelations* consists 'for the chief part, [of] very clever hits at the follies, fashions, and manners of the year 1823'.[8] Among the fashions of the period was that of phrenology, which Banim satirises. He did not, however, spare the literary profession. It was the age of reviewing and Banim satirises both contemporary reviewers and newspaper critics. And so Banim's utopian satire, set in the future, connects to Madden's *Memoirs of the Twentieth Century*, exposing and satirising folly wherever it manifests itself while alluding to improvements in taste, art and society to be revealed in future times.

Both Thompson and Doyle Wheeler presented a different utopian mode of enquiry. Using the analytical tools of a philosopher, Thompson questions why inequality exists and wonders about the possibilities of human beings finding happiness. He wonders why in the midst of the plenty enjoyed by the idle classes was there such poverty. And why are the institutions of society reluctant to give power to the people? In 1825 he and Doyle Wheeler cooperated on one of the first books in Ireland to express the rudiments of a socialist feminist position. *The Appeal of One Half the Human Race, Women, Against the Pretensions of the Other Half, Men, to Retain Them in Political and Thence in Civil and Domestic Slavery* explains the causes of the subordination of women, causes which permeate through all of contemporary society's institutions. The remedies that would remove sexual inequality are also outlined. The visit of Doyle Wheeler's collaborator Robert Owen to Ireland in 1823 led directly to the development of a cooperative experiment on the Vandeleur estate at Ralahine, County Clare. Owen held a series of public meetings at the Rotunda in Dublin, attended by John Scott Vandeleur, who was impressed by Owen's account of New Lanark. In his essay 'An Irish Utopia' (1910), James Connolly refers to Owen's visit undertaken, as Connolly notes, with 'the purpose of explaining the principles of Socialism to the people of that city'.[9] Owen presented an outline of the possibilities that a system of socialist cooperation could produce. The result of this proposal was the establishment of an association styling itself the 'Hibernian Philanthropic Society', formed with the aim of carrying out Owen's ideas. A sum of money was subscribed to aid the society, and Owen himself subscribed £1,000. The society was short-lived, but Connolly records how Vandeleur was impressed with what he had seen and heard of the possibilities of Owenite socialism. The Owenite moment, in turn, provided the impetus for the establishment of his cooperative at Ralahine. Vandeleur came to believe that Ralahine could become the agricultural equivalent of New Lanark. Early in 1831 he travelled to England to seek an assistant for his project, and recruited E.T. Craig following an interview in a Manchester hotel. In *An Irish Commune: the history of Ralahine*, Craig describes Ralahine upon his arrival:

> I found the estate admirably adapted for the purposes of a co-operative farm. It consisted of 618 acres, about one-half of which was under tillage, with suitable farm buildings and situated between the two main roads from Limerick to Ennis. A bog of sixty-three acres supplied fuel. A lake on the borders of the estate gave a constant and available supply of water power.[10]

While the cooperative at Ralahine lasted a short two years, its legacy continued to generate commentary. In his introduction to the edition of Craig's *An Irish Commune* published in 1920, the intellectual idealist George Russell lauds Craig's endeavours at Ralahine, and comments on the then current development of cooperatives in Ireland and beyond:

> We are moving rapidly to the creation of co-operative communities all over Ireland. We have co-operation in purchase, manufacture and sale in every country, and I hear with pleasure that societies for co-operative farming on the Italian model will soon be established, and these Italian co-operative land cultivation societies are the nearest things in Europe to the Ralahine community; and in Italy I am told they regard that long-vanished society at Ralahine as the pioneer or morning star of their own fascinating movement.[11]

Moreover, Connolly, in 'An Irish Utopia', concludes that 'Ralahine was an Irish point of interrogation erected amidst the wilderness of capitalist thought and feudal practice'.[12] In writing about Ralahine, Connolly reveals an understanding of the historic tradition of Irish utopianism. From a twentieth-century vantage point his appraisal of the Ralahine cooperative and its historical and social context shows that the utopian tradition on which he drew was no tradition of idle dreaming but a plan for future political engagement that could be both transformative and emancipatory. This was first set out in his early pamphlet *Erin's Hope* (1897), a very uncompromising statement of the socialist case. It begins by invoking the common ownership of land, which Connolly maintained characterised the Celtic clan system and which lasted longer than similar systems elsewhere. He believed that the conflict between the rival systems of land ownership was the pivot around which all the Irish struggles and rebellions revolved. He argues that different elements of Irish society fused in a compact nationality, and during this process a new class arose that accepted the social system of the invader. This was the new middle class, which was viewed as compromising and betraying the hopes of the Irish people. This is the most vital aspect of the pamphlet, and it is the theme that Connolly developed further in his major work *Labour in Irish History*.[13]

The utopian propensity in Irish culture emerged over many centuries, and its longevity is matched by its variety. As this book has demonstrated, Irish utopianism is multifaceted: it can be found in the literary realms of novels and poetry, in political manifestos, in art and architecture, in speeches and songs, in the pamphlets and works of eighteenth-century improving societies, in the lived traditions of nineteenth-century communal enterprises, and in the cultural and political nationalisms of the twentieth century. The case for 'a national being' as a prerequisite for an improved and better Ireland was expressed in a utopian mode by Russell, who believed that national ideals 'must be built up with the same conscious deliberation of purpose as the architect of the Parthenon conceived its lofty harmony of shining marble lines, or as the architect of Rheims Cathedral designed its intricate magnificence and mystery'.[14] The international developments in science, in chemistry and physics, as well as in art, prompted Russell to enquire into the nature of both his environment in Ireland and in the world beyond, for Russell was not simply receptive to emerging trends in global thought: he actively developed new modes of discussion. His belief in self-help and the moral benefits that accrued from industrial, as well as psychological, decolonisation contributed to his own programme of national reconstruction. As an agent of economic and national revolution in Ireland, as a painter and author of pamphlets, poetry and prose, Russell was a utopian thinker capable of rigorous practicality. The Ireland in which he and others wrote from 1890 to 1930 was a society experiencing relentless change.

The history of Irish utopianism has its own peculiarity and uniqueness, but it is a peculiarity and uniqueness that must be assessed in terms of the contingencies of history. There is no doubt that the continuum of utopianism from earliest times to the present day ensures that the prospect of a society transformed and reconfigured lies always ahead. Somewhere between Yeats' 'vague utopia' and Craig's 'city on a hill', it is a utopian ideal – an ideal we have not realised and might never attain, and yet it pervades our daily existence.

Notes and References

Chapter 1

1 See Ethna Carbery [pseudonym of Anna MacManus née Johnson (1866–1902)], *The Four Winds of Eirinn: poems of Ethna Carbery*, ed. Séumas MacManus (Dublin: M.H. Gill & Son; [and] Jas. Duffy, 1906).

2 See Micheál Coimín, *Laoi Oisín ar Tír na nÓg* [*The Lay of Oisín in the Land of Youth*] (1750), ed. Tomás Ó Flannghaile (London: City of London Book Depot; Dublin: M.H. Gill & Son, 1896).

3 See 'Cider' by Paul Muldoon in *Mules* (London: Faber & Faber, 1977).

4 This excerpt is from Seán Ó Ríordáin's poem 'Cúl an Tí':
> Tá Tír na nÓg ar chúl an tí,
> Tír álainn trína chéile.

It translates as 'Tír na nÓg is at the back of the house'. An Ulster or Connacht translator might render the poet's words in the second line as 'A lovely through-other country'. The poet is speaking about the backyard of his own house in Inniscarra, County Cork. For my purposes I see a move in this poem towards a connection between the concept of the actual space of home and the possibility that the utopian imagination can find in such a space, a Celtic otherworld or a utopian vista. It inhabits two landscapes – one that is utopian and one that is just the backyard of the poet's house. For the complete collection of Ó Ríordáin's poetry, see *Seán Ó Ríordáin: na dánta*, ed. Seán Ó Coileáin, with illustrations by Seán Ó Flaithearta (Galway: Cló Iar-Chonnacht, 2011).

5 The author of this pamphlet is unknown. The reference to that 'memorable day, October 9th 1753', is curious. Swift died on 19 October 1745. It is possible that the date on the pamphlet is a misprint and that the author was actually referring to 19 October. This would mean that the memorable day referred to in the title is 19 October 1753, the eighth anniversary of Swift's death. Swift had a long association with St Patrick's Cathedral: he had been appointed dean in 1713, a position he held until his death in 1745. While Swift was buried in St Patrick's, Prior was buried in the local churchyard in Rathdowney, County Laois (then called Queen's County). A monument was erected to him in Christchurch Cathedral in 1756, with an epitaph inscribed by George Berkeley. It was appropriate that the sculptor of the monument should have been J. Van Nost, who from the earliest years of the Dublin Society was associated with its successful efforts to develop an Irish school of sculpture.

6 Anon., *A Dialogue Between Dean Swift and Thomas Prior, Esq. in the Isles* [*sic*] *of St Patrick's Church, Dublin, on that Memorable Day, October 9th, 1753* (Dublin: G. & A. Ewing, 1753), p. 64.

7 Ibid., p. 3.

8 Ibid.

9   Ibid., p. 4.
10 Ibid.
11 Ibid.
12 Ibid., p. 5.
13 Ibid.
14 Ibid.
15 Ibid.
16 Ibid., pp. 6–7.
17 Ibid., p. 7.
18 Ibid., p. 9.
19 Ibid.
20 Ibid., p. 14.
21 Ibid., p. 17.
22 Ibid., p. 19.
23 Ibid., p. 23.
24 Ibid.
25 Ibid., p. 52.
26 Ibid., p. 53.
27 Ibid.
28 Ibid.
29 Ibid.
30 Ibid.
31 Ibid., p. 62.
32 Ibid., p. 66.
33 Ibid., p. 67.
34 Ibid., p. 68.
35 Ibid., p. 21.
36 Ibid.
37 Jürgen Habermas, *The Structural Transformation of the Public Sphere; an inquiry into a category of bourgeois society,* trans. Thomas Burger with Frederick Lawrence (Cambridge, MA: MIT Press, 1991), p. 58.
38 Thomas More, *Utopia,* in *The Complete Works of St. Thomas More,* eds S.J. Edward Surtz and J.H. Hexter (New Haven, CT: Yale University Press, 1965), p. 21.
39 William Winstanley (*c.* 1628–98), *Lives of the Most Famous Poets* (1687), p. 48.
40 Lyman Tower Sargent, *Utopianism: a very short introduction* (Oxford: Oxford University Press, 2010), p. 5.
41 See also Lyman Tower Sargent, 'The Three Faces of Utopianism Revisited', *Utopian Studies,* vol. 5, no. 1 (1994), and 'Utopia', *New Dictionary of the History of Ideas* (2004).
42 Sargent, 'The Three Faces of Utopianism Revisited', p. 1.
43 Ibid., p. 3.
44 Lyman Tower Sargent, 'Theorizing Intentional Community in the Twenty-First Century', in Eliezer Ben Rafael, Yaacov Oved and Menahem Topel (eds), *The*

Communal Idea in the 21st Century (Leiden: Brill, 2012), p. 54; idem., 'What is a Utopia?', *Morus: Utopia e Renascimento*, no. 2 (2005), pp. 153–60.

45 Timothy Miller, 'A Matter of Definition: just what is an intentional community?', *Communicatio Socialis*, vol. 30, no. 1 (2010), p. 7.

46 Philip B. Gove, *The Imaginary Voyage in Prose Fiction, 1700–1800: a history of its criticism and a guide for its study, with an annotated check list of 215 imaginary voyages from 1700 to 1800* (London: Holland Press, 1961), p. 75.

47 James T. Presley, 'Bibliography of Utopias and Imaginary Travels and Histories,' quoted in Gove, *The Imaginary Voyage*, p. 76.

48 Joyce Oramel Hertzler, *The History of Utopian Thought* (New York: Macmillan, 1923), p. 2.

49 R.W. Gibson and J. Max Patrick (compilers), *St. Thomas More: a preliminary bibliography of his works and of Moreana to the year 1750* (New Haven, CT: Yale University Press, 1961), p. 293.

50 On heresy and utopianism, see, for example, Thomas Molnar, *Utopia: the perennial heresy* (New York: Sheed & Ward, 1967).

51 J.C. Davis, *Utopia and the Ideal Society: a study of English utopian writing, 1516–1700* (Cambridge: Cambridge University Press, 1981), pp. 19–20.

52 J.C. Davis, 'Thomas More's *Utopia*: sources, legacy and interpretation', in Gregory Claeys (ed.), *The Cambridge Companion to Utopian Literature* (Cambridge: Cambridge University Press, 2010), p. 47.

53 Jacqueline Dutton, '"Non-western" Utopian Traditions', in Gregory Claeys (ed.), *The Cambridge Companion to Utopian Literature* (Cambridge: Cambridge University Press, 2010), p. 223.

54 Ruth Levitas, *The Concept of Utopia* (Hemel Hempstead: Philip Allan, 1990), p. 1.

55 Ibid., p. 122.

56 Fredric Jameson, *Marxism and Form* (Princeton, NJ: Princeton University Press, 1971), p. 111.

57 See Fredric Jameson, 'Comments', *Utopian Studies*, vol. 9, no. 2 (1998), pp. 74–8.

58 Tom Moylan, *Scraps of the Untainted Sky: science fiction, utopia, dystopia* (Boulder, CO: Westview, 2000), p. 85.

59 Levitas, *The Concept of Utopia*, p. 7. For more on 'the education of desire', see Ruth Levitas, 'Educated Hope: Ernst Bloch on abstract and concrete Utopia', *Utopian Studies*, vol. 1, no. 2 (1990), pp. 13–26.

60 Levitas, *The Concept of Utopia*, p. 8.

61 Fátima Vieira, 'The Concept of Utopia', in Gregory Claeys (ed.), *The Cambridge Companion to Utopian Literature* (Cambridge: Cambridge University Press, 2010), p. 23.

62 Ibid.

63 Marie Louise Berneri, *Journey Through Utopia* (London: Freedom Press, 1982), p. 2.

64 See Vincent Geoghegan 'Remembering the Future', *Utopian Studies*, vol. 1, no. 2 (1990), p. 53.

65 For commentary on Roland Schaer and Lyman Tower Sargent's essays in

Roland Schaer, Gregory Claeys and Lyman Tower Sargent (eds), *Utopia: the search for the ideal society in the Western world*, trans. Nadia Benabid (New York, Oxford: New York Public Library/Oxford University Press, 2000), see Zhang Longxi, 'The Utopian Vision, East and West', *Utopian Studies*, vol. 13, no. 1 (2002), pp. 1–20.

66   Frank Manuel and Fritzie P. Manuel, *Utopian Thought in the Western World* (Cambridge, MA: Belknap Press of Harvard University Press, 1979), p. 5.

67   Chlöe Houston, 'Utopia, Dystopia or Anti-Utopia? *Gulliver's Travels* and the Utopian mode of discourse', *Utopian Studies*, vol. 18, no. 3 (2007), p. 425.

68   Lyman Tower Sargent, *Utopianism: a very short introduction* (Oxford: Oxford University Press), p. 104.

69   Darko Suvin, *Metamorphoses of Science Fiction: on the poetics and history of a literary genre* (New Haven, CT: Yale University Press, 1979), p. 49.

70   Ibid., p. 41.

71   Ibid., p. 39.

72   Moylan, *Scraps of the Untainted Sky*, p. 76.

73   Bertolt Brecht quoted in Suvin, *Metamorphoses of Science Fiction*, p. 374.

74   Suvin, *Metamorphoses of Science Fiction*, p. 375.

75   Lucy Sargisson, 'Strange Places: estrangement, utopianism and intentional communities, *Utopian Studies*, vol. 18, no. 3 (2007), p. 394.

76   Vincent Geoghegan, *Utopianism and Marxism* (London: Methuen, 1987), pp. 1–2.

77   Kenneth M. Roemer, 'Paradise Transformed: varieties of nineteenth-century Utopias', in Gregory Claeys (ed.), *The Cambridge Companion to Utopian Literature* (Cambridge: Cambridge University Press, 2010), p. 79.

78   Northrop Frye, 'Varieties of Literary Utopias', in Frank E. Manuel (ed.), *Utopias and Utopian Thought* (Boston, MA: Beacon Press, 1965; republished London: Souvenir Press, 1973), p. 25.

79   Ibid., p. 26.

80   Manuel and Manuel, *Utopian Thought in the Western World*, p. 23.

81   Sargent, *Utopianism*, p. 6.

82   Barbara Goodwin, *The Philosophy of Utopia* (London: Routledge, 2001), p. 10.

83   Miquel A. Ramiro Avilés and J.C. Davis (eds), *Utopian Moments* (London: Bloomsbury, 2012), p. xvii.

Chapter 2

1   John Mitchel, *Jail Journal* (Dublin: M.H. Gill, 1913), p. 83.

2   Daniel Corkery, 'Love Consecrate', in *I Bhreasail: a book of lyrics* (London: Elkin Mathews, 1921), p. 71.

3   Daniel Corkery, *The Hidden Ireland* (Dublin: Gill & Macmillan, 1967; first published 1924), p. 128.

4   Joseph McMinn, 'Literature and Religion in Eighteenth-century Ireland: a

critical survey', in Robert Welch (ed.), *Irish Writers and Religion* (Gerrards Cross: Colin Smythe, 1992), pp. 25–6.

5   Breandán Ó Buachalla, 'Irish Jacobitism and Irish Nationalism: the literary evidence', in Michael O'Dea and Kevin Whelan (eds), *Nations and Nationalisms: France, Britain, Ireland and the eighteenth-century context*, Studies on Voltaire and the Eighteenth Century, vol. 335 (Oxford: Voltaire Foundation, 1996), p. 109.

6   On nostalgia, see William Fiennes, *The Snow Geese* (London: Picador, 2002), especially pp. 122–3.

7   Sean O'Faolain, *An Irish Journey: with illustrations by Paul Henry* (London: Longmans, Green & Co. Ltd, 1940), p. 127.

8   Corkery, *The Hidden Ireland*, p. 135.

9   Hy Brasil is Hiberno-English orthography for *Uí Bhreasail* (the descendants of Bresal or Bresail). On the University College Cork website CELT, the Corpus of Electronic Texts, an online resource for Irish history, literature and politics (www.ucc.ie/celt/index.html), the name Bresal appears thirty times, the first being from AD 435. I also found records of the name Breasail and the Uí Breasail clan (AD 536). For an explanation of the name and analysis of accounts in Irish folklore, see Dáithí Ó hÓgáin, 'The Mystical Island in Irish Folklore" in Patricia Lysaght, Séamus Ó Catháin and Dáithí Ó hÓgáin (eds), *Islanders and Water-dwellers* (Dublin: Four Courts Press, 1999), pp. 247–60. Also see Donald S. Johnson, *Phantom Islands of the Atlantic: the legends of seven lands that never were* (London: Souvenir Press, 1997), pp. 113–28, and Walter B. Scaife, 'Brazil, as a Geographical Appellation', *Modern Language Notes*, vol. 5, no. 4 (1890), pp. 105–7. Another possible explanation for the meaning of Hy Brasil is derived from Old/Middle Irish of around the tenth century. Hy is a variation of *Í*, which means island, and this could explain why we find the written form I-Brasil, or the island of Brasil. For a comprehensive study of Hy Brasil, see Barbara Freitag, *Hy-Brasil: the metamorphosis of an island: from cartographic error to Celtic Elysium* (Amsterdam and New York: Rodopi, 2013).

10   The edition I use is the revised text, literal translation, new metrical version, notes and vocabulary of *Laoi Oisín ar Tír na nÓg* by Micheál Coimín, ed. Tomás Ó Flannghaile (London: City of London Book Depot; Dublin: M.H. Gill & Son, 1896).

11   On Elysium and the Islands of the Blest, see Frank Manuel and Fritzie P. Manuel, *Utopian Thought in the Western World* (Cambridge, MA: Belknap Press of Harvard University Press, 1979), especially pp. 75–8, and Gregory Claeys and Lyman Tower Sargent (eds), *The Utopia Reader* (New York: New York University Press, 1999), especially pp. 12–13.

12   Coimín, *Laoi Oisín ar Tír na nÓg*, ll. 13–16.

13   Ibid., ll. 41–4.

14   Ibid., ll. 105–8.

15   On the association between Utopia and the city, see Lewis Mumford, 'Utopia, the City and the Machine', in Frank E. Manuel (ed.), *Utopias and Utopian Thought* (Boston, MA: Beacon Press, 1965; republished London: Souvenir

Press, 1973), pp. 3–24. On John Winthrop and a 'citty upon a hill', see Lyman Tower Sargent, 'Colonial and Postcolonial Utopias', in Gregory Claeys (ed.), *The Cambridge Companion to Utopian Literature* (Cambridge: Cambridge University Press, 2010), p. 206.

16 Jonathan Swift, *A Tale of a Tub. Written for the universal improvement of mankind* (Dublin: G. Faulkner, 1771), p. 106.

17 Sir D. Wilson, *The Lost Atlantis and other Ethnographic Studies* (Edinburgh: David Douglas, 1892), p. 35.

18 Walter B. Scaife, 'Brazil, as a Geographical Appellation', *Modern Language Notes*, vol. 4 (1890), p. 209.

19 Ibid.

20 Ibid.

21 See Freitag, *Hy-Brasil*, p. 5.

22 Ibid., p. 6.

23 Ibid.

24 Jason H. Pearl, *Utopian Geographies and the Early English Novel* (Charlottesville, VA and London: University of Virginia Press, 2014), p. 19.

25 See Freitag, *Hy-Brasil*, p. 6.

26 See ibid., p. 9.

27 See Fortescue Hitchins and Samuel Drew (eds), *The History of Cornwall: from the earliest records and traditions to the present times* (London: Penaluna, 1824), vol. 2, p. 206.

28 See W. Harrison (ed.), *A History of the Isle of Man Written by William Blundell 1648–56* (Douglas, Isle of Man: Manx Society, 1876), pp. 58–9.

29 The medical treatise to which Westropp alludes is known as The Book of the O'Lees or The Book of Hy-Brasil, and is held among the medieval manuscripts collection of the Royal Irish Academy. It is written in Irish with some Latin. It contains a translation from Latin into Irish of a highly organised medical treatise, with forty-four tables providing details of diseases. The manuscript was bought for the Academy from the O'Lee family, hereditary physicians to the O'Flahertys, and the name 'P. Lee' is inscribed on page 47. In the course of the seventeenth century a member of the O'Lee family told a 'wild story' of his having been transported to the enchanted island of Hy Brasil and having obtained supernatural knowledge of medical cures, which he recorded in his book. The unusual appearance of the book convinced some of the validity of his story.

30 W.G. Wood-Martin, *Traces of the Elder Faiths of Ireland: a folklore sketch; a handbook of Irish pre-Christian tradition*, 2 vols (London: Longmans, Green & Co., 1902), vol. 1, p. 217.

31 See Thomas Johnson Westropp's account in 'Brasil and the Legendary Islands of the North Atlantic: their history and fable. A contribution to the "Atlantis" problem', *Proceedings of the Royal Irish Academy*, vol. 30, sect. C (Dublin: Hodges Figgis, 1912), p. 35.

32 Wood-Martin, *Traces of the Elder Faiths of Ireland*, vol. 1, p. 217.

33   Ibid.
34   James Shirley, *No Wit, No Help Like a Woman's* (1653), quoted in Andrew Carpenter (ed.), *Verse in English from Tudor and Stuart Ireland* (Cork: Cork University Press, 2003), p. 214.
35   Anon. [William Winstanley], *Poor Robin's Vision: wherein is described, the present humours of the times; the vices and fashionable fopperies thereof; and after what manner men are punished for them hereafter; discovered in a dream* (London: printed for and sold by Arthur Boldero, 1677), p. 31.
36   Calhoun Winton, 'Richard Head and Origins of the Picaresque in England', in S. Benito-Vessels and M. Zappala (eds), *The Picaresque: a symposium on the rogue's tale* (Newark, DE: University of Delaware Press, 1994) p. 81.
37   William Winstanley, *The Lives of the Most Famous English Poets, 1687: a facsimile reproduction with an introduction by William Riley Parker* (Gainesville, FL: Scholars Facsimiles & Reprints, 1963), p. 208.
38   Ibid.
39   Richard Head, *The English Rogue Described, in the Life of Meriton Latroon, a Witty Extravagent, Being a Compleat History of the Most Eminent Cheats of Both Sexes* (London: printed for Henry Marsh, 1665), p. 12.
40   Winstanley, *The Lives of the Most Famous English Poets*, p. 208.
41   Ibid., p. 209.
42   See Richard Head, *Hic et Ubique: or, the humours of Dublin* (London: printed by R.D. for the author, 1663). For more on this, see Christopher J. Wheatley, *Beneath Iërne's Banners: Irish Protestant drama of the Restoration and eighteenth century* (Notre Dame, IN: University of Notre Dame Press, 1999), pp. 15–28; Michael J. Griffin, 'Offshore Irelands; or, Hy-Brazil Hybridized: utopian colonies and anti-colonial Utopias, 1641–1760', in Eóin Flannery and Angus Mitchell (eds), *Enemies of Empire* (Dublin: Four Courts Press, 2007), especially pp. 134–6.
43   Wheatley, *Beneath Iërne's Banners*, p. 16.
44   Ibid.
45   Head, *Hic et Ubique*, ll. 29–9.
46   Ibid., l. 29.
47   Wheatley, *Beneath Iërne's Banners*, p. 20.
48   Head, *Hic et Ubique*, l. 23.
49   Ibid., l. 3.
50   Ibid., l. 23.
51   Ibid., l. 24.
52   See Richard Head, *The Western Wonder: or, O Brazeel, an inchanted island discovered; with a relation of two ship-wracks in a dreadful sea-storm in that discovery. To which is added, a description of a place, called Montecapernia, relating the nature of the people, their qualities, humours, fashions, religion, etc.* (London, 1674), pp. 1–17.
53   Ibid., pp. 5–6.
54   Ibid., p. 6.

55 Ibid., p. 7.
56 Ibid.
57 Ibid., p. 21.
58 Ibid., p. 32.
59 Ibid., p. 34.
60 See Griffin, 'Offshore Irelands', p. 135.
61 Manus O'Donnel, *A Voyage to O'Brazeel: or, the sub-marine island. Giving a brief description and a short account of the customs, manners, government, law, and religion of the inhabitants* (*Ulster Miscellany*, 1753), p. 3.
62 Ibid.
63 For a detailed analysis and contextualisation of *The Ulster Miscellany* and the *Voyage to O'Brazeel*, see Michael Griffin and Breandán MacSuibhne, 'Da's Boat; or, Can the Submarine Speak? *A Voyage to O'Brazeel* (1752) and other glimpses of the Irish Atlantis', *Field Day Review*, no. 2 (2006), pp. 110–27.
64 Ibid., p. 119.
65 O'Donnel, *A Voyage to O'Brazeel*, p. 6.
66 Ibid., p. 7.
67 Ibid., p. 15.
68 Ibid., p. 9.
69 Ibid., p. 19.
70 Ibid., p. 54.
71 Ibid.
72 Ibid., pp. 54–5.
73 Ibid., p. 55.
74 Ibid., p. 64.
75 Ibid.
76 Ibid., p. 9.
77 Apropos of colonialism, see Sargent, 'Colonial and Postcolonial Utopias', pp. 200–2.
78 Ibid., p. 200.
79 O'Donnel, *A Voyage to O'Brazeel*, p. 20.
80 Ibid.
81 Ibid., p. 22.
82 Ibid.
83 Ibid.
84 Ibid., p. 25.
85 Griffin and MacSuibhne, 'Da's Boat', p. 124.
86 O'Donnel, *A Voyage to O'Brazeel*, p. 27.
87 Ibid., p. 9.
88 Donald S. Johnson, *Phantom Islands of the Atlantic: the legends of the seven lands that never were* (London: Souvenir Press, 1997), p. 114.
89 Ibid.
90 Anon., *Old Ireland's Misery at an End, or the English Empire in the Brazils Restored* (Rhode Island and Boston, MA, 1752), p. 4.

91   Ibid., pp. 5–6.
92   Ibid., p. 5.
93   Ibid., p. 6.
94   Ibid., p. 7.
95   Ibid.
96   Ibid.
97   Ibid., p. 8.
98   Ibid.
99   Kerby Miller, 'Revd James MacSparran's America Dissected (1753): eighteenth-century emigration and constructions of "Irishness"', *History Ireland*, vol. 11, no. 4 (winter 2003), p. 18.
100 Ibid., p. 20.
101 Wheatley, *Beneath Iërne's Banners*, p. 17.
102 Toby Barnard, *The Kingdom of Ireland, 1641–1760* (Houndmills: Palgrave Macmillan, 2004), p. 12.

Chapter 3

1   Query 313 in George Berkeley, *The Querist Containing Several Queries, Proposed to the Consideration of the Public in Three Parts*, pt 1 (Dublin: R. Reilly for G. Risk, G. Ewing and W. Smith, booksellers, 1735, 1736; printed by R. Reilly for J. Leathley, bookseller, 1737).
2   *The Querist* originally appeared in 1735 as an anonymous publication. A continuation designated part II was issued in 1736, and a further instalment, part III, in 1737. In 1746 it is said that Dean Gervais 'could not find one in the shops, for my Lord Lieutenant [Lord Chesterfield], at his desire'; George Berkeley, *The Works of George Berkeley D.D.; formerly Bishop of Cloyne: including his posthumous works*, 4 vols, ed. Alexander Campbell Fraser (Oxford: Clarendon Press, 1901), vol. 4, p. 247. It is possible that this circumstance encouraged Berkeley to print a second edition of *The Querist* in 1750, with some queries added and many omitted.
3   On Richard Warburton's comments made in 1750, see Noah Porter, *The Two-hundredth Birthday of Bishop George Berkeley: a discourse given at Yale College on 12th March 1885* (New York: Charles Scribner's Sons, 1885), p. 55.
4   *Catalogue of Manuscripts, Books and Berkeleiana Exhibited in the Library of Trinity College Dublin on the Occasion of the Commemoration of the Bicentenary of the Death of George Berkeley, Held on 7–12 July 1953* (Dublin: Dublin University Press, 1953), p. 9.
5   Desmond Clarke, *Thomas Prior, 1681–1751: founder of the Royal Dublin Society* (Dublin: published for the Royal Dublin Society by At the Sign of the Three Candles, 1951).
6   Berkeley, *Works* (ed. Fraser), vol. 4, p. 259.
7   Ibid., pp. 257–64.
8   Ibid., p. 264.

9 The use by Henry Lewis Younge in his *Utopia: or, Apollo's golden days* in 1747 of the word dystopia (spelled as 'dustopia') as a clear contrast to Utopia is the earliest usage of the word that I have noted. The poem was reprinted in *The Gentleman's Magazine and Historical Chronicle* in September 1748, with the word spelled as 'Dystopia' on pages 400–1, and with a footnote on page 400 defining the word as 'an unhappy country'. On the contrast between the two versions, see V[esselin] M. Budakov, 'Dystopia: an earlier eighteenth-century use', *Notes and Queries*, vol. 57, no. 1 (March 2010), pp. 86–8. See also Kenneth M. Roemer, 'Clearing up "Dystopia"', *Utopus Discovered* (April 2010), pp. 2–3.

10 George Berkeley, *The Works of George Berkeley*, ed. Joseph Stock, 2 vols (Dublin: 1784), vol. 1, p. 2.

11 J.V. Luce, 'Dublin Societies Before the R.D.S.', a discourse delivered at a joint meeting of the Royal Dublin Society and the Dublin Philosophical Society, 10 December 1981 (Dublin: Royal Dublin Society, 1981), p. 2.

12 David Berman, *Berkeley and Irish Philosophy* (London: Continuum, 2005), p. 80.

13 Thomas Duddy, *A History of Irish Thought* (London: Routledge, 2002), p. 126.

14 Ibid.

15 Berkeley, *Works* (ed. Stock), vol. 1, p. 47.

16 Denis Donoghue, *We Irish: essays on Irish literature and society* (Oakland, CA: University of California Press, 1988), p. 17.

17 Duddy, *A History of Irish Thought*, p. 128.

18 Quoted in Benjamin Rand, *Berkeley and Percival: the correspondence of Berkeley and Sir John Percival* (Cambridge, MA: Harvard University Press, 1914), p. 80.

19 George Berkeley, *The Works of George Berkeley*, eds A.A. Luce and T.E. Jessop, 9 vols (London: Thomas Nelson & Sons, 1948–57), vol. 2, p. 282.

20 Berman, *Berkeley and Irish Philosophy*, p. 150.

21 Quoted in H. Lyons, *The Royal Society 1660–1940: a history of its administration under its charters* (Cambridge: Cambridge University Press, 1944), p. 41.

22 J.G. Simms, *William Molyneux of Dublin: a life of the seventeenth-century political writer and scientist*, ed. P.H. Kelly (Dublin: Irish Academic Press, 1982).

23 Theodore Hoppen, *The Common Scientist in the Seventeenth Century: a study of the Dublin Philosophical Society, 1683–1708* (Charlottesville, VA: University Press of Virginia, 1970), p. 21.

24 Quoted in Simms, *William Molyneux of Dublin*, p. 37.

25 See Hoppen, *The Common Scientist in the Seventeenth Century*, p. 23. Hoppen is quoting from Capel Molyneux's *An Account of the Family and Descendants of Sir Thomas Molyneux, Kt., Chancellor of the Exchequer in Ireland to Queen Elizabeth* (Evesham: privately printed, 1820), pp. 63–4.

26 Irvin Ehrenpreis, *Swift: the man, his works, and the age*, 3 vols (London: Methuen, 1962; republished 1983), vol 1, p. 79.

27   Jonathan Swift, *Gulliver's Travels*, ed. Robert Demaria Jnr (London: Penguin, 2003), p. 105.
28   Hoppen, *The Common Scientist in the Seventeenth Century*, p. 176.
29   Quoted in James Meehan and Desmond Clarke (eds), *The Royal Dublin Society, 1731–1981* (Dublin: Gill & Macmillan, 1981), p. 1.
30   Ibid., p. 16.
31   Ibid., pp. 21–2.
32   Ibid., pp. 32–3.
33   Ibid., p. 6.
34   Ibid., p. 7.
35   Ibid.
36   Quoted in Constantia Maxwell, *Dublin Under the Georges, 1714–1830* (London: G.G. Harrap, 1936), p. 173.
37   Luce, 'Dublin Societies Before the R.D.S.', p. 5.
38   Leszek Kolakowski, 'The Death of Utopia Reconsidered', in Sterling M. McMurrin (ed.), *The Tanner Lectures on Human Value*, vol. 4 (Salt Lake City, UT: University of Utah Press/Cambridge: Cambridge University Press, 1983), pp. 227–47, reprinted in Kolakowski, *Modernity on Endless Trial* (Chicago, IL: University of Chicago Press, 1990), pp. 131–45.
39   Raymond Williams, *Marxism and Literature* (London: Oxford University Press, 1977), p. 132.
40   Ibid.
41   Michael Griffin, 'Offshore Irelands; or, Hy-Brazil Hybridized: utopian colonies and anti-colonial Utopias, 1641–1760', in Eóin Flannery and Angus Mitchell (eds), *Enemies of Empire* (Dublin: Four Courts Press, 2007), p. 131.
42   J.M. Hone and M.M. Rossi, *Bishop Berkeley: his life, writings and philosophy with an introduction by W.B. Yeats* (London: Faber & Faber, 1931), p. 30.

Chapter 4

1   Stanza four of George Berkeley's poem 'On America; or the Muse's Refuge: a prophecy in six verses'. It was enclosed in a letter from Berkeley to John Percival in February 1726. See Benjamin Rand, *Berkeley and Percival: the correspondence of Berkeley and Sir John Percival* (Cambridge, MA: Harvard University Press, 1914), pp. 230–1.
2   John Mitchel, *Jail Journal* (Dublin: M.H. Gill, 1913), p. 55.
3   Jonathan Swift, 'Journal to Stella', in *The Works of Jonathan Swift in Two Volumes* (London: Henry Washbourne, 1841), vol. 1, p. 274. On 12 April 1713 Swift brought Berkeley to the Court of St James, where he presented him to Lord Berkeley of Stratton, who in February 1700 has appointed Swift as vicar of Laracor in the diocese of Meath. Henceforward, Swift and Lord Berkeley remained best acquaintances. Interestingly, Lord Berkeley of Stratton was a distant kinsman of George Berkeley; see J.M. Hone and M.M. Rossi, *Bishop Berkeley: his life, writings and philosophy with an introduction by W.B. Yeats*

(London: Faber & Faber, 1931), p. 89: 'My Lord [said Swift on this occasion] here is a fine young gentleman of your family. I can assure your Lordship, it is a much greater honour to you to be related to him, than it is to him to be related to you.'

4   Swift, *Works*, vol. 3, p. 173.

5   George Berkeley, *The Works of George Berkeley*, eds A.A. Luce and T.E. Jessop, 9 vols (London: Thomas Nelson & Sons, 1948–57), vol. 6, p. 84.

6   Hone and Rossi, *Bishop Berkeley*, pp. 131–2.

7   George Berkeley, *The Works of George Berkeley D.D.; formerly Bishop of Cloyne: including his posthumous works*, 4 vols, ed. Alexander Campbell Fraser (Oxford: Clarendon Press, 1901), vol. 4, p. 343.

8   Rand, *Berkeley and Percival*, pp. 207–8.

9   Ibid., p. 208.

10 Ibid., p. 217.

11 George Berkeley, *The Works of George Berkeley*, ed. Joseph Stock, 2 vols (Dublin: 1784), vol. 1, pp. 68–9.

12 Swift, *Works*, vol. 4, pp. 344–5.

13 Ibid.

14 Carole Fabricant, 'George Berkeley the Islander: some reflections on Utopia, race, and tar-water', in Felicity A. Nussbaum (ed.), *The Global Eighteenth Century* (Baltimore, MD: Johns Hopkins University Press, 2003), p. 263.

15 Jonathan Swift, *The Correspondence of Jonathan Swift*, ed. Harold Williams, vol. 1 (Oxford: Clarendon Press, 1963), pp. 203–4.

16 Ibid., p. 204.

17 Ibid., p. 205.

18 Rand, *Berkeley and Percival*, p. 205.

19 Ibid., p. 206.

20 Ibid., p. 207.

21 Ibid., p. 225.

22 Lyman Tower Sargent, *Utopianism: a very short introduction* (Oxford: Oxford University Press, 2010), p. 13.

23 See Hesiod, *Works and Days*, trans. Jack Lindsay, in T.F. Higham and C.M. Bowra (eds), *The Oxford Book of Greek Verse in Translation* (Oxford: Clarendon Press, 1938), p. 133.

24 Jean Delumeau, *History of Paradise: the Garden of Eden in myth and tradition* (Chicago, IL: University of Illinois Press, 2000), p. 6.

25 See Ovid, *Metamorphoses*, Book 1, ll. 89–112, trans. Mary M. Innes (Harmondsworth: Penguin, 1955), pp. 33–4.

26 Berkeley, *Works* (ed. Fraser), vol. 4, p. 343.

27 Hone and Rossi, *Bishop Berkeley*, p. 132.

28 The broadside bears neither a date nor a place of publication; drawing on the contemporary correspondence, however, it was probably published in Dublin in 1723. It is quoted by Edwing Gaustad in *George Berkeley in America* (New Haven, CT and London: Yale University Press, 1979), pp. 29–30. Gaustad

notes Revd Dr Berkeley's purported response to the 'beautiful young lady's' petition (p. 30):

> Dear Miss, I thank you for your kind surrender,
> I doubt not but you'r Soft, and young and Tender, As for your Dex'trous
>   Faculty of Breeding,
> Your Species seldom fail of well succeeding:
> Since Eden once was lost by Woman's base Device, Who'd bring a Woman
>   to his Paradise?
> I live an Easy, Sweet, and Graceful Life,
> My Study, my Companion, my books, my wife.

29   The second revised edition was printed in Dublin in 1725. A postscript announces the grant of a charter, and gives a list of persons to whom subscriptions should be sent. It is the only one of the three editions mentioning the proposed college in the title: *A Proposal for the Better Supplying of Churches in Our Foreign Plantations, and for Converting the Savage Americans to Christianity, by a College to be Erected in the Summer Islands, Otherwise Called the Isles of Bermuda.* The third edition, printed in London in 1725, was the same in content as the second edition, but with the shorter title of the first edition.

30   Berkeley, *Works* (ed. Fraser), vol. 4, p. 346.

31   Ibid.

32   Donald S. Johnson, *Phantom Islands of the Atlantic: the legends of the seven lands that never were* (London: Souvenir Press, 1997), p. xvi.

33   Berkeley, *Works* (ed. Fraser), vol. 4, p. 348.

34   Ibid.

35   Ibid., p. 349.

36   Hone and Rossi, *Bishop Berkeley*, pp. 136–7.

37   Berkeley, *Works* (ed. Fraser), vol. 4, p. 356.

38   Ibid., p. 356.

39   Ibid.

40   Ibid., p. 357.

41   Ibid.

42   Rand, *Berkeley and Percival*, p. 231.

43   Ibid., p. 230.

44   George Berkeley, *Miscellany* (1752), pp. 186–7.

45   Edmund Waller, 'The Battle of the Summer Islands' (canto 1, ll. 44–7), in George Gilfillan, *The Poetical Works of Edmund Waller and Sir John Denham: with memoir and critical dissertation* (Edinburgh: J. Nichol, 1857), p. 27.

46   Horace, epode 16, ll. 41–56, quoted in Deborah Boedeker and David Sider (eds), *The New Simonides Contexts of Praise and Desire* (Oxford: Oxford University Press, 2001), p. 269.

47   Quoted in Jessie L. Weston, *The Chief Middle English Poets* (Cambridge, MA: Riverside Press, 1914), p. 58.

48   Carlos Fuentes, 'This is America', in Carol Christensen and Thomas Christensen

(eds), *The Discovery of America and Other Myths: a New World reader* (San Francisco: Chronicle Books, 1992), p. 94.

49 Noah Porter, *The Two-Hundredth Birthday of Bishop George Berkeley: a discourse given at Yale College on 12th March 1885* (New York: Charles Scribner's Sons, 1885), p. 29.

50 Joseph-Marie Degerando, 'Considérations sur les Divers Methods à Suivre dans l'Observation des Peuples Sauvages', in Jean Copans and Jean Jamin (eds), *Aux Origins de l'Anthropologies Française. Les mémoires de la Société des Observateurs de l'Homme* (Paris: Jean-Michel Place, 1978), pp. 131–2.

51 Rexmond C. Cochrane, 'Bishop Berkeley and the Progress of Arts and Learning: notes on a literary convention', *Huntington Library Quarterly*, vol. 17, no. 3 (1953–54), p. 230.

52 Ibid.

53 Ibid., p. 231.

54 David Berman, *George Berkeley: idealism and the man* (Oxford: Clarendon, 1994), p. 117.

55 Ibid.

56 A.A. Luce, *Berkeley's Bermuda Project and His Benefactions to American Universities* (Dublin: Hodges Figges, 1934–35), p. 99.

57 Berkeley, *Works* (eds Luce and Jessop), vol. 8, p. 189.

58 Quoted in Benjamin Rand, *Berkeley's American Sojourn* (Cambridge, MA: Harvard University Press, 1932), pp. 15–16.

59 The letter is reprinted in Benjamin Rand, *Berkeley and Percival: the correspondence of Berkeley and Sir John Percival* (Cambridge, MA: Harvard University Press, 1914).

60 Wilkins Updike, *A History of the Episcopal Church in Narragansett, Rhode Island* (New York: Onderdonk, 1847), p. 76.

61 Berkeley, *Works* (eds Luce and Jessop), vol. 8, p. 194.

62 Quoted in Benjamin Rand, *Berkeley's American Sojourn*, p. 20.

63 Ibid., pp. 13–14.

64 Berkeley, *Works* (eds Luce and Jessop), p. 102.

65 Ibid., p. 102.

66 Ibid.

67 H.P. Thompson, *Thomas Bray* (London: SPCK, 1954), pp. 92–3.

68 Rand, *Berkeley and Percival*, p. 275.

69 Berkeley, *Works* (ed. Stock), vol. 1, p. 23.

70 Berkeley, *Works* (eds Luce and Jessop), vol. 8, p. 212.

71 Berman, *George Berkeley*, p. 106.

72 Ibid.

73 Berkeley, *Works* (eds Luce and Jessop), vol. 7, p. 358.

74 Raymond W. Houghton, David Berman and Maureen T. Lapan, *Images of Berkeley* (Dublin: National Gallery of Ireland, Wolfhound Press, 1986).

75 Berkeley, *Works* (eds Luce and Jessop), vol. 7, p. 212.

76 Berman, *George Berkeley*, p. 108.

77   George Berkeley, *Alciphron, or the Minute Philosopher in Seven Dialogues. Containing an apology for the Christian religion, against those who are called free-thinkers* (Dublin: printed for Thomas Watson, bookseller, 1755), dialogue vi.

78   David Bjelajac, *American Art: a cultural history* (London: Laurence King, 2000), p. 103.

79   Ibid., p. 104.

80   Johnson, *Phantom Island of the Atlantic,* p. 91.

81   Zhang Longxi, 'The Utopian Vision, East and West', *Utopian Studies*, vol. 13, no. 1 (2002), p. 1.

82   The folded engraving illustrating Berkeley's plan for the 'City of Bermuda Metropolis of the Summer Islands' appeared in the first collected edition of Berkeley's *Works*, printed in two volumes in 1784. The engraving appeared in Berkeley, *Works* (ed. Stock), vol. 2, p. 419.

83   Hone and Rossi, *Bishop Berkeley*, p. 134.

84   Lewis Mumford, 'Utopia, the City and the Machine', in Frank E. Manuel (ed.), *Utopias and Utopian Thought: a timely appraisal* (Boston, MA: Beacon Press, 1967), p. 13.

85   David Harvey, *Spaces of Hope* (Edinburgh: Edinburgh University Press, 2002), p. 182.

86   A.A. Luce, 'Berkeley's Bermuda Project and His Benefactions to American Universities, with Unpublished Letters and Extracts from the Egmont Papers', *Proceedings of the Royal Irish Academy*, vol. 42, sect. C (1934), read 14 May 1934, published 22 August 1934 (Dublin: Hodges, Figgis, & Co.; London: Williams & Norgate, 1935), p. 97.

87   Ibid.

88   Hone and Rossi, *Bishop Berkeley*, p. 164.

89   Luce, 'Berkeley's Bermuda Project', p. 107.

90   Frank Manuel and Fritzie P. Manuel, *Utopian Thought in the Western World* (Cambridge, MA: Belknap Press of Harvard University Press, 1979), p. 15.

91   See Patrick Pearse, *The Sovereign People* (1916), quoted in Ruth Dudley Edwards, *Patrick Pearse: the triumph of failure* (London: Victor Gollancz, 1977), p. 260.

92   Fredric Jameson, *Archaeologies of the Future: the desire called Utopia and other science fictions* (London: Verso, 2005), p. xi.

93   Lyman Tower Sargent, 'Colonial and Postcolonial Utopias', in Gregory Claeys (ed.), *The Cambridge Companion to Utopian Literature* (Cambridge: Cambridge University Press, 2010), p. 204.

94   Carla H. Hay, 'The Making of a Radical: the case of James Burgh', *Journal of British Studies*, vol. 18. no. 2, p. 103.

95   See Theobald Wolfe Tone, *The Life of Theobald Wolfe Tone: written by himself and continued by his son*, ed. William Wolfe Tone, 2 vols (1826).

96   Ibid., vol. 1, p. 27.

97   Ibid., p. 36.

98   Ibid., p. 535.

99   Ibid., p. 520.
100 Nigel Leask, 'Irish Republicans and Gothic Eleutherarchs: Pacific Utopias in the writing of Theobald Wolfe Tone and Charles Brockden Brown', in Robert M. Manquis (ed.), *British Radical Culture of the 1790s* (San Marino, CA: Huntington Library Press, 2002), p. 95.
101 Tone, *The Life of Theobald Wolfe Tone*, vol. 1, p. 524.
102 Ibid., p. 522.
103 Leask, 'Irish Republicans and Gothic Eleutherarchs', p. 96.
104 Quoted in Constantia Maxwell, *Dublin Under the Georges, 1714–1830* (London: G.G. Harrap, 1936), p. 32.
105 Quoted in Marianne Elliot, *Partners in Revolution: the United Irishmen and France* (New Haven, CT and London: Yale University Press, 1982), p. 23.
106 Tone, *The Life of Theobald Wolfe Tone*, vol. 1, p. 520.

Chapter 5

1   See Carola Baumgardt, *Johannes Kepler: life and letters* (New York: Philosophical Library, 1951), pp. 155–6.
2   See 'A Voyage to Laputa', in Jonathan Swift, *Gulliver's Travels*, ed. Robert Demaria Jnr (London: Penguin, 2003), p. 146.
3   Janet Todd in *Rebel Daughters: Ireland in conflict, 1798* (London: Viking, 2003) mentions Dublin-born Margaret King's utopian novel *Selene*, written in the early 1820s, in which she imagined an ideal society set on the moon based on a classical republican government. The three-volume unpublished manuscript of *Selene* is part of the Carl H. Pforzheimer Collection of Shelley and His Circle held in New York Public Library. I am indebted to Dr Anne Markey of Trinity College, Dublin for providing me with much information and assistance in relation to *Selene*. In her ongoing research and analysis of the manuscript, she says that it would be accurate to describe it as 'a novel that incorporates a lunar Utopian narrative'; email communication, Anne Markey, August 2012.
4   Robert Elliott, *The Power of Satire: magic, ritual, art* (New Jersey: Princeton University Press, 1960), pp. 8–9.
5   Ibid., p. 9.
6   Lyman Tower Sargent, *Utopianism: a very short introduction* (Oxford: Oxford University Press, 2010), p. 24.
7   Lyman Tower Sargent, 'The Three Faces of Utopianism Revisited', *Utopian Studies*, vol. 5, no. 1 (1994), p. 9.
8   Northrop Frye, 'Varieties of Literary Utopias', in Frank E. Manuel (ed.), *Utopias and Utopian Thought* (Boston, MA: Beacon Press, 1965; republished London: Souvenir Press, 1973), p. 39.
9   [Francis Gentleman], *The Theatres: a poetical dissection. By Sir Nicholas Nipclose, Baronet* (London: printed for J. Bell, 1772), p. 5.
10 Jonathan Swift, *A Full and True Account of the Battel Fought Last Friday Between the Antient and Modern Books in St. James's Library* (1697), p. 172.

11   Anon., *The Antisatyrist: a dialogue. To which is prefixed, a short dissertation on panegyric, and satyr* (Dublin: George Faulkner, 1750), pp. 4–5.

12   Nicole Pohl, 'Utopianism after More: the Renaissance and Enlightenment', in Gregory Claeys (ed.), *The Cambridge Companion to Utopian Literature* (Cambridge: Cambridge University Press, 2010), p. 53.

13   Ibid., p. 54.

14   Majorie Hope Nicolson, *Voyages to the Moon* (New York: Macmillan, 1960), p. 7.

15   Peter Leighton, *Moon Travellers* (London: Oldbourne Book Co. Ltd, 1960), p. 5.

16   Ibid., p. 13.

17   Frank Manuel and Fritzie P. Manuel, *Utopian Thought in the Western World* (Cambridge, MA: Belknap Press of Harvard University Press, 1979), p. 22.

18   Nicolson, *Voyages to the Moon*, p. 46.

19   Brian Aldiss, *Billion Year Spree: the history of science fiction* (London: Corgi, 1975), pp. 69–70.

20   Nicolson, *Voyages to the Moon*, p. 81.

21   Francis, Godwin, *The Man in the Moone* (London: printed by John Norton for Joshua Kirton and Thomas Warren, 1638; Hereford: *Hereford Times*, 1959), p. 13.

22   Jonathan Swift, *The Correspondence of Jonathan Swift*, ed. Harold Williams, vol. 1 (Oxford: Clarendon Press, 1963), p. 87.

23   Swift, *Gulliver's Travels*, p. 42.

24   Quoted in Brendan McWilliams, 'Privateer's Life Was a Blueprint for Fiction', *Irish Times*, 24 March 2004.

25   William Le Fanu, *A Catalogue of Books Belonging to Dr. Jonathan Swift, Dean of St Patrick's, Dublin, Aug. 19. 1715* (Cambridge: Cambridge Biographical Society, 1988), p. 16.

26   Robert Boyle, *Occasional Reflections on Several Subjects, Whereto is Premis'd a Discourse About Such Kind of Thoughts* (London, 1665), pp. 350–1.

27   Swift, *Gulliver's Travels*, p. 46.

28   A.L. Morton, *The English Utopia* (London: Lawrence & Wishart, 1978), pp. 80–1.

29   Nicolson, *Voyages to the Moon*, p. 190.

30   Swift, *Gulliver's Travels*, p. 259.

31   Ibid.

32   Ibid., p. 261.

33   Ibid., p. 262.

34   Ibid., pp. 263–4.

35   Ibid., p. 264.

36   Ibid., p. 266.

37   Ibid., p. 271.

38   Ibid., p. 272.

39   Ibid., p. 273.

40 Ibid., p. 274.

41 Ibid., p. 278.

42 Ibid.

43 Ibid., pp. 283–4.

44 Declan Kiberd, *Irish Classics* (London: Granta Books, 2000), p. 93.

45 Swift, *Gulliver's Travels*, p. 287. William Wood (1671–1730) was an English hardware manufacturer and mint master who received a contract to strike an issue of Irish coinage from 1722–24. Wood thought this would be profitable, and purchased the royal patent for £10,000. Wood's coinage was extremely unpopular in Ireland. Swift in his *Drapier's Letters* (writing under the guise of 'M.B. Drapier', a Protestant shopkeeper), a series of seven pamphlets written during 1724–25, wrote against the measure whereby a private individual should be awarded the patent to mint. After the Irish parliament objected to Wood's patent, Swift began his campaign against 'the deluge of brass'. Robert Walpole (1676–1745) revoked the patent in 1725, and Wood was privately compensated. See Swift, *The Drapier's Letters*, ed. Herbert Davis (Oxford: Clarendon Press, 1935). An example of Wood's halfpence (1722) can be found in Fintan O'Toole, *A History of Ireland in 100 Objects* (Dublin: *Irish Times* and the Royal Irish Academy, 2013).

46 These paragraphs were not printed in the first edition of 1726, the second edition of 1727 or the revised edition of 1735, presumably because the publishers feared political repercussions. They remained unprinted until 1896. This shows how particular political and historical events could come to be evident in the composition of *Gulliver's Travels*.

47 Swift, *Gulliver's Travels*, p. 292.

48 Ibid.

49 Ibid., p. 295.

50 Ibid., p. 166.

51 Ibid., p. 298.

52 Ibid., p. 301.

53 Ibid., pp. 306–7.

54 Thomas Duddy, *A History of Irish Thought* (London: Routledge, 2002), p. 161.

55 Ibid., p. 162.

56 Quoted in Morton, *The English Utopia*, p. 82.

57 Francis Bacon, *The Works of Francis Bacon, Baron of Verulum, Viscount St. Albans, and Lord High Chancellor of England*, 10 vols (London: printed for W. Baynes & Son, 1824), vol. 2, p. 3.

58 Ibid., p. 21.

59 Swift, *Gulliver's Travels*, p. 278.

60 Ibid., p. 324.

61 Richard Whately, *'A Lost Leaf of Gulliver's Travels': miscellaneous remains from the commonplace book of Richard Whately, D.D. late archbishop of Dublin, being a collection of notes and essays made during the preparation of his various works,*

ed. Miss E.J. Whately, new edn with additions (London: Longman, Green, Longman, Roberts & Green, 1865), p. 320.

62   Ibid., p. 321.

63   Ibid., p. 325.

64   It is probable that Whately is referring to actual advances in medicine. In 1796 Edward Jenner observed that the mild disease cowpox gave immunity against smallpox, and established the practice of vaccination. Whately would have been cognisant of such medical advances, and retrospectively incorporated them into the work of the medical projectors Gulliver meets on his return visit to the academy. Whately was also a promoter of homeopathy, an alternative medicine based on the theory that 'like cures like'. He was vice-president of the London Homeopathic Hospital in 1850.

65   Ibid., p. 325.

66   Ibid., p. 326.

67   Ibid.

68   Ibid.

69   Ibid., p. 327.

70   Ibid.

71   Jonathan Swift, *A Tale of a Tub. Written for the universal improvement of mankind* (Dublin: G. Faulkner, 1771), p. 50.

72   Peter Ruppert, *Reader in a Strange Land: the activity of reading literary Utopias* (Athens, GA and London: University of Georgia Press, 1986), p. 8.

73   Ibid., p. 16.

74   Charles Henry Wilson, *Swiftiana* (London: R. Phillips, 1804), p. 73.

75   Swift, *Gulliver's Travels*, p. 162.

76   Ibid., p. 153.

77   Ibid.

78   Wilson, *Swiftiana*, pp. 171–2.

79   Gregory Claeys and Lyman Tower Sargent (eds), *The Utopia Reader* (New York: New York University Press, 1999), p. 141.

80   Jeanne K. Welcher and George Edward Bush Jnr (eds), *Gulliveriana*, vol. 1 (Gainesville, FL: Scholars' Facsimiles and Reprints, 1970), p. v.

81   McDermot's work was first printed by Christopher Dickson in Dublin in 1727. It was reprinted by J. Roberts in London in 1728. The Dublin and London editions conclude with 'the end of the first part', but nothing more was ever published.

82   Murtagh McDermot, *A Trip to the Moon. Containing some observations and reflections, made by him during his stay in that planet, upon the manners of the inhabitants* (Dublin: Christopher Dickson 1727; reprinted in London, for J. Roberts, 1728), p. 91.

83   Ibid., p. 90.

84   Ibid., p. 6.

85   Ibid., p. 9.

86   Ibid., pp. 10–11.

87   Ibid., p. 16.

88   Ibid., p. 21–2.

89   Ibid., p. 82.

90   Ibid., p. 83.

91   Ibid., p. 21.

92   Jonathan Swift, *The Prose Works of Jonathan Swift*, ed. Herbert Davis, 14 vols (Oxford: Basil Blackwell, 1939–68), vol. 1, p. 174.

93   McDermot, *A Trip to the Moon*, p. 38.

94   Ibid., p. 3.

95   Ibid., p. 44.

96   Ibid., p. 58.

97   Rolf Loeber and Magda Loeber (eds), *A Guide to Irish Fiction* (Dublin: Four Courts Press, 2006), p. 811.

98   McDermot, *A Trip to the Moon*, p. 84.

99   Ibid., p. 89.

100   Ibid., pp. 89–90.

101   Ibid., pp. 2–3.

102   Ibid., p. 94.

103   Ibid.

104   Francis Gentleman, *The Modish Wife: a comedy* (London: T. Evans & J. Bell, 1775), p. 6.

105   Ibid., pp. 15–16.

106   Ibid., p. 1.

107   Ibid., p. 2.

108   Ibid., p. 5.

109   Ibid., p. 12.

110   Ibid., pp. 13–14.

111   Ibid., p. 17.

112   Ibid., pp. 16–17.

113   Ibid., p. 20.

114   Ibid., p. 27.

115   Ibid., p. 21.

116   Ibid.

117   Ibid., p. 14.

118   Ibid., p. 24. The well called the Notlam, or Spring of Purification, is a reversal of Malton, the town near York in England where Gentleman lived for about four years and where he wrote both volumes of *A Trip to the Moon*. There are many other such examples throughout *A Trip to the Moon*, most notably in volume 1. Bishop Wilkins' title Namredal is an anagram of alderman. The House of Justice, called Requecex, needs only to be reworked and given an extra letter to form Exchequer. Each of these techniques – added letters, foreign-sounding words, anagrams – form part of the pattern found in Gulliverian works.

119   Ibid., p. 25.

120   Ibid.

121   Ibid., pp. 26–7.
122   Ibid., p. 28.
123   Ibid., p. 29.
124   Ibid., p. 32.
125   Ibid., p. 34.
126   Ibid., p. 40.
127   Ibid.
128   Ibid., p. 42.
129   Ibid., p. 43.
130   Ibid.
131   Ibid.
132   Ibid.
133   Ibid., p. 57.
134   Ibid., p. 58.
135   Ibid., p. 67.
136   Ibid., p. 77.
137   Ibid., p. 69.
138   Ibid., p. 79.
139   Ibid., p. 98.
140   Ibid.
141   Ibid., p. 99.
142   Ibid.
143   Ibid., p. 97.
144   Ibid.
145   Ibid.
146   Ibid.
147   Ibid., p. 82.
148   Ibid., pp. 203–4.
149   Ibid., pp. 149–50.
150   Ibid., pp. 204–5.
151   Francis Gentleman, *A Trip to the Moon. Containing an account of the island of Noibla. Its inhabitants, religious and political customs, &c. By Sir Humphrey Lunatic, Bart*, vol. 2 (London: printed for S. Crowder et al., 1765), p. 1.
152   Ibid., p. 98.
153   Ibid., p. 85.
154   Ibid., p. 212.
155   Ibid., vol. 1 (York: printed by A. Ward for S. Crowder et al., 1764), p. 52.
156   There is no indication that this pamphlet is a reprint or of there being a London imprint. As the Dublin imprint is the only one listed, that would seem to indicate that it was an Irish work printed in Dublin by John Hillary of Castle Street in 1782. While it was printed in Dublin in 1782, it was therefore most likely written during the period when William Cradock was dean of St Patrick's, a position he held from 1775 until his death in 1793. Meanwhile, Fowler had been appointed archbishop of Dublin in 1779; thus, the author could have

been anticipating Fowler's nascent machinations in promoting the ecclesiastical career of his son Robert.

157   Anon., *A History of the Customs, Manners, and Religion of the Moon. To which are annexed several specimens of lunar poetry; and the characters of the most distinguished personages* (Dublin: John Hillary, 1782), pp. 7–8.
158   Ibid., p. 9.
159   Ibid., pp. 9–10.
160   Ibid., p. 10.
161   Ibid., p. 11.
162   Ibid., pp. 14–15.
163   Ibid., p. 23.
164   Ibid., p. 26.
165   Ibid., p. 32.
166   Ibid.
167   Ibid., p. 50.
168   Ibid., pp. 51–2.
169   Ibid., pp. 52–3.
170   Ibid., p. 86.
171   Ibid.
172   Ibid., p. 87.
173   Ibid.
174   Ibid.
175   Ibid., p. 90.
176   Ibid., pp. 5–6.
177   Ibid., p. 37.
178   Ibid., p. 41.
179   Ibid., p. 44.
180   Kenneth Milne, 'The end of the old order, 1745–1846', in John Crawford and Raymond Gillespie (eds), *St Patrick's Cathedral, Dublin: a history* (Dublin: Four Courts Press, 2009), p. 247.
181   A.P. W. Malcomson, *Archbishop Charles Agar: churchmanship and politics in Ireland, 1760–1810* (Dublin: Four Courts Press, 2002), p. 413.
182   Anon, *A History of the Customs, Manners, and Religion of the Moon*, p. 12.
183   Janet Todd, 'Ascendancy: Lady Mount Cashell, Lady Moira, Mary Wollstonecraft and the Union pamphlets', *Eighteenth-century Ireland/Iris an dá Chultúr*, vol. 18 (2003), p. 102.
184   Claire Connolly, *A Cultural History of the Irish Novel, 1790–1829* (Cambridge: Cambridge University Press, 2012), p. 195.
185   Anne Markey, 'Literary Labours, Lunar Landscapes, and Lady Mount Cashell's *Selene*', symposium, Trinity College, Dublin, 22 October 2012, p. 4.
186   Ibid.
187   Barbara M. Benedict, 'Readers, Writers, Reviewers', in Thomas Keymer and Jon Mee (eds), *The Cambridge Companion to English Literature, 1740–1830* (Cambridge: Cambridge University Press, 2004), p. 6.

188   The 'long eighteenth century' is a phrase often used by historians to cover a more natural historical period than the standard calendar definition. They expand it to include the larger historical movements, with their subsequent 'long eighteenth century' extending from the Glorious Revolution of 1688 to the Battle of Waterloo in 1815. Other definitions, perhaps those with a more social or global interest, extend the period further – for example, 1660–1830.

Chapter 6

1   Samuel Madden, *Memoirs of the Twentieth Century. Being original letters of state, under George the Sixth: relating to the most important events in Great-Britain and Europe, as to Church and state, arts and sciences, trade, taxes, and treaties, peace, and war: and characters of the greatest persons of those times; from the middle of the eighteenth, to the end of the twentieth century, and the world. Received and revealed in the year 1728; and now published, for the instruction of all eminent statesmen, churchmen, patriots, politicians, projectors, papists and Protestants* (London: printed for Osborn, Longman, Davis & Battey et al., 1733), 6 vols, vol. 1, p. 3. Only one volume of the work appeared, and whether any more were ever really intended is uncertain.

2   Ibid., p. 15.

3   Lyman Tower Sargent, 'Three Faces of Utopianism Revisited', *Utopian Studies*, vol. 5, no. 1 (1994), p. 9.

4   Samuel Madden, *A Proposal for the General Encouragement of Learning in Dublin-College. Dedicated to His Grace the lord primate; and humbly offer'd to the consideration of all that wish well to Ireland* (Dublin: George Faulkner, 1732, second edn), pp. 10–11.

5   Ibid., p. 10.

6   Richard Robert Madden, *The History of Irish Periodical Literature, from the End of the 17th to the Middle of the 19th Century: its origin, progress, and results; with notices of remarkable persons connected with the press in Ireland during the past two centuries* (London: T.C. Newby, 1867), vol. 2, p. 286.

7   Angélique Day (ed.), *The Correspondence of Mary Delany, 1731–68: letters from Georgian Ireland* (Belfast: Friar's Bush Press, 1991), pp. 494–5.

8   See H. Davis (ed.), *The Prose Writing of Jonathan Swift*, 14 vols (Oxford: Oxford University Press, 1939–68), vol. x, p. 84.

9   See Anon., *A Letter to the Right Honourable Robert Walpole* (1716), p. 6; Anon., *The Woeful Treaty* (London, 1716), p. 4; Anon., *The Character and Principles of the Present Set of Whigs* (London, 1711), p. 15.

10   Isaac Kramnick, *Bolingbroke and His Circle: the politics of nostalgia in the age of Walpole* (Ithaca, NY and London: Cornell University Press, 1968), p. 12.

11   Ibid., p. 18.

12   See Samuel Johnson, *The Lives of the Most Eminent English Poets*, 4 vols (London, 1783), vol. 4, p. 337.

13 Laurence Hanson, *Government and the Press, 1695–1763* (Oxford: Clarendon Press, 1967, lithographical reprint of the 1936 edn), p. 108.

14 J.H. Plumb, *Sir Robert Walpole*, 2 vols: vol. 1, *The Making of a Statesman* (London: Cresset Press, 1956); vol. 2, *The King's Minister* (London: Allen Lane the Penguin Press, 1960), p. 141.

15 See Tone Sundt Urstad, *Sir Robert Walpole's Poets: the use of literature as pro-government propaganda, 1721–1742* (Newark, DE: University of Delaware Press, 1999), p. 114.

16 Ibid.

17 Anon. [William Pulteney, Earl of Bath], *A Letter from the Right Hon. W----m P------y, Esq: to the Right Honourable Sir R-----t W-----e; with regard to the observations on the writings of the craftsman* (1733), p. 1.

18 Ibid., p. 2.

19 Ibid., p. 1.

20 Jonathan Swift, *The Correspondence of Jonathan Swift*, ed. F.E. Ball, 6 vols (London: 1910–14), vol. 3, p. 388.

21 Jonathan Swift, *Gulliver's Travels*, ed. Robert Demaria Jnr (London: Penguin, 2003), p. 83.

22 [Francis Gentleman] *The Dramatic Censor: or, Critical Companion*, 2 vols (London: printed for J. Bell, London and C. Etherington, York, 1770), vol. 1, p. 120.

23 Ibid., pp. 120–1.

24 See Urstad, *Sir Robert Walpole's Poets*, p. 15.

25 Ibid. Urstad cites British Library, Holland House Papers, additional manuscript, 51396, fol. 84r (Hervey to Henry Fox, 25 January 1733).

26 On what Bertrand Goldgar has termed an opposition 'argot', see his *Walpole and the Wits: the relation of politics to literature, 1722–1742* (Lincoln: University of Nebraska Press, 1976).

27 See Urstad, *Sir Robert Walpole's Poets*, p. 73. Urstad notes that this letter from Madden to Walpole is held in Cambridge University Library, Cholmondeley (Houghton) correspondence, 1507 (Madden to Walpole, September, no year).

28 See John Nichols, *Biographical and Literary Anecdotes of William Bowyer, Printer, F.S.A. and of His Learned Friends Containing an Incidental View of the Progress and Advancement of Literature in the Kingdom* (London: printed by and for the author, 1782), pp. 82–3. John Nichols (1745–1826) was apprenticed at twelve years of age to William Bowyer, often referred to as 'the last of the learned printers'.

29 Ibid., p. 83.

30 Madden, *Memoirs of the Twentieth Century*, p. iii.

31 Ibid., p. iv.

32 Ibid.

33 Ibid.

34 Ibid., p. v.

35 Ibid., p. vi.

36 Ibid., p. ix.

37 Ibid.

38 Ibid., p. 29.

39 Madden is referring to Jean-Louis Guez de Balzac (1597–1654), born probably in Balzac, near Angoulême, France. He was an author and critic best known for his epistolary essays that were widely circulated and read in his day. He was one of the original members of the Académie Française. Swift's library contained a copy of de Balzac's *Oeuvres Diverses* (1664). See William Le Fanu, *A Catalogue of Books Belonging to Dr. Jonathan Swift, Dean of St Patrick's, Dublin, Aug. 19. 1715* (Cambridge: Cambridge Biographical Society, 1988), p. 12.

40 Madden, *Memoirs of the Twentieth Century*, pp. 9–10. The sacred text of *The Comte de Gabalis* was anonymously published in 1670 under the title *Comte de Gabalis*, a French 'novel of ideas'. The first English translation was printed in 1680. Only in later publishings did the name Abbé de Villars (b. 1635) become associated with it as author of the work. The book describes an encounter with a mysterious Comte de Gabalis, who is a master of the occult sciences. De Gabalis initiates de Villars into the secrets of elemental beings: the sylphs of the air, the undines of the water, the gnomes of the earth, the salamanders of fire. Alexander Pope was influenced by the *Comte de Gabalis* in *The Rape of the Lock*, his Rosicrucian poem first published in 1712.

41 Ibid., pp. 1–2.

42 Ibid., p. 3.

43 Ibid., pp. 10–11. Hermann Thyräus (1532–91) was a German Jesuit theologian and preacher. His *Confessio Augustana* appeared in 1567. He also left several volumes of sermons.

44 Ibid., p. 11.

45 Ibid.

46 Ibid., p. 12.

47 Ibid.

48 Ibid.

49 Ibid.

50 Ibid., p. 14.

51 Ibid., p. 15.

52 Ibid., p. 17.

53 Ibid.

54 Ibid., p. 18.

55 Ibid., p. 19.

56 Ibid.

57 Ibid., p. 22.

58 Ibid., p. 23.

59 Ibid., p. 24.

60 Ibid., p. 25.

61 Ibid., p. 27.

62 Ibid.

63 Ibid., p. 28. Madden here refers to the actual historical event of the earth-quake that struck Port Royal, Jamaica on 7 June 1692. Port Royal was then the unofficial capital of Jamaica, and one of the busiest and wealthiest ports of the West Indies. The earthquake caused most of the city to sink below sea level, and around 2,000 people died as a result of the earthquake and the following tsunami.

64 Ibid., p. 215.

65 Ibid., p. 216.

66 Ibid., p. 222.

67 Ibid., p. 227.

68 Ibid., p. 234.

69 Ibid., p. 235, my emphasis.

70 Ibid., p. 238.

71 Ibid., p. 250.

72 Ibid., p. 252. Vincent Wing (1619–68) was an English astrologer and astrono-mer. In 1649 he published *A Dreadful Prognostication* containing astrological predictions. His major work, *Astronomia Britannica* (1652; second edn 1669), was a complete compendium of astronomy on Copernican principles. Madden may well have been familiar with Wing's work, and refers to him as his 'learned friend' in Memoirs. He is also alluding to the long tradition of almanac-making. As an antidote to seemingly bogus almanac-makers, Swift, in January 1708 (as Isaac Bickerstaff), published his *Predictions for the Year 1708*, the initial instalment of his satirical attack on the astrologer and alma-nac-maker John Partridge. Conversely, Madden, in his references to political astrology and in his positive appraisal of Wing, is clearly presenting Wing as an almanac-maker and astrologer in a positive light.

73 Ibid., p. 507.

74 Ibid., p. 509.

75 Ibid., p. 513.

76 Ibid.

77 Ibid., p. 527.

78 Ibid., p. 2.

79 Ibid.

80 Ibid., p. 3.

81 Ibid.

82 Ibid., p. 5.

83 Ibid., p. 6.

84 Ibid., p. 8.

85 Ibid., p. 10.

86 Ibid., p. 13.

87 Ibid., p. 14.

88 Ibid., p. 17.

89 Ibid., p. 133.

90 Ibid., p. 136.

91   Ibid., p. 137.
92   Ibid., p. 138.
93   Ibid., pp. 138–9.
94   Ibid., p. 141.
95   Ibid., p. 142.
96   Ibid., p. 143.
97   Ibid., p. 145.
98   Ibid., p. 28.
99   Ibid., pp. 28–9.
100   Ibid., p. 29.
101   Ibid., p. 30.
102   Ibid.
103   Ibid.
104   Ibid., p. 34.
105   Ibid.
106   Ibid., p. 37.
107   Ibid.
108   Ibid., p. 40.
109   Ibid., p. 41.
110   Ibid., p. 42.
111   Ibid., p. 44.
112   Ibid.
113   Ibid., p. 47.
114   Ibid., pp. 49–50.
115   Ibid., pp. 51–2.
116   Ibid., p. 52.
117   Ibid.
118   Ibid.
119   Ibid.
120   Ibid., p. 99.
121   Ibid., p. 102.
122   Ibid., p. 99.
123   Ibid., p. 105.
124   Ibid., p. 106.
125   Ibid., p. 105.
126   Ibid., p. 55.
127   Ibid.
128   Ibid., p. 69.
129   Ibid., p. 72.
130   Ibid., p. 339.
131   Ibid., p. 80.
132   Ibid., p. 75.
133   Ibid., p. 78.
134   Ibid.

135 Ibid., p. 84.
136 Ibid., p. 85.
137 Ibid., p. 434.
138 Ibid.
139 Ibid.
140 Ibid., p. 423.
141 Ibid., p. 424.
142 Ibid.
143 Ibid.
144 Ibid., p. 425.
145 Madden, *A Proposal for the General Encouragement of Learning in Dublin-College*, p. 12.
146 Madden, *Memoirs of the Twentieth Century*, p. 425.
147 Ibid.
148 Ibid., p. 426.
149 Ibid., p. 309.
150 Ibid., p. 311.
151 Ibid.
152 Ibid., p. 313.
153 Ibid., p. 334.
154 Ibid., p. 475.
155 Ibid., p. 496.
156 Ibid., p. 495.
157 Ibid., p. 485.
158 Ibid.
159 Ibid., p. 486.
160 Ibid., p. 75.
161 Ibid.
162 Ibid.
163 Ibid., pp. 75–6.
164 Ibid., p. 77.
165 Ibid.
166 Ibid., p. 78.
167 Ibid.
168 Ibid.
169 Ibid., p. 79.
170 Ibid., p. 83.
171 Ibid., p. 80.
172 Ibid., p. 84.
173 Ibid., p. 85.
174 Ibid., p. 90.
175 Ibid., p. 289.
176 Ibid., p. 290.
177 Ibid.

178   Ibid., p. 291.
179   Ibid., p. 368.
180   Ibid., p. 371.
181   Ibid., p. 372.
182   Ibid.
183   Ibid.
184   Ibid., pp. 372–3.
185   Ibid., p. 373.
186   Ibid.
187   Ibid., p. 375.
188   Ibid., p. 379.
189   Quoted in Urstad, *Sir Robert Walpole's Poets*, p. 59.
190   Ibid.
191   Ibid., p. 90.
192   Ibid.
193   Ibid.
194   Eric S. Martin, H. Greenberg and Joseph D. Olander (eds), *No Place Else: explorations in utopian and dystopian fiction* (Carbondale, IL: Southern Illinois UP, 1983), p. vii.
195   Paul Alkon, *Origins of Futuristic Fiction* (Athens, GA: Georgia UP, 1987), p. 93.
196   Ibid., p. 96.
197   Ibid., p. 109.
198   Ibid., p. 197. See Peter Fitting, 'Utopia, Dystopia and Science Fiction', in Gregory Claeys (ed.), *The Cambridge Companion to Utopian Literature* (Cambridge: Cambridge University Press, 2010), p. 138. Mercier's work has often been noted as an inaugural time-travel Utopia, in which the narrator falls asleep and wakes up 700 years later in a transformed Paris.
199   Alkon, *Origins of Futuristic Fiction*, p. 3.
200   Samuel Madden, *A Letter to the Dublin Society, on the Improving Their Fund; and the Manufactures, Tillage, &c. in Ireland* (Dublin: printed by R. Reilly for G. Ewing, 1739), p. 2.
201   Ibid., p. 5.
202   Ibid., p. 6.
203   Ibid., p. 7.
204   Ibid., p. 8.
205   Ibid., p. 35.
206   Ibid., p. 49.
207   Ibid., p. 53.
208   The term '*Tír na nÓg* of intellect and imagination' was used by Seamus Heaney and applied by him to Vaclav Havel in an address given on 13 November 2003. I have taken his usage and applied it in an eighteenth-century Irish context to Samuel Madden.

Chapter 7

1   This poem is from *The Winding Stair and Other Poems* (London: Macmillan & Co., 1933). It is set in Lissadell, a late-Georgian house, home to the Gore-Booths. Political change was an integral feature of early twentieth-century Ireland. On the shift to national independence, I see this poem and, most notably, the lines quoted as representative of the unease that such change wrought. The hopeful visions for the future that Yeats represents as 'some vague utopia' (ll. 10–13) are ultimately those out of which an evolving independent Ireland, grappling with colonialism and its legacy, must emerge.

2   See E.T. Craig, *An Irish Commune: the history of Ralahine. Adapted from the Narrative of E.T. Craig, secretary and trustee of the association. With an introduction by George Russell (AE) and notes by Diarmuid Ó Cobhthaigh* (Dublin: Martin Lester, 1920), p. 80.

3   Edward Mangin, *Utopia Found: being an apology for Irish absentees addressed to a friend in Connaught. By an absentee residing in Bath* (Bath: Gye & Son, 1813), pp. 1–2.

4   Ibid., p. 14.

5   Ibid., p. 84.

6   John Banim, *Revelations of the Dead Alive* (London: W. Simpkin & R. Marshall, 1824), p. 7.

7   Ibid., p. 335.

8   Patrick Joseph Murray, *The Life of John Banim, the Irish Novelist, with Extracts from His Correspondence, General and Literary* (London: William Lay, 1857), p. 141.

9   James Connolly, 'An Irish Utopia', in *Labour in Ireland* (Dublin: Maunsel, 1922; republished Dublin: Irish Transport and General Workers' Union, 1944), p. 129.

10   Craig, *An Irish Commune*, p. 11.

11   Ibid., p. v.

12   Connolly, 'An Irish Utopia', p. 143.

13   James Connolly, *Labour in Irish History*, reproduced in idem., *Labour in Ireland* (Dublin: Maunsel, 1922; republished Dublin: Irish Transport and General Workers' Union, 1944), p. 143.

14   Æ [George Russell], *The National Being: some thoughts on an Irish polity* (Dublin and London: Maunsel, 1918), pp. 6–7.

Bibliography

Primary sources

Æ [George Russell], *The National Being: some thoughts on an Irish polity* (Dublin and London: Maunsel, 1918)

Anon., *A Dialogue Between Dean Swift and Thomas Prior in the Isles [sic] of St. Patrick's Church, Dublin, on that Memorable Day, October 9th 1753. By a friend to the peace and prosperity of Ireland* (Dublin: G. & A. Ewing, 1753)

____, [Advocate for Justice], *Oppression Unmasked: being a narrative of the proceedings in a case between a great corporation, and a little fishmonger, relative to some customs for fish, demanded by the former as legal, but refused by the latter, as exactions and extortions* (Dublin, 1784)

____, *A History of the Customs, Manners, and Religion of the Moon. To which are annexed several specimens of lunar poetry; and the characters of the most distinguished personages* (Dublin: John Hillary, 1782)

____, *A Letter to G...... W...... Esq; concerning the present condition of the college of Dublin, and the late disturbances that have been therein* (Dublin, 1734)

____, *A Letter from Utopia: with a character of the candidates for that famous metropolis* (Dublin, 1749)

____, *A List of the Members of the Dublin-Society, for the Improvement of Husbandry and Other Useful Arts, for the Year 1733* (printed by A. Rhames, printer to the Dublin Society, 1734)

____, *A Long Ramble, or Several Years Travels, in the Much Talk'd of, But Never Before Discovered, Wandering Island of O-Brazil, Containing a Full Description of that Whimsical Country* (London, 1712)

____, Book of the O'Lees [Book of Hy-Brasil], Royal Irish Academy MS 23 P10(ii): cat. no. 453

____, *Catalogue of Manuscripts, Books and Berkeleiana Exhibited in the Library of Trinity College Dublin on the Occasion of the Commemoration of the Bicentenary of the Death of George Berkeley, Held on 7–12 July 1953* (Dublin: Dublin University Press, 1953)

____, *Instructions for Planting and Managing Hops, and for Raising Hop-poles: drawn up and Published by Order of the Dublin Society* [attributed to Thomas Prior] (Dublin: A. Rhames, 1733)

____ [Lucas Bennet, pseudonym possibly used by Eliza Fowler Haywood], *Memoirs of the Court of Lilliput. Written by Captain Gulliver. Containing an account of the intrigues, and some other particular transactions of the nation, omitted in the two volumes of his travels. Published by Lucas Bennet, with a preface, showing how these papers fell into his hands* (Dublin: printed by S.P. for George Risk, George Ewing and William Smith, 1727)

____, *Some Thoughts on the Tillage of Ireland: humbly dedicated to the parliament* (Dublin, 1738)

_____, *Taciturna and Jocunda: or, Genius Alaciel's journey through those two islands. A satirical work*, written in English; trans. from French (London: printed for R. Withy & J. Cork)

_____, *The Antisatyrist. A dialogue. To which is prefixed, a short dissertation on Panegyric and Satyr* (Dublin: George Faulkner, 1750)

_____, *The Irish Blasters: or, the votaries of Bacchus* (Dublin: 1738), sometimes attributed to George Berkeley

_____, *The State Dunces Inscribed to Mr. Pope* (London: W. Dickenson, 1733)

_____, *The Reign of George VI, 1900–1925: a forecast written in the year 1763* (London: W. Nicholl, 1763; republished with preface and notes by C. Oman, London: Rivingtons, 1899), misattributed to Samuel Madden

_____, [William Pulteney, Earl of Bath], *A Fourth Letter from the Rt Hon W-----m P-----y, Esq: to the Rt. Hon. Sir R----t W-----e; with regard to the observations on the writings of the craftsman; being a continuation of remarks on the history of England from the minutes of Mr. Oldcastle* (1733)

_____, [William Pulteney, Earl of Bath], *A Letter from the Right Hon. W----m P------y, Esq: to the Right Honourable Sir R-----t W-----e; with regard to the observations on the writings of the craftsman* (1733)

Bacon, Francis, *The Works of Francis Bacon, Baron of Verulam, Viscount St. Albans, and Lord High Chancellor of England*, 10 vols (London: printed for W. Baynes & Son, 1824), vol. 2

Banim, John, *Revelations of the Dead-alive* (London: W. Simpkin & R. Marshall, 1824)

Beckett, Samuel, *Waiting for Godot* (London: Folio Society, 2000)

_____, *Dream of Fair to Middling Women*, eds E. O'Brien and E. Fournier (New York: Arcade Publishing; Dublin: Riverrun Press, 1992)

Berkeley, George, *A Proposal for the Better Supplying of Churches in Our Foreign Plantations, and for Converting the Savage Americans to Christianity, by a College to be Erected in the Summer Islands, Otherwise Called the Isles of Bermuda* (Dublin: George Grierson, 1725)

_____, *The Querist Containing Several Queries, Proposed to the Consideration of the Public*, in three parts (Dublin: printed by R. Reilly for G. Risk, G. Ewing and W. Smith, booksellers, 1735, 1736; printed by R. Reilly for J. Leathley, bookseller, 1737)

_____, *The Works of George Berkeley*, ed. J. Stock, 2 vols (Dublin: 1784)

_____, *The Works of George Berkeley D.D.; formerly bishop of Cloyne; including his posthumous works*, ed. Alexander Campbell Fraser, 4 vols (Oxford: Clarendon Press, 1901)

_____, *The Works of George Berkeley*. eds A.A. Luce and T.E. Jessop, 9 vols (London: Thomas Nelson & Sons, 1948–57)

Boyle, Robert, *Occasional Reflections Upon Several Subjects, Whereto is Premis'd a Discourse About Such Kinds of Thoughts* (London: W. Wilson for Henry Herringman, 1665)

Connolly, James, *Labour in Ireland: 1. Labour in Irish History; 2. The Reconquest of*

Ireland (Dublin: Maunsel, 1922; republished by Irish Transport and General Workers' Union, 1944, with intro. by Robert Lynd)

____, *Erin's Hope: the end and the means (first published 1897), and The New Evangel Preached to Irish Toilers (first published 1901)*, intro. Joseph Deasy (Dublin, Belfast: New Books Publications, 1972)

Corkery, Daniel, *I Bhreasail: a book of lyrics* (London: Elkin Mathews, 1921)

____, *The Hidden Ireland* (Dublin: Gill & Macmillan, 1967; first published 1924)

Cotgrave, Randle, *A Dictionarie of the French and English Tongues* (London: Adam Islip, 1611)

Cullen, Emily, *No Vague Utopia* (Galway: Annir Publishing, 2003)

Dobbs, Arthur, *An Essay on the Trade and Improvement of Ireland* (Dublin: A. Rhames, 1729–31)

Edge, John H., *An Irish Utopia: a story of a phase in the land problem* (Dublin: Hodges Figgis, 1906)

____, *Private Notes on the Second and Third Editions of* An Irish Utopia (1911)

Fortescue Hitchins and Samuel Drew (eds), *The History of Cornwall: from the earliest records and traditions to the present times*, vol. 11 (London: 1824)

Froude, J.A., *The English in Ireland in the Eighteenth Century*, 3 vols (1872–74)

Gavin, Antonio, *A Master-key to Popery. Containing, I. The Damages Which the Mass Causeth, & c. II. A Catalogue of Miracles Wrought by the Consecrated Wafer. III. The Miracles of Many Living Persons. IV. The Revelations of Three Nuns. V. The Life of the Good Primate, and Metropolitan Aragon, & c. Omitted in the Second Volume by the Reverend Mr. Gavin, & c* (Dublin: 1726)

[Gentleman, Francis], *A Trip to the Moon. Containing an account of the island of Noibla. Its inhabitants, religious and political customs, etc. by Sir Humphrey Lunatic, Bart*, 2 vols (vol. 1, York: printed by A. Ward for S. Crowder et al., 1764; vol. 2, London: printed for S. Crowder et al., 1765); reprinted in Jeanne Welcher and George E. Bush Jnr (eds), *Gulliveriana*, vol. 1 (Gainesville, FL: Scholars' Facsimiles and Reprints, 1970)

[____], *The Dramatic Censor: or, critical companion*, 2 vols (London: printed for J. Bell, London and C. Etherington, York, 1770)

[____], *The Favourite: an historical tragedy* (London: printed for J. Bell, London and C. Etherington, York, 1770)

[____], *The Theatres: a poetical dissection. By Sir Nicholas Nipclose, Baronet* (London: printed for J. Bell, 1772)

Godwin, Francis, *The Man in the Moone* (London: printed by John Norton for Joshua Kirton and Thomas Warren, 1638; Hereford: *Hereford Times*, 1959)

Goldsmith, Oliver, 'The Proceedings of Providence Vindicated. An eastern tale', *Royal Magazine*, December 1759, pp. 296–99. The index lists the title as 'Asem, the misanthrope, history of', republished without a title in his essays (London: printed for W. Griffin, 1765), pp. 126–39. Published separately as *Asem. The man-hater: an eastern tale* (London: Griffith & Farran, 1877)

Gregory, Lady Augusta, 'The Jester', in *The Wonder Plays* (London, New York: G.P. Putnam's Sons, 1923)

Gulliver, Martin, *The Censoriad* (1730)

Harrison, W. (ed.), *A History of the Isle of Man Written by William Blundell, 1648–56* (Douglas, Isle of Man: Manx Society, 1876)

Haywood, Eliza Fowler, *Memoirs of a Certain Island Adjacent to the Kingdom of Utopia. Written by a celebrated author of that country, now translated in English*, 2 vols (London: printed and sold by the booksellers of London and Westminster, 1725; Dublin: single volume for R. Gunne & P. Dugan, 1725; second edn, 2 vols: London: printed and sold by the booksellers of London and Westminster, 1726)

Head, Richard, *Hic et Ubique: or, the humours of Dublin: a comedy; acted privately with general applause* (London: printed by R.D. for the author, 1663)

____, *The English Rogue Described, in the Life of Meriton Latroon, a Witty Extravagent, Being a Compleat History of the Most Eminent Cheats of Both Sexes* (London: printed for Henry Marsh, 1665)

____, *The Floating Island: or, a new discovery relating the strange adventure on a late voyage from Lambethana to Villa Franca, alias Ramallia, to the eastward of Terra del Templo, by three ships, viz.* the Pay-naught, the Excuse, the Least-in-Sight, *under the conduct of Captain Robert Owe-much: describing the nature of the inhabitants, their religion, laws and customs, published by Frank Careless* [pseud.], *one of the discoverers* (1673); Francis Kirkman has been suggested as an alternative to Head as the author

____, *The Western Wonder; or, O Brazeel, an inchanted island discovered; with a relation of two ship-wracks in a dreadful Sea-storm in that discovery. To which is added, a description of a place, called, Montecapernia, relating the nature of the people, their qualities, humours, fashions, religion, &c.* (London: 1674)

____, *O-Brazile, or the Inchanted Island: being a perfect relation of the late discovery and wonderful dis-inchantment of an island on the north of Ireland: with an account of the riches and commodities thereof, communicated by a letter from London-Derry, to a friend in London* (London: 1675)

Heaney, Seamus, speech delivered at the presentation of the inaugural Amnesty International 'Ambassador of Conscience' Award to Vaclav Havel, 13 November 2003, Abbey Theatre, Dublin

Hesiod, *Works and Days*, trans. Jack Lindsay, in T.F. Higham and C.M. Bowra (eds), *The Oxford Book of Greek Verse in Translation* (Oxford: Clarendon Press, 1938)

Hogg, William, *The History of the Inchanted-Island of O'Brazile: giving an account of the country, religion, government, marriages, funerals, their customs, also of the strange birds and beasts that are there, and of his own landing in Galloway* (Dublin, 1724)

Hutchinson, John (ed.), *The Paradise*, catalogue of exhibition, nos 1–10, Douglas Hyde Gallery, Dublin (May 2001–January 2003)

Johnson, Samuel, *The Lives of the Most Eminent English Poets: with critical observations on their works*, 4 vols (London: printed for C. Bathurst, J. Buckland, W. Strahan et al., 1781)

Joyce, James, *Finnegans Wake* (London: Faber & Faber, 1939)

Larminie, William, *Glanlua and Other Poems* (London: Kegan Paul, Trench & Co., 1889)

Lecky, W.E.H., *A History of Ireland in the Eighteenth Century*, 5 vols (London: Longmans, Green & Co., 1892–1896)

Llanover, the Rt Hon. Lady (ed.), *Autobiography and Correspondence of Mary Granville, Mrs. Delany*, vols 1–6 (London: Richard Bentley, 1861–62)

Locke, John, *An Essay Concerning Human Understanding* [1689], ed. Peter H. Nidditch (Oxford: Oxford University Press, 1975)

_____, *Two Treatises on Government*, ed. Peter Laslett (Cambridge: Cambridge University Press, 1967)

Luce, A.A., 'Berkeley's Bermuda Project and His Benefactions to American Universities, with Unpublished Letters and Extracts from the Egmont Papers', *Proceedings of the Royal Irish Academy*, vol. 42, sect. C (1934), read 14 May 1934, published 22 August 1934 (Dublin: Hodges, Figgis & Co., 1934; London: Williams & Norgate, 1935)

Luce, J.V., 'Dublin Societies Before the R.D.S', a discourse delivered at a joint meeting of the Royal Dublin Society and the Dublin Philosophical Society on 10 December 1981 (Dublin: Royal Dublin Society, 1981)

MacNeice, Louis, *Holes in the Sky: poems 1944–1947* (London: Faber & Faber, 1948)

MacSparran, James, *America Dissected, Being a Full and True Account of All the American Colonies* (Dublin: S. Powell, 1753)

Madden, Richard Robert, *The History of Irish Periodical Literature, from the End of the 17th Century to the Middle of the 19th Century, its Origin, Progress, and Results: with notices of remarkable persons connected with the press in Ireland during the past two centuries*, vol. 11 (London: T.C. Newby, 1867)

Madden, Samuel, *Themistocles, the Lover of His Country* (Dublin: printed by S. Powell for George Risk, George Ewing & William Smith, 1729)

_____, *A Proposal for the General Encouragement of Learning in Dublin-College. Dedicated to His Grace the lord primate: and humbly offer'd to the consideration of all that wish well to Ireland.* second edn (Dublin: George Faulkner, 1732)

Madden, Samuel, *Memoirs of the Twentieth Century. Being original letters of state, under George the Sixth: relating to the most important events in Great-Britain and Europe, as to Church and state, arts and sciences, trade, taxes, and treaties, peace, and war: and characters of the greatest persons of those times; from the middle of the eighteenth, to the end of the twentieth century, and the world. Received and revealed in the year 1728; and now published, for the instruction of all eminent statesmen, churchmen, patriots, politicians, projectors, papists and Protestants* (London: printed for Osborn, Longman, Davis & Battey et al., 1733)

_____, *Memoirs of the Twentieth Century Being Original Letters of State under George the Sixth. With a new introduction for the Garland edition by Malcolm J. Bosse* (New York and London: Garland, 1972)

_____, *Reflections and Resolutions Proper for the Gentlemen of Ireland, as to Their Conduct for the Service of Their Country, as Landlords, as Masters of Families, as Protestants, as Descended from British Ancestors, as Country Gentlemen and Farmers, as Justices of the Peace, as Merchants, as Members of Parliament* (Dublin: printed by R. Reilly, 1738)

____, *A Letter to the Dublin Society on the Improving Their Fund; and the Manufactures, Tillage, &c. in Ireland* (Dublin: printed by R. Reilly for G. Ewing, 1739)

Maginn, William, *Whitehall: or the days of George IV* (London: William Marsh, 1827)

Mangin, Edward, *Utopia Found: being an apology for Irish absentees. Addressed to a friend in Connaught. By an absentee residing in Bath* (Bath: Gye & Son, 1813)

Maple, William, *A Method of Tanning Without Bark* (Dublin: A. Rhames, 1729)

McDermot, Murtagh, *A Trip to the Moon. Containing some observations and reflections, made by him during his stay in that planet, upon the manners of the inhabitants* (Dublin: Christopher Dickson, 1727; reprinted in London for J. Roberts, 1728)

McKenna, Stephen, *Et In Arcadia Ego*, exhibition catalogue, Douglas Hyde Gallery, Dublin (7 February–29 March 2003)

McWilliams, Brendan, 'Privateer's Life Was a Blueprint for Fiction', *Irish Times*, 24 March 2004)

Méliès, Georges (dir.), *Le Voyage dans la Lune [A Trip to the Moon]* (1902), silent film

Mercier, Louis Sébastien, *Memoirs of the Year Two Thousand Five Hundred*, trans. W. Hooper, MD (Dublin: W. Wilson, 1772)

Mitchel, John, *Jail Journal* (Dublin: M.H. Gill, 1913)

Molyneux, Capel, *An Account of the Family and Descendants of Sir Thomas Molyneux, Kt., Chancellor of the Exchequer in Ireland to Queen Elizabeth* (Evesham: privately printed, 1820)

More, Thomas, *Utopia: the complete works of St. Thomas More*, English translation, vol. 4, eds Edward Surtz, S.J. and J.H. Hexter (New Haven, CT: Yale University Press, 1965)

Morris, William, *News from Nowhere* (reprinted London: Reeves & Turner, 1890)

Nichols, John, *Literary Anecdotes of the Eighteenth Century*, 9 vols (London: printed for the author by Nichols, Son & Bentley, 1812–15); facsimile edn edited by Colin Clair (London: Centaur Press Ltd, 1967)

____, *Literary Anecdotes of the Eighteenth Century. Comprizing biographical memoirs of William Bowyer, printer, F.S.A., and many of his learned friends*, vol. 3 (Cambridge: Cambridge University Press, 2014)

Ó Colmáin, Domhnall, *Párliament na mBan [The Parliament of Women]* (c. 1703), in *Field Day Anthology of Irish Literature: Vols 4–5: Irish Women's Writings and Tradition* (Cork: Cork University Press in association with Field Day, 2002)

O'Donnel, Manus, *A Voyage to O'Brazeel: or, the sub-marine island. Giving a brief description and a short account of the customs, manners, government, law, and religion of the inhabitants* (*Ulster Miscellany*, 1753)

O'Faolain, Sean, *An Irish Journey with Illustrations by Paul Henry* (London: Longmans, Green & Co. Ltd, 1940)

O'Flaherty, Roderic, *A Chorographical Description of West or H-Iar Connaught* (Dublin: M.H. Gill, 1846)

____, *Ogygia, or, a Chronological Account of Irish Events*, 3 vols (Dublin: W. M'Kenzie and G. Faulkner, 1775/1793)

O'Grady, Standish James, *Sun and Wind* (Dublin: University College Dublin Press, 2004; first published 1928)

Ó hÓgáin, Dáithí, *Cogar: ar thóir Hy Brasil*, TG4 documentary (2006)

Ovid, *Metamorphoses*, vol. 1, trans. Mary M. Innes (Harmondsworth: Penguin, 1955)

Plaine, Timothy, *Tom Tell-Truth, of the Island of Utopia's Letter to Mr. Nobody, Num. 1. Newly translated from the Utopian language* (Dublin, 1737)

Plato, *The Republic*, trans. R. Waterfield (Oxford: Oxford University Press, 1993)

Pope, Alexander, *Of the Use of Riches: an epistle to the Right Honourable Allen Lord Bathurst* (London: reprinted in Dublin by and for George Faulkner, 1733)

_____, 'Epilogue to the *Satires*', dialogue 11 in *Pope: poetical works*, ed. H. Davis (Oxford: Oxford University Press, 1966)

Porter, Noah, *The Two-hundredth Birthday of Bishop George Berkeley: a discourse given at Yale College on 12th March 1885* (New York: Charles Scribner's Sons, 1885)

Prior, Thomas, *A List of the Absentees of Ireland, and the Yearly Value of Their Estates and Incomes Spent Abroad. With Observations on the Present Trade and Condition of That Kingdom* (Dublin: printed for R. Gunne, 1729)

_____, *Observations on Coin in General: with some proposals for regulating the value of coin in Ireland* (Dublin: printed by A. Rhames for R. Gunne, 1729)

Raspe, Erich Rudolf [Baron Munchausen], *Gulliver Revived: containing singular travels, campaigns, voyages, and adventures in Russia, the Caspian Sea, Iceland, Turkey, Egypt, Gibraltar, up the Mediterranean, on the Atlantic Ocean, and through the centre of Mount Etna into the South Sea: also an account of a voyage into the moon and Dog-Star, with many extraordinary particulars, relative to the cooking animal in those planets, which are here called the human species* (Dublin: P. Byrne, Grafton Street, 1788)

Roche, Charles Francois de la Tiphaigne, *Giphantia: or, a view of what has passed, what is now passing, and during the present century what will pass in the world* (London: printed for Robert Horsfield, 1761)

Sheridan, Richard Brinsley, *The School for Scandal and Other Plays*, ed. Michael Cordner (Oxford: Oxford University Press, 1998)

Skelton, Philip, *A Letter to the Authors of Divine Analogy, and of the Minute Philosophers from an Officer* (Dublin, 1733)

Smedley, Jonathan, *Gulliveriana: or, a fourth volume of miscellanies: being a sequel of the three volumes published by Pope and Swift: to which is added, Alexanderiana; or, a comparison between the ecclesiastical and poetical Pope: and many things, in verse and prose, relating to the latter: with an ample preface; and a critique on the third volume of miscellanies lately publish'd by those two facetious writers* (London: J. Roberts, 1728)

Stoppard, Tom, *The Coast of Utopia: Part I: Voyage; Part II: Shipwreck; Part III: Salvage* (London: Faber & Faber, 2002)

Swift, Jonathan, *A Tale of A Tub. Written for the universal improvement of mankind. To which is added, an account of a battel between the antient and modern books in St. James's Library. The second edition corrected* (London: John Nutt, 1704)

_____, *Gulliver's Travels*, ed. Robert Demaria Jnr (London: Penguin, 2003)

_____, *The Works of Jonathan Swift*, ed. W. Scott, 19 vols (London: Bickers & Son, 1883)

____, *The Prose Works of Jonathan Swift*, ed. Herbert Davis, 14 vols (Oxford: Basil Blackwell, 1939–68)

____, *The Tale of a Tub and Other Works by Jonathan Swift*, ed. Henry Morley (London: Carlsbrooke Library, George Routledge & Sons, 1889)

____, *The Writings of Jonathan Swift*, eds Robert A. Greenberg and William B. Piper (New York: W.W. Norton & Co, 1973)

____, *The Drapier's Letters to the People of Ireland*, ed. Herbert Davis (Oxford: Clarendon Press, 1935)

____, *The Correspondence of Jonathan Swift*, ed. F.E. Ball, 6 vols (London: 1910–1914), vol. 3

____, *The Correspondence of Jonathan Swift*, ed. Harold Williams, vol. 1 (Oxford: Clarendon Press, 1963)

Thinking Allowed, 'Utopia', BBC Radio 4, 3 January 2011

Tone, Theobald Wolfe, *The Life of Theobald Wolfe Tone: written by himself, and continued by his son; with his political writings, and fragments of his diary, whilst agent to the general and sub-committee of the Catholics of Ireland, and secretary to the delegation who presented their petition to His Majesty George III. Edited by his son, William Theobald Wolfe Tone in two volumes* (Washington: Gales & Seaton, 1826)

Townley, Richard, *A Journal kept in the Isle of Man, Giving an Account of the Wind and Weather, and Daily Occurrences, for Upwards of Eleven Months: with observations on the soil, clime and natural productions of the island* (Whitehaven: J. Ware, 1791)

Twiss, Richard, *A Tour in Ireland in 1775*, third edn (Dublin: printed for Sheppard, Corcoran, Potts et al., 1777)

Updike, Wilkins, *A History of the Episcopal Church in Narragansett, Rhode Island (volume 1, pt 1): including a history of other Episcopal Churches in the state* (New York: Onderdonk, 1847)

Webb, Alfred, *A Compendium of Irish Biography Comprising Sketches of Distinguished Irishmen, Eminent Persons Connected with Ireland by Office or by their Writings* (Dublin: M.H. Gill & Son, 1878)

Westropp, Thomas Johnson, 'Brasil and the Legendary Islands of the North Atlantic: their history and fable. A contribution to the "Atlantis" problem', *Proceedings of the Royal Irish Academy*, vol. 30, sect. C, read 10 June 1912, published 12 August 1912 (Dublin: Hodges, Figgis, 1912)

Whately, Richard, *Account of an Expedition to the Interior of New Holland*, ed. Lady Mary Fox (London: Richard Bentley, 1837), reprinted in Gregory Claeys (ed.), *Modern British Utopias, 1700–1850*, 8 vols (London: Pickering & Chatto, 1997), vol. 7

____, 'A Lost Leaf of Gulliver's Travels': *Miscellaneous remains from the commonplace book of Richard Whately, D.D. late archbishop of Dublin, being a collection of notes and essays made during the preparation of his various works*, ed. Miss E.J. Whately, new edition with additions (London: Longman, Green, Longman, Roberts & Green, 1865)

Wilson, Henry Charles, *Swiftiana* (London: R. Phillips, 1804)

Winstanley, William, *The Lives of the Most Famous English Poets, 1687: a facsimile reproduction with an introduction by William Riley Parker* (Gainesville, FL: Scholars Facsimiles & Reprints, 1963)

____ [attributed to Winstanley], *Poor Robin's Vision: wherein is described, the present humours of the times; the vices and fashionable fopperies thereof; and after what manner men are punished for them hereafter; discovered in a dream* (London: printed for and sold by Arthur Boldero, 1677)

Wood-Martin, W.G., *Traces of the Elder Faiths of Ireland: a folklore sketch: a handbook of Irish pre-Christian tradition*, 2 vols (London: Longmans, Green & Co., 1902)

Wordsworth, William, *The Complete Poetical Works* (London: Macmillan and Co., 1888)

Yeats, William Butler, *The Wanderings of Oisin and Other Poems* (London: Kegan Paul & Trench, 1889)

Younge, Lewis Henry, *Utopia: or, Apollo's golden days* (Dublin: George Faulkner, 1747)

Young, Arthur, *A Tour in Ireland, 1776–1779* (London: Cassell & Company, 1887)

Secondary sources

Adams, John, 'Outer Space and the New World in the Imagination of Eighteenth-century Europeans', *Eighteenth Century Life*, vol. 19, no. 1 (1995)

Aldiss, Brian, *Billion Year Spree: the history of science fiction* (London: Corgi, 1975)

Alkon, Paul, *Origins of Futuristic Fiction* (Athens, GA: Georgia UP, 1987)

Andrews, Charles M., 'Introduction', in various authors (Rousseau, More, Bacon and Campanella), *Famous Utopias: being the complete text of Rousseau's Social Contract, More's Utopia, Bacon's New Atlantis, Campanella's City of the Sun* (New York: Tudor Publishing Company, n.d)

Appadurai, Arjun, *Modernity at Large: cultural dimensions of globalization* (Minneapolis, MN: University of Minnesota Press, 1998)

Appelbaum, Robert, *Literature and Utopian Politics in Seventeenth-century England* (Cambridge: Cambridge University Press, 2002)

Ashe, Geoffrey, *Land to the West: St. Brendan's voyage to America* (New York: Viking, 1962)

Aviles Ramiro, Miquel A. and J.C. Davis (eds), *Utopian Moments* (London: Bloomsbury Academic, 2012)

Babcock, William H. *Legendary Islands of the Atlantic: a study in medieval geography* (New York: American Geographical Society, 1922)

Balasopoulos, Antonis, 'Unworldly Worldliness: America and the trajectories of utopian expansionism', *Utopian Studies*, vol. 15, no. 2 (2004)

Balderston, Katharine (ed.), *The Collected Letters of Oliver Goldsmith* (Cambridge: Cambridge University Press, 1928)

Barnard, Toby, *The Kingdom of Ireland, 1641–1760* (Houndmills: Palgrave Macmillan, 2004)

____, *Improving Ireland? Projectors, prophets and pamphleteers, 1641–1786* (Dublin: Four Courts Press, 2008)

_____, 'St Patrick's Cathedral in the Age of Swift, 1690–1745', in John Crawford and Raymond Gillespie (eds), *St Patrick's Cathedral, Dublin: a history* (Dublin: Four Courts Press, 2009)

Barthes, Roland, 'The Death of the Author', in *The Rustle of Language*, trans. Richard Howard (Oxford: Basil Blackwell, 1986)

Bartlett, Thomas, David Dickson, Dáire Keogh and Kevin Whelan (eds), *1798: a bicentenary perspective* (Dublin: Four Courts Press, 2003)

Bauman, Zygmunt, *Liquid Modernity* (Cambridge: Polity Press, 2000)

Baumgardt, Carola, *Johannes Kepler: life and letters* (New York: Philosophical Library, 1951)

Bayly, Christopher, *Imperial Meridian: the British Empire and the world, 1780–1830* (London: Longman, 1989)

Benedict, Barbara M., 'Readers, Writers, Reviewers', in Thomas Keymer and Jon Mee (eds), *The Cambridge Companion to English Literature, 1740–1830* (Cambridge: Cambridge University Press, 2004)

Benjamin, Walter, *Illuminations*, intro. Hannah Arendt, trans. Harry Zohn (London: Fontana, 1992)

Benson, Charles and Siobhán Fitzpatrick (eds), *That Woman! Studies in Irish bibliography. A festschrift for Mary 'Paul' Pollard* (Dublin: Lilliput Press for the Library Association of Ireland, Rare Books Group, 2005)

Berman, David, *Berkeley and Irish Philosophy* (London: Continuum, 2005)

_____, *George Berkeley: Idealism and the Man* (Oxford: Clarendon, 1994)

Berman, David, 'George Berkeley: pictures by Goldsmith, Yeats, Luce', *Heramathena*, vol. 139 (Winter 1985)

_____, 'Frances Hutcheson on Berkeley and the Molyneux Problem', *Proceedings of the Royal Irish Academy*, vol. 74, sect. C (1974)

Berneri, Marie Louise, *Journey through Utopia* (London: Freedom Press, 1982)

Berry, Henry F., *A History of the Royal Dublin Society* (London: Longmans, Green and Co., 1915)

Bestor, Arthur Eugene, *Backwoods Utopias: the sectarian and Owenite phases of communitarian socialism in America, 1663–1829* (Philadelphia: University of Pennsylvania Press, 1950; second edn 1970)

Black, Jeremy, *Robert Walpole and the Nature of Politics in Early Eighteenth-entury Britain* (London: Macmillan, 1990)

Blake, James J., 'Yeats, Oisín and Irish Gaelic Literature', in Brigit Bramsbäck and Martin Croghan (eds), *Anglo-Irish and Irish Literature: aspects of language and culture*, vol. 1 (Uppsala: University of Uppsala, 1988)

Bliss, Alan (ed.), *A Dialogue in Hybernian Stile Between A & B & Irish Eloquence by Jonathan Swift* (Dublin: Cadenus Press, 1977)

Bloch, Ernst, *The Principle of Hope*, trans. Neville Plaice and Stephen Plaice (Berkeley: University of California, 1991)

Bourke, Eoin (ed.), *Poor Green Erin: German travel writers' narratives on Ireland from before the 1798 rising to after the Great Famine* (Frankfurt am Main: Peter Lang, 2012)

Boyce, George, Robert Eccleshall and Vincent Geoghegan (eds), *Political Thought in Ireland Since the Seventeenth Century* (London: Routledge, 1993)
____ and Alan O'Day (eds), *The Making of Modern Irish History Revisionism and the Revisionist Controversy* (London: Routledge, 1996)
Boyle, Frank T., 'Chinese Utopianism and Gulliverian Narcissism in Swift's Travels', in Aileen Douglas, Patrick Kelly and Ian Ross (eds), *Locating Swift* (Dublin: Four Courts Press, 1998)
Brady, Ciaran, *James Anthony Froude: an intellectual biography of a Victorian prophet* (Oxford: Oxford University Press, 2013)
Brady, Joseph and Anngret Simms (eds), *Dublin Through Space and Time (c. 900–1900)* (Dublin: Four Courts Press, 2002)
Bramsbäck, Brigit and Martin Croghan (eds), *Anglo-Irish and Irish Literature: aspects of language and culture. Proceedings of the ninth international congress of the International Association for the Study of Anglo-Irish Literature*, Uppsala University, 4–7 August 1986, 2 vols
Brearton, Fran and Eamonn Hughes (eds), *Last Before America: Irish and American writing: essays in honour of Michael Allen* (Belfast: Blackstaff Press, 2001)
Brown, Michael, 'Configuring the Irish Enlightenment: reading *the Transactions of the Royal Irish Academy*', in James Kelly and Martyn J. Powell (eds), *Clubs and Societies in Eighteenth-century Ireland* (Dublin: Four Courts Press, 2010)
Burgh, James, 'An Account of the First Settlement, Laws, Form of Government, and Police, of the Cessares, A People of South America (1764)', in Gregory Claeys (ed.), *Utopias of the British Enlightenment* (Cambridge: Cambridge University Press, 1994)
Burke, Mary, 'Hy-Brasil', in David Marcus (ed.), *The Faber Book of Best New Irish Short Stories, 2004–2005* (London: Faber & Faber, 2005)
Calvino, Italo, *The Uses of Literature* (New York: Harcourt Brace & Company, 1986)
Campbell, W.E., 'The Utopia of Sir Thomas More', in Richard O'Sullivan (ed.), *The King's Good Servant: papers read to the Thomas More Society of London* (Oxford: Basil Blackwell, 1948)
Cantarino, Geraldo, 'An Island Called Brazil', *History Ireland*, vol. 16, no. 4 (July/August 2008)
Carpenter, Andrew (ed.), *Verse in English from Tudor and Stuart Ireland* (Cork: Cork University Press, 2003)
Chart, D.A. (ed.), *The Drennan Letters: being a selection from the correspondence which passed between William Drennan, M.D. and his brother-in-law and sister Samuel and Martha McTier. During the years 1776–1819* (Belfast: His Majesty's Stationery Office, 1931)
Claeys, Gregory (ed.), *Utopias of the British Enlightenment* (Cambridge: Cambridge University Press, 1994)
____ (ed.), *The Cambridge Companion to Utopian Literature* (Cambridge: Cambridge University Press, 2010)
____, *Searching for Utopia: the history of an idea* (London: Thames & Hudson, 2011)
____ and Lyman Tower Sargent (eds), *The Utopia Reader* (New York: New York University Press, 1999)

Clarke, Desmond, *Thomas Prior, 1681–1751: founder of the Royal Dublin Society* (Dublin: published for the Royal Dublin Society by At the Sign of the Three Candles, 1951)

Cochrane, Rexmond C., 'Bishop Berkeley and the Progress of Arts and Learning: notes on a literary convention', *Huntington Library Quarterly*, vol. 17, no. 3 (1953–54)

Coimín, Micheál, *Laoi Oisín ar Tír na nÓg* [*The Lay of Oisín in the Land of Youth*], ed. Tomás Ó Flannghaile (London: City of London Book Depot; Dublin: M.H. Gill & Son, 1896)

Connolly, Claire, *A Cultural History of the Irish Novel, 1790–1829* (Cambridge: Cambridge University Press, 2012)

Connolly, S.J., *Religion, Law, and Power: the making of Protestant Ireland, 1660–1760* (Oxford: Clarendon Press, 1995; originally published 1992)

_____, 'Eighteenth-century Ireland: colony or *ancien regime?*', in D. George Boyce and Alan O'Day (eds), *The Making of Modern Irish History Revisionism and the Revisionist Controversy* (London: Routledge, 1996)

Connolly, S.J. *Divided Kingdom: Ireland, 1630–1800* (Oxford: Oxford University Press, 2008)

Coombes, James, *Utopia in Glandore* (Butlerstown, Co. Cork: Muintir na Tíre, 1970)

Coxe, William, *Memoirs of the Life and Administration of Sir Robert Walpole, Earl of Oxford. With original correspondence and authentic papers, never before published, in three volumes. Volume the third: Containing the Correspondence from 1730 to 1745* (London: printed for T. Cadell and W. Davies, 1798)

Craig, E.T., 'Early History of Co-operation', *Co-operative News*, no. 16 (1888)

_____, *An Irish Commune: the history of Ralahine. Adapted from the narrative of E.T. Craig, secretary and trustee of the association. With an introduction by George Russell (AE) and notes by Diarmuid Ó Cobhthaigh* (Dublin: Martin Lester, 1920)

_____, *An Irish Commune: the experiment at Ralahine, Co. Clare, with essays by James Connolly (1910) and Cormac Ó Gráda (1974)* (Dublin: Irish Academic Press, 1983)

Crane, Verner W., 'A Lost Utopia of the First American Frontier', *Sewanee Review*, vol. 27, no. 1 (1919)

Crawford, John and Raymond Gillespie (eds), *St. Patrick's Cathedral, Dublin: a history* (Dublin: Four Courts Press, 2009)

Cronin, James, 'An "Island" of Cosmopolitan Culture: Anson's voyage round the world and the library at Bowen's Court, Co. Cork', *History Ireland*, vol. 5, no. 19 (2011)

Crookshank, Ann and David Webb, *Paintings and Sculptures in Trinity College Dublin* (Dublin: Trinity College Dublin Press, 1990)

Cullen, Fintan (ed.), *Sources in Irish Art: a reader* (Cork: Cork University Press, 2000)

Cunningham, Graham R.B., *A Vanished Arcadia: being some account of the Jesuits in Paraguay, 1607–1767 (first published in 1901). With an introduction by Philip Healy* (London: Century, 1988)

Davis, J.C., *Utopia and the Ideal Society: a study of English utopian writing, 1516–1700* (Cambridge: Cambridge University Press, 1981)

_____, 'Thomas More's *Utopia*: sources, legacy and interpretation', in Gregory Claeys (ed.), *The Cambridge Companion to Utopian Literature* (Cambridge: Cambridge University Press, 2010)

Day, Angélique (ed.), *The Correspondence of Mary Delany, 1731–68: letters from Georgian Ireland* (Belfast: Friar's Bush Press, 1991)

de Búrca, Éamonn, *The Three Candles Collection: a bibliographical catalogue* (Áth Cliath: de Búrca, 1998)

Degerando, Joseph-Marie, 'Considérations sur les Divers Methods á Suivre dans l'Observation des Peuples Sauvages', in Jean Copans and Jean Jamin (eds), *Aux Origins de l'Anthropologies Française. Les Mémoires de la Société des Observateurs de l'Homme* (Paris, 1978)

Delumeau, Jean, *History of Paradise: the Garden of Eden in myth and tradition* (Chicago, IL: University of Illinois Press, 2000)

Dickson, David, *Old World Colony: Cork and South Munster, 1630–1830* (Cork: Cork University Press, 2005)

_____ and Cormac Ó Gráda, *Refiguring Ireland* (Dublin: Lilliput Press, 2003)

Dooley, Dolores, *Equality in Community: sexual equality in the writings of William Thompson and Anna Doyle Wheeler* (Cork: Cork University Press, 1996)

Donnelly, J.S. and Kerby A. Miller (eds), *Irish Popular Culture, 1650–1850* (Dublin: Irish Academic Press, 1998)

Donner, H.W., *Introduction to Utopia* (London: Sidgwick & Jackson, 1945)

Donoghue, Denis (ed.), *We Irish* (Berkeley, CA: University of California Press, 1986)

Douglas, Aileen, Patrick Kelly and Ian Ross (eds), *Locating Swift: essays from Dublin on the 250th anniversary of the death of Jonathan Swift, 1667–1745* (Dublin: Four Courts Press, 1998)

Duddy, Thomas, *A History of Irish Thought* (London: Routledge, 2002)

Dudley Edwards, Ruth, *Patrick Pearse: the triumph of failure* (London: Victor Gollancz, 1977)

Durey, Michael, *Transatlantic Radicals and the Early American Republic* (Lawrence, KS: University Press of Kansas, 1997)

Dutton, Jacqueline, '"Non-western" Utopian Traditions', in Gregory Claeys (ed.), *The Cambridge Companion to Utopian Literature* (Cambridge: Cambridge University Press, 2010)

Eagleton, Terry, 'The Irish Sublime', speech, University of Limerick, November 2003

Edmond, Rod and Vanessa Smith (eds), *Islands in History and Representation* (London: Routledge, 2003)

Ehrenpreis, Irvin, *Swift the Man, His Works and the Age. Vol. One: Mr. Swift and his Contemporaries* (London: Methuen, 1962)

Elliot, Marianne, *Partners in Revolution: the United Irishmen and France* (New Haven, CT and London: Yale University Press, 1982)

_____, *Wolfe Tone: prophet of Irish independence* (New Haven, CT and London: Yale University Press, 1989)

Elliott, Robert, *The Power of Satire: magic, ritual, art* (New Jersey: Princeton University Press, 1960)

Engel, Morris S., *Wittgenstein's Doctrine of the Tyranny of Language: a historical and critical examination of his Blue Book* (The Hague: Martinus Nijhoff, 1975)

Evans, J.E. and J.N. Wall (eds), *A Guide to Prose Fiction in* The Tatler *and* The Spectator (New York: Garland Pub, 1977)

Fabricant, Carole, 'George Berkeley the Islander: some reflections on Utopia, race, and tar-water', in Felicity A. Nussbaum (ed.), *The Global Eighteenth Century* (Baltimore, MD: Johns Hopkins University Press, 2003)

_____, 'Eighteenth-century Travel Literature', in John Richetti (ed.), *The Cambridge History of English Literature, 1660–1780* (Cambridge: Cambridge University Press, 2005)

Fabricant, Carole and Robert Mahony (eds), *Swift's Irish Writings: selected prose and poetry* (London: Palgrave Macmillan, 2010)

Fanning, Bryan, 'Patrick Pearse Predicts the Future', *Dublin Review of Books*, www.drb.ie/essays/patrick-pearse-predicts-the-future (accessed 24 May 2015)

Fiennes, William, *The Snow Geese* (London: Picador, 2002)

Firestone, Clark B., *The Coasts of Illusion: a study of travel tales* (New York: Harper, 1924)

Fischer, Joachim, '"Kultur – and our need of it": the image of Germany and Irish national identity, 1890–1920', *Irish Review*, no. 24 (1999)

Fitting, Peter, 'Utopian Effect/Utopian Pleasure', *Utopian Studies*, vol. 4 (1991)

_____, 'Urban Planning/Utopian Dreaming: Le Corbusier's Chandigarh today', *Utopian Studies*, vol. 13, no. 1 (2002)

_____, 'Narrating Utopian Space', *Science Fiction Studies*, vol. 30 (2003)

_____, 'A Short History of Utopian Studies', *Science Fiction Studies*, vol. 36, no. 1 (2009)

_____, 'Utopia, Dystopia and Science Fiction', in Gregory Claeys (ed.), *The Cambridge Companion to Utopian Literature* (Cambridge: Cambridge University Press, 2010)

Flannery, Eóin and Angus Mitchell (eds), *Enemies of Empire* (Dublin: Four Courts Press, 2007)

_____, *Ireland and Postcolonial Studies: theory, discourse, Utopia* (Houndmills: Palgrave Macmillan, 2009)

Foster, R.F., *Vivid Faces: the revolutionary generation in Ireland, 1890–1923* (London: Allen Lane, 2014)

France, Peter (ed.), *The New Oxford Companion to Literature in French* (Oxford: Clarendon Press, 1995)

Freitag, Barbara, *Hy Brasil: the metamorphosis of an island from cartographic error to Celtic Elysium* (Amsterdam and New York: Rodopi, 2013)

_____, 'The Discovery of an Imaginary Island: Irish fiction visits Hy Brasil', in Sandra Mayer, Julia Novak and Margarete Rubik (eds), *Ireland: in drama, film and popular culture* (Trier: WVT, 2012)

Friedman, Arthur (ed.), *The Collected Works of Oliver Goldsmith*, 5 vols (Oxford: Clarendon Press, 1966)

Frye, Northrop, 'Varieties of Literary Utopias', in Frank E. Manuel (ed.), *Utopias and*

Utopian Thought (Boston, MA: Beacon Press, 1965; reprinted London: Souvenir Press, 1973)

Fuentes, Carlos, 'This is America', in Carol Christensen and Thomas Christensen (eds), *The Discovery of America and Other Myths: a New World reader* (San Francisco, CA: Chronicle Books, 1992)

Garnett, R.G., *Co-operation and the Owenite Socialist Communities in Britain, 1825– 45* (Manchester: Manchester University Press, 1972)

Gaustad, Edwin, *George Berkeley in America* (New Haven, CT and London: Yale University Press, 1979)

Geoghegan, Vincent, *Utopianism and Marxism* (London: Methuen, 1987)

_____, 'Remembering the Future', *Utopian Studies*, vol. 1, no. 2 (1990)

Geoghegan, Vincent, 'Ralahine: an Irish Owenite community (1831–1833)', *International Review of Social History*, vol. 36, no. 3 (1991)

Gilbert, J.T., *A History of the City of Dublin,* 3 vols (Dublin, London, Edinburgh: McGlashan, Orr, Menzies, 1854–59)

Gillis, John, *Islands of the Mind* (New York: Palgrave, 2004)

_____, 'Taking History Offshore: Atlantic islands in European minds, 1400–1800', in Rod Edmond and Vanessa Smith (eds), *Islands in History and Representation* (London: Routledge, 2003)

Goldgar, Bertrand A., *Walpole and the Wits: the relation of politics to literature, 1722– 1742* (Lincoln: University of Nebraska Press, 1976)

_____, *The Philosophy of Utopia* (London: Routledge, 2001)

Gove, Philip B., *The Imaginary Voyage in Prose Fiction: a history of its criticism and a guide for its study, with an annotated check list of 215 imaginary voyages from 1700 to 1800* (New York: Columbia University Press, 1941)

Graham, Colin, *Deconstructing Ireland* (Edinburgh: Edinburgh University Press, 2001)

Graham, Gargett and Geraldine Sheridan (eds), *Ireland and the French Enlightenment, 1700–1800* (London: Macmillan, 1999)

Green Stopford, Alice, *The Making of Ireland and its Undoing, 1200–1600* (Dublin and London: Maunsel & Company Ltd, 1920)

Griffin, Dustin, *Authorship in the Long Eighteenth Century* (Newark, DE: University of Delaware Press, 2014)

_____, *Satirists in Dialogue* (Cambridge: Cambridge University Press, 2010)

Griffin, Michael, 'Oliver Goldsmith and François-Ignace Espiard de la Borde: an instance of plagiarism', *Review of English Studies*, new ser., vol. 50, no. 197 (1999)

_____, 'Delicate Allegories, Deceitful Mazes: Goldsmith's landscapes', *Eighteenth-Century Ireland: Iris an dá Chultúr*, vol. 16 (2001)

_____, 'Utopian Music and the Problem of Luxury', *Utopian Studies*, vol. 16, no. 2 (2005)

_____, 'Offshore Irelands; or, Hy-Brazil Hybridized: utopian colonies and anti-colonial Utopias, 1641–1760', in Eóin Flannery and Angus Mitchell (eds), *Enemies of Empire* (Dublin: Four Courts Press, 2007)

Griffin, Michael J. and Breandán MacSuibhne, 'Da's Boat, or, Can the Submarine

Speak? *A Voyage to O'Brazeel* (1752) and other glimpses of the Irish Atlantis', *Field Day Review*, vol. 2 (2006)

Griffin, Michael J. and Tom Moylan (eds), *Exploring the Utopian Impulse: essays on utopian thought and practice* (Bern, Oxford: Peter Lang, 2007)

Griffin, Michael, *Enlightenment in Ruins: the geographies of Oliver Goldsmith* (Lewisburg: Bucknell University Press, 2013)

Hanson, Laurence, *Government and the Press, 1695–1763* (lithographical reprint of 1936 edn: Oxford: Clarendon Press, 1967)

Harbison, Peter, *William Burton Conyngham and His Irish Circle of Antiquarian Artists* (New Haven, CT: Yale University Press, 2012)

Hardt, Michael and Antonio Negri, *Empire* (Cambridge, MA: Harvard University Press, 2000)

Harrison, Alan, *The Dean's Friend: Anthony Raymond, 1675–1726: Jonathan Swift and the Irish language* (Dublin: Éamonn de Búrca [publisher], 1999)

Hartley, Harold (ed.), *The Royal Society: its origins and founders* (London: Royal Society, 1960)

Harvey, David, *Spaces of Hope* (Edinburgh: Edinburgh University Press, 2002)

Hay, Carla H., 'The Making of a Radical: the case of James Burgh', *Journal of British Studies*, vol. 18, no. 2 (1979)

Heaney, Seamus, 'The Disappearing Island', in *The Haw Lantern*, no. 50 (London: Faber & Faber, 1987)

_____, *The Redress of Poetry: Oxford lectures* (London: Faber & Faber, 1995)

Herlihy, Kevin (ed.), *The Irish Dissenting Tradition, 1650–1750* (Dublin: Four Courts Press, 1995)

Hertzler, Joyce Oramel, *The History of Utopian Thought* (New York: Macmillan, 1923)

Hexter, J.H., *More's Utopia: the biography of an idea* (New York: Princeton University Press, 1952)

Hickey, Raymond, 'English in Eighteenth-century Ireland', in Raymond Hickey (ed.), *Eighteenth-century English Ideology and Change* (Cambridge: Cambridge University Press, 2010)

Higgins, Michael D., *Renewing the Republic* (Dublin: Liberties Press, 2011)

Hinkson, Tynan Katharine (ed.), *The Cabinet of Irish Literature: Volumes I–IV* (London: Gresham Publishing Company, 1905)

Hone, J.M. and M.M. Rossi, *Bishop Berkeley: his life, writings and philosophy with an introduction by W.B. Yeats* (London: Faber & Faber, 1931)

Hoppen, Theodore, *The Common Scientist in the Seventeenth Century: a study of the Dublin Philosophical Society, 1683–1708* (Charlottesville, VA: University Press of Virginia, 1970)

Houghton, Raymond W., David Berman and Maureen T. Lapan, *Images of Berkeley* (Dublin: National Gallery of Ireland, Wolfhound Press, 1986)

Houston, Chlöe, 'Utopia, Dystopia or Anti-Utopia? *Gulliver's Travels* and the utopian mode of discourse', *Utopian Studies*, vol. 18, no. 3 (2007)

_____, *The Renaissance Utopia Dialogue: travel and the ideal society* (Surrey: Ashgate, 2014)

Jameson, Fredric, *Marxism and Form* (Princeton, NJ: Princeton University Press, 1971)

_____, 'Comments', *Utopian Studies*, vol. 9, no. 2 (1998)

_____, *Archaeologies of the Future: the desire called Utopia and other science fictions* (London: Verso, 2005)

Jeffares, Norman A. (ed.), *Swift: modern judgements* (London: Macmillan, 1969)

_____, *Parameters of Irish Literature in English* (Buckinghamshire: Colin Smythe, 1986)

_____, *W.B. Yeats: man and poet* (Dublin: Gill & Macmillan, 1996)

Johnson, Donald S., *Phantom Islands of the Atlantic: the legends of the seven lands that never were* (London: Souvenir Press, 1997)

Kateb, George, *Utopia and its Enemies* (New York: Free Press of Glencoe, 1963)

Kelly, James and Martyn J. Powell (eds), *Clubs and Societies in Eighteenth-century Ireland* (Dublin: Four Courts Press, 2010)

_____, 'Jonathan Swift and the Irish Economy in the 1720s', *Eighteenth-century Ireland/ Iris an dá Chultúr*, no. 6 (1991)

Kiberd, Declan, *Irish Classics* (London: Granta Books, 2000)

Kolakowski, Leszek, 'The Death of Utopia Reconsidered', in Sterling M. McMurrin (ed.), *The Tanner Lectures on Human Value*, vol. 4 (Salt Lake City, UT: University of Utah Press/Cambridge: Cambridge University Press, 1983); reprinted in idem., *Modernity on Endless Trial* (Chicago, IL: University of Chicago Press, 1990)

Kramnick, Isaac, *Bolingbroke and His Circle: the politics of nostalgia in the age of Walpole* (Ithaca, NY and London: Cornell University Press, 1968)

Kumar, Krishan, *Utopia and Anti-Utopia in Modern Times* (Oxford: Basil Blackwell, 1978)

Kumar, Krishan, *Utopianism* (Minneapolis, MN: University of Minnesota Press, 1991)

Laird, Heather (ed.), *Daniel Corkery's Cultural Criticism: selected writings* (Cork: Cork University Press, 2012)

Latané, David, *William Maginn and the British Press: a critical biography* (Surrey: Ashgate, 2013)

Leadbeater, Mary, *Memoirs and Letters of Richard and Elizabeth Shackleton, Late of Ballitore, Ireland* (London: Charles Gilpin; Dublin: J.B. Gilpin, 1849)

Leask, Nigel, 'Irish Republicans and Gothic Eleutherachs: Pacific Utopias in the writings of Theobald Wolfe Tone and Charles Brockden Brown', *Huntington Library Quarterly*, vol. 63, no. 3 (2000)

Lee, David, *Ralahine: land war and the co-operative* (Limerick: Bottom Dog Assoc. Co-op Books, 1981)

Leerssen, Joep, *Mere Irish and Fíor-Ghael* (Cork: Cork University Press, 1996)

Le Fanu, William, *A Catalogue of Books Belonging to Dr. Jonathan Swift, Dean of St Patrick's, Dublin, Aug. 19. 1715* (Cambridge: Cambridge Biographical Society, 1988)

Lefebvre, Henri, *The Production of Space*, trans. Donald Nicholson Smith (Oxford: Blackwell, 1991)

Leighton, Peter, *Moon Travellers* (London: Oldbourne Book Co. Ltd, 1960)

Leslie, Marina, *Renaissance Utopias and the Problem of History* (Ithaca, NY: Cornell University Press, 1998)

Levitas, Ruth, *The Concept of Utopia* (Hemel Hempstead: Philip Allan; Syracuse, NY: Syracuse University Press, 1990)

____, 'Educated Hope: Ernst Bloch on abstract and concrete Utopia', *Utopian Studies*, vol. 1, no. 2 (1990)

____, 'The Imaginary Reconstitution of Society or Why Sociologists and Others Should Take Utopia More Seriously', lecture, University of Bristol, 24 October 2005

____, *Utopia as Method: the imaginary reconstitution of society* (Houndmills: Palgrave Macmillan, 2013)

Livesey, James, 'The Dublin Society in Eighteenth-century Political Thought', *Historical Journal*, vol. 47, no. 3 (2004)

Livesey, James, 'A Kingdom of Cosmopolitan Improvers: the Dublin Society, 1731–1798', in Koen Stapelbroek and Jani Marjanen (eds), *The Rise of Economic Societies in the Eighteenth Century* (Houndmills: Palgrave Macmillan, 2012)

Loeber, Rolf and Magda Loeber (eds), *A Guide to Irish Fiction* (Dublin: Four Courts Press, 2006)

____ (eds), *Irish Poets and Their Pseudonyms in Early Periodicals* (Dublin: Edmund Burke Publisher, 2007)

Luce, A.A., 'More Unpublished Berkeley Letters and New Berkeleiana', *Hermathena*, vol. 23 (1933)

____, 'Is There a Berkeleian Philosophy?' *Hermathena*, vol. 25 (1936)

Lynch, Sean, 'Preliminary Sketches for the Reappearance of HyBrazil', *Utopian Studies*, vol. 21, no. 1 (2010)

Lyons, H., *The Royal Society, 1660–1940: a history of its administration under its charters* (Cambridge: Cambridge University Press, 1944)

Lysaght, Patricia, Séamus Ó Catháin and Dáithí Ó hÓgáin (eds), *Islanders and Water-dwellers* (Dublin: Four Courts Press, 1999)

Magennis, Eoin, *The Irish Political System, 1740–1765: the golden age of undertakers* (Dublin: Four Courts Press, 2000)

Malcomson, Anthony, *Archbishop Charles Agar: churchmanship and politics in Ireland, 1760–1810* (Dublin: Four Courts Press, 2002)

Manguel, Alberto, *A History of Reading* (London: Flamingo, 1997)

____ and Gianni Guadalupi, *The Dictionary of Imaginary Places* (St Albans and London: Granada Publishing Limited, 1980)

Maniquis, Robert M. (ed.), *British Radical Culture of the 1790s* (San Marino, CA: Henry E. Huntington Library, 2002)

Mansoor, M., *The Story of Irish Orientalism* (London: Longmans, Green & Co. Ltd, 1944)

Manuel, Frank, *The Prophets of Paris* (New York: Harper Torchbook, 1965)

____ and Fritzie P. Manuel, *French Utopias: an anthology of ideal societies* (Toronto, ON: Free Press, 1966)

____, *Utopian Thought in the Western World* (Cambridge, MA: Belknap Press of Harvard University Press, 1979)

Marin, Louis, *Utopics: the semiological play of textual spaces*, trans. Robert A. Volrath (Atlantic Highlands, NJ: Humanities Press, 1984)

Markey, Anne, 'Literary Labours, Lunar Landscapes, and Lady Mount Cashell's *Selene*', symposium, Trinity College, Dublin, 22 October 2012

Matteson, Robert S., *A Large Private Park: the collection of Archbishop William King 1650–1729*, 2 vols (Cambridge: LP Publications, 2003)

Maxwell, Constantia, *Dublin Under the Georges, 1714–1830* (London: George G. Harrap, 1936)

_____, *The Stranger in Ireland: from the reign of Elizabeth to the Great Famine* (London: Jonathan Cape, 1954)

McAleer, Edward, *The Sensitive Plant: a life of Lady Mount Cashell* (Chapel Hill, NC: University of North Carolina Press, 1958)

McBride, Ian, *Eighteenth-century Ireland: the isle of slaves* (Dublin: Gill & Macmillan, 2009)

_____, 'Catholic Politics in the Penal Era: Father Sylvester Lloyd and the Devlin address of 1725', *Eighteenth-century Ireland*, vol. 1 (2011)

_____, 'Burke and Ireland', in David Dwan and Christopher Insole (eds), *The Cambridge Companion to Edmund Burke* (Cambridge: Cambridge University Press, 2013)

McCarthy, Muriel and Ann Simmons (eds), *Marsh's Library: a mirror on the world: law, learning and libraries, 1650–1750* (Dublin: Four Courts Press, 2009)

McGuire, James and James Quinn, *Dictionary of Irish Biography*, 9 vols (Cambridge: Cambridge University Press, 2009)

McMinn, Joseph, 'Literature and Religion in Eighteenth-century Ireland: a critical survey', in Robert Welch (ed.), *Irish Writers and Religion* (Gerrards Cross: Colin Smthe, 1992)

_____, *Jonathan's Travels: Swift and Ireland* (Belfast: Appletree Press, 1994)

Meehan, James and Desmond Clarke (eds), *The Royal Dublin Society, 1731–1981* (Dublin: Gill & Macmillan, 1981)

Miller, Timothy, 'A Matter of Definition: just what is an intentional community?' *Communicatio Socialis*, vol. 30, no. 1 (2010)

Miller, Kerby A., 'Revd James MacSparran's America Dissected (1753): eighteenth-century emigration and constructions of "Irishness"', *History Ireland*, vol. 11, no. 4 (winter 2003)

_____, Arnold Schrier, Bruce D. Boling and David N. Doyle (eds), *Irish Immigrants in the Land of Canaan: letters and memoirs from colonial and revolutionary America, 1675–1815* (Oxford: Oxford University Press, 2003)

Milne, Kenneth, 'The End of the Old Order, 1745–1846', in John Crawford and Raymond Gillespie (eds), *St Patrick's Cathedral, Dublin: a history* (Dublin: Four Courts Press, 2009)

Mitchell, Angus and Geraldo Cantarino, *Origins of Brazil: a search for the origins of the name Brazil* (London: Brazilian Embassy, 2000)

Molnar, Thomas, *Utopia: the perennial heresy* (New York: Sheed & Ward, 1967)

Moran, Gerard (ed.), *Radical Irish Priests, 1660–1970* (Dublin: Four Courts Press, 1998)

Morton, A.L., *The English Utopia* (London: Lawrence & Wishart, 1978)

Moylan, Tom, *Demand the Impossible: science fiction and the utopian imagination* (New York: Methuen, 1987)

_____, 'Utopia and Postmodernity: six theses', in Jeanne Randolph (ed.), *The City Within: rhetoric, Utopia, and technology* (Alberta: Banff Centre for the Arts, 1992)

_____, 'Introduction: Jameson and Utopia', *Utopian Studies*, vol. 9, no. 2 (1998)

_____, *Scraps of the Untainted Sky: science fiction, Utopia, dystopia* (Boulder, CO: Westview, 2000)

_____, 'To Stand with Dreamers: on the use value of Utopia', *Irish Review*, vol. 34, no. 34 (spring 2006)

_____, 'Irish Voyages and Visions: pre-figuring, re-configuring Utopia', *Utopian Studies*, vol. 18, no. 3 (2007)

_____, 'Utopia, Crisis, Justice', paper read at 'Steps of Renewed Praxis', Utopian Studies Society Conference, Nicosia, Cyprus, July 2011

_____ and Raffaella Baccolini (eds), *Utopia Method Vision: the use value of social dreaming* (Bern and New York: Peter Lang, 2007)

Mullan, John, *Anonymity: a secret history of English literature* (London: Faber & Faber, 2007)

Mulvihill, Mary, *Ingenious Ireland: a county-by-county exploration of Irish mysteries and marvels* (Dublin: Town House & Country House, 2002)

Mumford, Lewis, 'Utopia, the City and the Machine', in Frank E. Manuel (ed.), *Utopias and Utopian Thought: a timely appraisal* (Boston, MA: Beacon Press, 1967)

Munter, Robert, *The History of the Irish Newspaper, 1685–1760* (Cambridge: Cambridge University Press, 2010)

Murray, Patrick Joseph, *The Life of John Banim, the Irish Novelist, with Extracts from His Correspondence, General and Literary* (London: William Lay, 1857)

Negley, Glenn and J. Max Patrick, *The Quest for Utopia: an anthology of imaginary societies* (New York: Henry Schumann, 1952)

Nic Dhiarmada, Bríona, 'Aspects of Utopia, Anti-Utopia, and Nostalgia in Irish-Language Texts', *Utopian Studies*, vol. 18, no. 3 (2007)

Nicolson, Majorie Hope, *Voyages to the Moon* (New York: Macmillan, 1960)

_____ and Nora M. Mohler, 'The Scientific Background of Swift's "Voyage to Laputa"', in A.N. Jeffares (ed.), *Swift: modern judgements* (London: Macmillan, 1969)

Nisbet, Robert, *The Social Philosophers* (St Albans: Paladin, 1976)

Ó Buachalla, Breandán, 'Irish Jacobitism and Irish Nationalism: the literary evidence', in Michael O'Dea and Kevin Whelan (eds), *Nations and Nationalisms: France, Britain, Ireland and the eighteenth-century context*, Studies on Voltaire and the Eighteenth Century, vol. 335 (Oxford: Voltaire Foundation, 1996)

_____, *Aisling Ghéar* (Áth Cliath: An Clóchomhar, 1996)

Ó Cionnaith, Finnian, *Mapping, Measurement and Metropolis: how land surveyors shaped eighteenth-century Dublin* (Dublin: Four Courts Press, 2012)

O'Connor, Frank, *The Backward Look: a survey of Irish literature* (London, Melbourne and Toronto: Macmillan, 1967)

Ó Ríordáin, Seán, *Na Dánta* (Indreabhán, Conemara: Cló Iar-Chonnacht, 2011)

O'Toole, Fintan, *A History of Ireland in 100 Objects* (Dublin: *Irish Times* and Royal Irish Academy, 2013)

Pagden, Anthony, *European Encounters with the New World: from Renaissance to Romanticism* (New Haven, CT and London: Yale University Press, 1993)

Parrington, Vernon Louis, *American Dreams: a study of American Utopias* (Providence, RI: Brown University, 1947; second edn 1964)

Patrick, J. Max, 'Introduction', in R.W. Gibson and J. Max Patrick (compilers), 'Utopias and Dystopias, 1500–1750', sect. 9 of R.W. Gibson (compiler), *St. Thomas More: a preliminary bibliography of his works and of Moreana to the year 1750* (New Haven, CT: Yale University Press, 1961)

Paulin, Tom, *The Day-star of Liberty: William Hazlitt's radical style* (London: Faber & Faber, 1998)

Jason, Pearl H., *Utopian Geographies and the Early English Novel* (Charlottesville, VA and London: University of Virginia Press, 2014)

Pindar, David, *Visions of the City* (Edinburgh: Edinburgh University Press, 2005)

Plomer, Henry R., *A Dictionary of the Printers and Booksellers Who Were at Work in England, Scotland and Ireland from 1668 to 1725* (Oxford: printed for Biographical Society at Oxford University Press, 1922)

Plumb, J.H., *Sir Robert Walpole*, 2 vols: vol. 1, *The Making of a Statesman* (London: Cresset Press, 1956); vol. 2, *The King's Minister* (London: Allen Lane the Penguin Press, 1960)

Plunkett, Horace, *Noblesse Oblige: an Irish rendering* (Dublin: Maunsel & Co., 1908)

Pohl, Nicole and Brenda Tooley (eds), *Gender and Utopia in the Eighteenth Century* (England: Ashgate, 2007)

_____, 'Utopianism after More: the Renaissance and Enlightenment', in Gregory Claeys (ed.), *The Cambridge Companion to Utopian Literature* (Cambridge: Cambridge University Press, 2010)

Pordzik, Ralph, 'A Postcolonial View of Ireland and the Irish Conflict in Anglo-Irish Utopian Literature since the Nineteenth Century', *Irish Studies Review*, vol. 9, no. 3 (2001)

Rabkin, Eric S., Martin H. Greenberg and Joseph D. Olander (eds), *No Place Else: explorations in utopian and dystopian fiction* (Carbondale, IL: Southern Illinois UP, 1983)

Rand, Benjamin, *Berkeley and Percival: the correspondence of Berkeley and Sir John Percival* (Cambridge, MA: Harvard University Press, 1914)

_____, *Berkeley's American Sojourn* (Cambridge, MA: Harvard University Press, 1932)

Rawson, C.J., *Gulliver and the Gentle Reader: studies in Swift and our time* (London and Boston, MA: Routledge, 1972; second edn, Humanities Press, 1991)

_____, *Swift's Angers* (Cambridge: Cambridge University Press, 2014)

_____, *Swift and Others* (Cambridge: Cambridge University Press, 2015)

Real, Hermann J., 'Swift's Non-reading', in Charles Benson and Siobhán Fitzpatrick (eds), *THAT WOMAN! Studies in Irish Bibliography: a Festschrift for Mary 'Paul' Pollard* (Dublin: Lilliput Press for Library Association of Ireland, Rare Books Group, 2005)

Rees, Christine, *Utopian Imagination and Eighteenth-century Fiction* (London: Longman, 1996; republished London: Routledge, 2014)

Rennie, Neil, *Far-fetched Facts: the literature of travel and the idea of the South Seas* (Oxford: Clarendon Press, 1995)

Richman, Berdine, *American Historical Review*, vol. 11, no. 2 (1906)

Rielly, Edward J., 'Irony in *Gulliver's Travels* and Utopia', *Utopian Studies*, vol. 3, no. 1 (1992)

Roemer, Kenneth M., *The Obsolete Necessity: America in utopian writings, 1888–1900* (Kent, OH: Kent State University Press, 1976)

_____, *Utopian Audiences: how readers locate nowhere* (Amherst, MA: University of Massachusetts Press, 2003)

_____, 'Paradise Transformed: varieties of nineteenth-century Utopias', in Gregory Claeys (ed.), *The Cambridge Companion to Utopian Literature* (Cambridge: Cambridge University Press, 2010)

Rogers, Pat, *Eighteenth Century Encounters: studies in literature and society in the age of Walpole* (Sussex: Harvester Press, 1985)

Ruppert, Peter, *Reader in a Strange Land: the activity of reading literary Utopias* (Athens, GA and London: University of Georgia Press, 1986)

Said, Edward, *Orientalism* (New York: Vintage Books, 1979)

_____, *The World, the Text, and the Critic* (Cambridge, MA: Harvard University Press, 1983)

_____, *Culture and Imperialism* (New York: Vintage Books, 1994)

Sargent, Lyman Tower, 'Theorizing Utopia/Utopianism in the Twenty-first Century', in Artur Blaim and Ludmila Gruszewska-Blaim (eds), *The Spectres of Utopia: theory, practice, conventions* (Frankfurt am Main: Peter Lang, 2012)

_____, 'Theorizing Intentional Community in the Twenty-first Century', in Eliezer Ben Rafael, Yaacov Oved and Menahem Topel (eds), *The Communal Idea in the 21st Century* (Leiden: Brill, 2012)

_____, *Utopianism: a very short introduction* (Oxford: Oxford University Press, 2010)

_____, Lyman Tower, 'Colonial and Postcolonial Utopias', in Gregory Claeys (ed.), *The Cambridge Companion to Utopian Literature* (Cambridge: Cambridge University Press, 2010)

_____, 'Choosing Utopia: utopianism as an essential element in political thought and action', in Tom Moylan and Raffaella Baccolini (eds), *Utopia Method Vision: the use value of social dreaming*, vol. 1 (Bern: Peter Lang, 2007)

_____, Tower, 'The Problem of the "Flawed Utopia": a note on the costs of Utopia', in Raffaella Baccolini and Tom Moylan (eds), *Dark Horizons: science fiction and the dystopian imagination* (London: Routledge, 2003)

_____, Lyman Tower, 'The Three Faces of Utopianism Revisited', *Utopian Studies*, vol. 5, no. 1 (1994)

_____, *British and American Utopian Literature, 1516–1975: an annotated bibliography* (Boston, MA: G.K. Hall & Co., 1979)

Sargisson, Lucy, 'Strange Places: estrangement, utopianism, and intentional communities', *Utopian Studies*, vol. 18, no. 3 (2007)

_____, *Fool's Gold? Utopianism in the twenty-first century* (Basingstoke: Palgrave Macmillan, 2012)

Scaife, Walter B., 'Brazil, as a Geographical Appellation', *Modern Language Notes*, no. 4 (1890)

Schaer, Roland, 'Utopia, Space, Time, History', in Roland Schaer, Gregory Claeys and Lyman Tower Sargent (eds), *Trans. Nadia Benabid. Utopia: the search for the ideal society in the Western world* (New York and Oxford: New York Public Library/ Oxford University Press, 2000)

Seed, David, *Science Fiction: a very short introduction* (Oxford: Oxford University Press, 2011)

Simms, J.G., *William Molyneux of Dublin: a life of the seventeenth-century political writer and scientist*, ed. P.H. Kelly (Dublin: Irish Academic Press, 1982)

Small, Stephen, *Political Thought in Ireland, 1776–1798: republicanism, patriotism, and radicalism* (Oxford: Oxford University Press, 2002)

Sobel, Dava, *Galileo's Daughter: a drama of science, faith and love* (London: Fourth Estate, 1999)

Stillman, Peter [G.], 'Review Essay: recent studies in the history of utopian thought', *Utopian Studies*, vol. 1, no. 1 (1990)

Strijbosch, Clara, *The Seafaring Saint: sources and analogues of the twelfth-century voyage of Saint Brendan* (Dublin: Four Courts Press, 2000)

Suvin, Darko, 'Defining the Literary Genre of Utopia: some historical semantics, some genealogy, a proposal, and a plea', *Studies in the Literary Imagination*, vol. 6 (fall 1973), reprinted in idem., *Metamorphoses of Science Fiction: on the poetics and history of a literary genre* (New Haven, CT: Yale University Press, 1979)

_____, *Metamorphoses of Science Fiction: on the poetics and history of a literary genre* (New Haven, CT: Yale University Press, 1979)

_____, 'Locus, Horizon, and Orientation: the concept of possible worlds as a key to utopian studies', *Utopian Studies*, vol. 1, no. 2 (1990)

Tafuri, Manfredo, *Architecture and Utopia: design and capitalist development*, trans. Barbara Luigia La Penta (Cambridge, MA: MIT Press, 1979)

Thompson, H.P., *Thomas Bray* (London: SPCK, 1954)

Todd, Janet, *Rebel Daughters: Ireland in conflict, 1798* (London: Viking, 2003)

_____, 'Ascendancy: Lady Mount Cashell, Lady Moira, Mary Wollstonecraft and the Union pamphlets', *Eighteenth-century Ireland/Iris an Dá Chultúr*, vol. 18 (2003)

Tomlinson, Gary, *Music in Renaissance Magic: towards a historiography of others* (Chicago, IL: University of Chicago Press, 1993)

Trahair, Richard C.S., *Utopias and Utopians: an historical dictionary* (London and Chicago: Fitzroy Dearborn, 1999)

Unger, R., *Social Theory: its situation and its task* (Cambridge: Cambridge University Press, 1987)

Urstad, Tone Sundt, *Sir Robert Walpole's Poets: the use of literature as pro-government propaganda, 1721–1742* (Newark, DE: University of Delaware Press, 1999)

Vieira, Fátima, 'The Concept of Utopia', in Gregory Claeys (ed.), *The Cambridge Companion to Utopian Literature* (Cambridge: Cambridge University Press, 2010)

Wegemer, Gerard B., *Thomas More: a portrait of courage* (Dublin: Four Courts Press, 1998)

Wegner, Phillip, *Imaginary Communities: Utopia, the nation, and the spatial histories of modernity* (Berkeley, CA: University of California Press, 2002)

Weisbrod, Carol, *The Boundaries of Utopia* (New York: Pantheon, 1980)

Welch, Robert (ed.), *The Oxford Companion to Irish Literature* (Oxford: Oxford University Press, 1996)

Westcott, Isabel M., *Seventeenth-century Tales of the Supernatural* (Los Angeles, CA: William Andrews Clark Memorial Library, University of California, 1958)

Weston, Jessie L., *The Chief Middle English Poets* (Cambridge, MA: Riverside Press, 1914)

Wheatley, Christopher J., *Beneath Ierne's Banners: Irish Protestant drama of the Restoration and eighteenth century* (Notre Dame, IN: University of Notre Dame Press, 1999)

White, T.H., *Mistress Masham's Repose* (Middlesex: Penguin/Jonathan Cape, 1947)

Widdicombe, Toby Richard, 'Early Histories of Utopian Thought (to 1950)', *Utopian Studies*, vol. 3, no. 1 (1992)

Wilde, Oscar, 'The Soul of Man Under Socialism', in *Selected Essays and Poems* (London: Penguin, 1954)

Williams, Raymond, *Marxism and Literature* (London: Oxford University Press, 1977)

_____, *Keywords: a vocabulary of culture and society* (London: Fontana Press, 1988)

Winkler, Kenneth P. (ed.), *The Cambridge Companion to Berkeley* (Cambridge: Cambridge University Press, 2005)

Winton, Calhoun, 'Richard Head and Origins of the Picaresque in England', in Carmen Benito-Vessels and Michael Zappala (eds), *The Picaresque: a symposium on the rogue's tale* (Newark, DE: University of Delaware Press, 1994)

Zaki, Hoda, *Phoenix Renewed: the survival and mutation of utopian thought in North American science fiction, 1965–1982* (Mercer Island, WA: Starmont House, 1988)

Zhang, Longxi, 'The Utopian Vision, East and West', *Utopian Studies*, vol. 13, no. 1 (2002)

Zimmermann, George D., *The Irish Storyteller* (Dublin: Four Courts Press, 2001)

Index

Illustrations are indicated by page numbers in bold